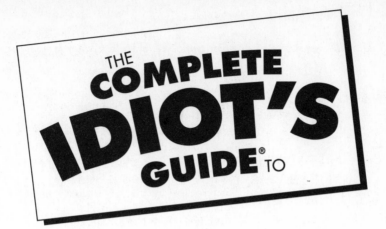

THE
COMPLETE
IDIOT'S
GUIDE® TO

Mary of Nazareth

by María Ruiz Scaperlanda

ALPHA

A member of Penguin Group (USA) Inc.

D1406529

For Judy M. Reilly, my sister seeker, whose confidence in Mother Mary inspires me.

ALPHA BOOKS

Published by the Penguin Group

Penguin Group (USA) Inc., 375 Hudson Street, New York, New York 10014, U.S.A.

Penguin Group (Canada), 10 Alcorn Avenue, Toronto, Ontario, Canada M4V 3B2 (a division of Pearson Penguin Canada Inc.)

Penguin Books Ltd, 80 Strand, London WC2R 0RL, England

Penguin Ireland, 25 St Stephen's Green, Dublin 2, Ireland (a division of Penguin Books Ltd)

Penguin Group (Australia), 250 Camberwell Road, Camberwell, Victoria 3124, Australia (a division of Pearson Australia Group Pty Ltd)

Penguin Books India Pvt Ltd, 11 Community Centre, Panchsheel Park, New Delhi—110 017, India

Penguin Group (NZ), cnr Airborne and Rosedale Roads, Albany, Auckland 1310, New Zealand (a division of Pearson New Zealand Ltd)

Penguin Books (South Africa) (Pty) Ltd, 24 Sturdee Avenue, Rosebank, Johannesburg 2196, South Africa

Penguin Books Ltd, Registered Offices: 80 Strand, London WC2R 0RL, England

International Standard Book Number: 1-59257-482-3
Library of Congress Catalog Card Number: 2005937202

08 07 06   8 7 6 5 4 3 2 1

Interpretation of the printing code: The rightmost number of the first series of numbers is the year of the book's printing; the rightmost number of the second series of numbers is the number of the book's printing. For example, a printing code of 06-1 shows that the first printing occurred in 2006.

Printed in the United States of America

Note: This publication contains the opinions and ideas of its author. It is intended to provide helpful and informative material on the subject matter covered. It is sold with the understanding that the author and publisher are not engaged in rendering professional services in the book. If the reader requires personal assistance or advice, a competent professional should be consulted.

The author and publisher specifically disclaim any responsibility for any liability, loss, or risk, personal or otherwise, which is incurred as a consequence, directly or indirectly, of the use and application of any of the contents of this book.

Most Alpha books are available at special quantity discounts for bulk purchases for sales promotions, premiums, fund-raising, or educational use. Special books, or book excerpts, can also be created to fit specific needs.

For details, write: Special Markets, Alpha Books, 375 Hudson Street, New York, NY 10014.

Publisher: *Marie Butler-Knight*
Editorial Director: *Mike Sanders*
Senior Managing Editor: *Jennifer Bowles*
Senior Acquisitions Editor: *Randy Ladenheim-Gil*
Development Editor: *Nancy D. Lewis*
Production Editor: *Megan Douglass*
Copy Editor: *Molly Schaller*

Illustrator: *Jody Shaeffer*
Book Designer: *Trina Wurst*
Cover Designer: *Bill Thomas*
Indexer: *Brad Herriman*
Layout: *Brian Massey*
Proofreading: *John Etchison*

Contents at a Glance

Contents

Appendixes

Introduction

For more than 2,000 years, Mary of Nazareth, mother of Jesus, has been written about, analyzed, theologized, adored, despised, forgotten, respected, made fun of, venerated, cast aside, and honored. How can one Jewish woman from an unremarkable town in Roman times continue to cause such a stir? If you picked up this book, you, too, are trying to understand.

Mary of Nazareth is a fundamental and indispensable character in the Christian story of salvation. Without her, there is no Nativity story! But Mary has been much more than simply one more element in the story. From the time of Jesus and through the early years of the Church, Mary was Mother to the community of Christian believers—and that mothering relationship is still vibrant today.

This book will tell you the facts and figures about Mary, and it will also introduce you to her character, her disposition to God, and her faithful spirit. It is here that you will come to know Mary of Nazareth.

How This Book Is Organized

This book is presented in six parts:

Part 1, "Presenting Mary," sets the stage for our discussion by presenting what we know about Mary of Nazareth. You will come to know all the particulars—from her place of birth to her family life—by examining the historical documents, the Bible references, and the noncanonical early texts (the ones that didn't make it into the Bible). We'll spend a little time familiarizing ourselves with Mary's Jewish culture in the Roman Empire and with the unfolding oral history of Jesus in what became known as the New Testament.

Part 2, "Encountering Mary—As Mother," is all about the first several references to Mary in the Gospels, the ones that directly describe her and present her in her mothering of Jesus. You will first read an overview of how Mary is portrayed by the different authors of the New Testament and then go into each specific story: the Annunciation; the Nativity; the presentation of Jesus according to Jewish law; Mary and Joseph's flight into Egypt; and searching for a lost 12-year-old Jesus in the Temple of Jerusalem. You will read about and understand each biblical text, and through it, become aware of what it shows about Mary's character.

Part 3, "Encountering Mary—As Disciple," continues the discussion of specific Scripture references in which Mary of Nazareth participates. But these three stories show her relationship with an adult Jesus, and therefore focus on her role as the first disciple of the Christian Messiah. Mary was present at the wedding feast at Cana, the passion and death of Jesus, and the descent of the Holy Spirit at Pentecost. And her presence speaks volumes about her and about her faith.

Part 4, "Knowing Mary," shifts focus from learning about Mary in Scripture to coming to know Mary through the names or titles that she has been given in the Christian church: the Lord's servant, Blessed, Mother of God, the first Christian, Mother of the Church. These names were not invented one day, but were birthed directly from the living relationship between Mary and the early Christians from the very beginning of the church.

Part 5, "Naming Mary," introduces you to the many names given to Mary of Nazareth, and why—and how—Christians over the centuries and throughout the world have personalized and claimed her as their own. It's all about ethnicity. It's all about personality and culture. It's all about a universal mother letting her children know she claims them.

Part 6, "Praying with Mary," offers you an experience of Mary through prayers, art, poetry, music, and literature. To know Mary of Nazareth today means to experience her, to be in relationship with her. By seeing how this has been true for others in the past 2,000 years, you, too, will be invited to take the final step in knowing Mary.

Things to Help You Out Along the Way

You will notice that throughout the chapters there are some special messages along the way.

Lord Knows
These tips will explain people, places, and stories that are related to Mary, but not necessarily obvious to her story.

Sunday School
Most of the words used in introducing Mary might be familiar to you. I have highlighted those that might be new to you and some that stand out as key concepts for you to pay attention to.

Holy Mother
These are quotes about Mary by people from all walks of life and all backgrounds—some contemporary, and many others from the past 2,000 years. I have also included a few short ancient Marian prayers that you might find fun and beautiful.

Acknowledgments

I would like to thank my agent, Marilyn Allen, for this project, who connected me with the great people at Alpha Books. And my writer friend, John Rosengreen, who introduced me to Marilyn! To Randy Ladenheim-Gil, senior acquisitions editor at Alpha, for her patience and guidance. And to Nancy D. Lewis, who never tired of explaining to me the process. ¡Muchas gracias!

I would also like to acknowledge my parents, family, and friends who have prayed for me and for this project, continually reminding me how important it is to introduce you to Mary! Special thanks to these communities who made it their calling to pray me through the writing of this book: Sister Ruth Miriam Irey and the discalced Carmelite nuns from the Carmel of St. Joseph in Piedmont, Oklahoma; Brother Kevin McGuire and the Benedictine monks from St. Gregory's Abbey in Shawnee, Oklahoma; my pastor Rev. Tom Boyer and the community of St. Mark the Evangelist in Norman, Oklahoma (thanks for the late-night use of the parish library!); and the catholicwriters list on Yahoo!, my colleagues and friends. Special thanks to my husband, Michael, and my children, Christopher, Anamaría, Rebekah, and Michelle, who understood often better than I did my need to buckle down and write—and to their friends at college and home, who adopted me in their prayers and love.

To the many experts from The Marian Library and the Mary Page online (www.udayton.edu/mary/marypage21.html), whose assistance and guidance was invaluable in my research. Thank you!

Thanks to Rev. Edward J. Weisenburger, pastor of the Cathedral of Our Lady of Perpetual Help in Oklahoma City, who granted permission and opportunity to photograph that beautiful sacred space.

I am indebted to Rev. Johann Roten and Rev. Bertrand Buby, both international Marian scholars associated with the Marian Library and the International Marian Research Institute, whose expertise they generously shared with me, and with all of you readers. A special note of thanks to Charles H. Miller, S.M., my dear friend and the first Marianist to grace my life!

Special Thanks to the Technical Reviewer

The Complete Idiot's Guide to Mary of Nazareth was reviewed by an expert, who double-checked the accuracy of what you learn here, to help ensure this book gives you everything you need to know. Special thanks are extended to Bertrand Buby, S.M.

Trademarks

All terms mentioned in this book that are known to be or are suspected of being trademarks or service marks have been appropriately capitalized. Alpha Books and Penguin Group (USA) Inc. cannot attest to the accuracy of this information. Use of a term in this book should not be regarded as affecting the validity of any trademark or service mark.

Part 1

Presenting Mary

The curtain rises, the drum rolls, and there she stands. She is young and beautiful, usually wearing a halo, and probably holding a baby. She might look sad or she might have no expression at all, with her hands piously folded. She is usually wearing simple, ordinary clothes, in a style that lets you know she lived over two millennia ago. Or she might be dressed in the most expensive and fancy linen you have ever seen—the type only a queen would wear.

How in the world are we supposed to get a visual of this Mary of Nazareth when the paintings and drawings of her are all so incredibly diverse?

We will start at the beginning, looking at the place and at the era when she was born and what we know about her. We will also look at our sources of information and what they reveal to us about Mary.

There Is Something About This Mary

In This Chapter

- An event that transformed history
- Mother of Jesus, the son of God
- Not just another Mary
- How can we get to know her?

She was there from the beginning. No, not the beginning of time, but from the beginning of what came to be called Christianity.

In both secular and religious terms, the birth of her child Jesus marked the beginning of a new epoch in history so momentous that our calendar even starts with that event!

What is the probability that a pregnant unwed Jewish teenager from a hick town in the Middle East would be remembered thirty years after her death, much less two millennia? Who is this woman we call Mary of Nazareth? And why are we still talking about her?

After two thousand years, this Mary remains a central figure in our world. Just take note of the countless number of churches, cities, businesses, and even streets in all cultures and countries around the globe named for Mary of Nazareth!

Within Christianity, Mary's importance in the Catholic and Orthodox faith traditions is clearly established and has been throughout their histories. Today, some Protestant Christians are also rediscovering Mary as an intricate part of their personal faith experience.

Some might argue that Mary is making a comeback, like a once popular but obscure sports' team that is suddenly thrust into the limelight and into fans' consciousness.

But in reality, Mary never left. As the mother of Jesus, her place in the Christian story is simply too vital, too fundamental.

In the next few chapters we will look at her unique place in the Christian story. In doing so, we will come to know Mary, the young Jewish woman with a courageous heart and a faith-filled spirit whose life and choices literally changed the course of history.

The Annunciation

Let's start at the very beginning.

We remember Mary of Nazareth first of all because she was the mother of Jesus the Christ. In a very literal sense, without Mary, there is simply no birth narrative, no nativity story!

But let's really begin at the beginning, nine months before the actual birth.

On an average day, in the nondescript town of Nazareth, in ancient Galilee, an *angel* of the Lord named Gabriel visited a young woman named Mary with some disturbing, yet amazing, "good news."

The long-awaited Jewish Messiah was finally coming to save the Jewish people. Not only that, but Mary had been chosen to give birth to him!

This moment and its announcement is called the *Annunciation*.

Later on in this book, you will hear more about angels and other heavenly announcements, and what it meant for Mary to respond to this message by declaring herself the handmaid of the Lord.

For now, the important thing to remember is that Mary not only got to hear this shocking news, but she also gave her assent to God's obviously unexpected and surprising plan for her life.

When told that she would give birth to the son of the Most High (Luke 1: 32), Mary simply and humbly replied, "I am the Lord's servant. Yes, let it be done to me according to God's will."

What Mary heard in this message was not just about her. She heard Gabriel announce that the creator of the world, the Lord of all, so loved his people that he wanted to be born of a human woman in order to be like us in all things (except sin).

Sunday School

In the Hebrew and Christian Scriptures, **angels** are spiritual, immortal creatures that glorify God without ceasing, assist in the divine plan, and serve God as messengers. The **Annunciation** is the name given to the moment when Mary of Nazareth learned from the angel Gabriel that she had been chosen to give birth to the Messiah. Those who accepted Jesus' message to follow him are called his **disciples**. The word *disciple* comes from the Latin *discipulus*, or pupil, from *discere*, to learn.

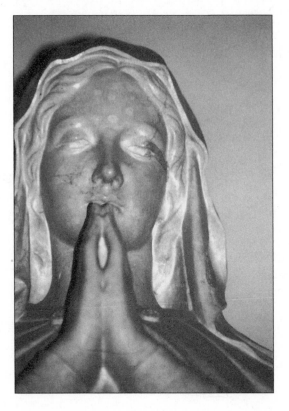

Image of Mary at the Cathedral of Our Lady of Perpetual Help in Oklahoma City.

© *Anamaría Scaperlanda-Ruiz*

And Mary believed this message to be true. Twenty centuries ago, Mary of Nazareth gave birth to a son and named him Jesus, the son of the Most High.

It is not an overstatement to say that since then, the world has not been the same. This one event transformed humanity's experience of God—and human history itself.

Mary's "yes," her simple but profound consent at the annunciation, is also the moment that made Mary the first *disciple*, the first believer that her son was the Messiah.

As the first person to hear and accept the good news sent by God, Mary was the first Christian; the first to recognize and acknowledge the truth that Jesus was the Christ, their Jewish Messiah.

Mother of God, Mother of the Church

Because Jesus was the Son of God, we call Mary the mother of God, a title that made her honored and respected from the beginning by early Christians. Much in the same spirit as I show consideration for and recognize the mother of my husband or the mother of a good friend, it simply made sense to the early believers to turn to Mary and to be thankful for her faith and her role as mother of Jesus.

As early as the fifth century A.D., the Christian church recognized the veracity of Jesus' identity as son of the Creator by officially and formally granting Mary the title of "Mother of God," a reality still acknowledged today. In Chapter 14, you will read more about this proclamation and why it was significant.

Sunday School

The word **ministry** comes from the Latin *ministerium* and *minister*, meaning servant. The word has come to mean an act or activity that involves serving. But it is also used to indicate the profession, duties, and services of a minister or Christian clergy.

Mary, the mother of Jesus, was at all the key events in her son's life, and she was prominently present at his crucifixion and death (see the image of Michelangelo's *Pietà* that follows). Because of her presence throughout Jesus' life and *ministry*, and because of her presence in the life of the early church, we also call Mary the mother of the whole church. For the first Christians, this recognition simply made sense. The Catholic and Orthodox traditions still recognize her as mother of the whole church.

Michelangelo's Pietà *portrays the anguish of a mother holding her dead son.*

© *Brian J. McMorrow*

Virgin and Mother

You have probably heard the mother of Jesus called the Blessed Virgin Mary. *Blessed* in this title recognizes, first of all, that as the mother of Jesus, Mary was, indeed, blessed and unique among all women. *Virgin* in the title acknowledges that Jesus was the son of God, conceived in Mary through the Holy Spirit, and not by a human act.

In Chapter 5, we will talk more in detail about the significance of Mary being both virgin and mother. But a beautiful and vivid artistic portrayal of this great mystery is found deep within the limestone cliffs of the mountain of Montserrat, 25 miles northwest of Barcelona, in the Catalonia region of Spain.

The monastery at Montserrat is best known for having one of the finest, and the oldest boys' choir in Europe—older than the Vienna Boys Choir! Yet the heart and spirit of this place truly reside with the image of Mary found inside the Montserrat monastery.

Thought by some to be the mountain sanctuary for the Holy Grail, the name Montserrat literally means *jagged mountain*, and it refers to the peculiar aspect of this strikingly pink rock formation. There are some fifteen hermitages (ancient chapels) scattered over Mount Montserrat, a few over 1,000 years old, as well as a vibrant community of *monks* still living in the monastery today.

Pilgrims have been traveling to Montserrat for centuries, coming to venerate a beautiful image of a Madonna and Child called *La Moreneta,* or *the dark little one* (see the image that follows).

Nuestra Señora de (Our Lady of) Montserrat, *Spain.*

© *Phillip Reilly*

At first glance, the mosaics of women saints that decorate the passageway, leading up the steps to the golden throne holding the image of Our Lady of Montserrat, appear to be nothing more than another display of awesome holy art in a beautiful sacred space.

But this grouping of images is anything but coincidental. On one side of the hall, there are holy women who were mothers, including Elizabeth (mother of John the Baptist), Helen (mother of Emperor Constantine), and Perpetua (a wife and mother martyred in 203). Across the stone passageway on the other wall, however, the holy women featured are women who are known to have professed a vow of virginity—such as Cecilia, Teresa of Avila, and Catherine of Siena.

Although throughout history holy women have been either virgins or mothers, only Mary of Nazareth has been given the privilege of being both virgin and mother simultaneously.

That is why the image of Our Lady of Montserrat is found in the community of all these holy women, yet symbolically and literally standing on its own at the end of the hallway in a small shrine.

What an amazing and vivid representation of the mysterious reality that makes up Mary from Nazareth!

Her Relevance After Two Millennia

As they have from the onset of Christianity, contemporary artists continue to discover Mary by exploring her roles and her attributes in their sculptures and other visual art forms. Across the centuries, thousands have created musical compositions inspired by and dedicated to Mary. Writers have authored countless numbers of books, poems, short stories, and novels exploring the heart and the spirit of Mary today.

A central character in Sue Monk Kidd's best-selling novel *The Secret Life of Bees* (Penguin, 2003), for example, was the wooden image of a Black Madonna who presided and guided over a household of three righteous sisters.

Persistently and deliberately, Mary and all things "Marian" continue to intrigue believers and nonbelievers alike, not to mention awaken the imagination and expand our comfort and discomfort zones. Why else would a quick search on Google.com for the specific words *Mary of Nazareth* produce an amazing 732,000+ hits!

Yet in too many Christian traditions Mary has become nothing more than one of the many decorative figures that are taken out yearly as part of the Christmas ornaments, alongside the shepherds, the camels, and the wise men.

As author Kathleen Norris says, "We dragged Mary out at Christmas ... denied [her] place in Christian tradition and were disdainful of the reverence displayed for her, so public and emotional, by Catholics."

Princeton professor Beverly Gaventa describes it this way: Mary has been the victim of a "Protestant conspiracy of silence: theologically, liturgically, and devotionally."

But not anymore, declared a recent *Time* magazine story that made the mother of Jesus its cover piece. As the article *Hail, Mary* in the March 21, 2005, issue noted, "a growing number of Christian thinkers who are neither Catholic nor Eastern Orthodox (another branch of faith to which Mary is central) have concluded that their various traditions have short-changed her in the very arena which Protestantism most prides itself: the careful and full reading of Scripture."

Mary is for everyone! And she is undoubtedly being discussed and explored with fervor in this new millennium.

Holy Mother

"And as a Jew, I cannot avoid seeing Mary as the sorrowful, Jewish mother whose guiltless son became the sacrifice of hatred for Jews. Especially today, after the incomprehensibility of the Holocaust, this aspect of the so-called Mariology could heal many wounds and lead to a more sympathetic attitude toward the people who are of the same race as Mary. We pray that the faithful Christian devotion to Mary might bear such fruit."

—David Flusser, *Mary: Images of the Mother of Jesus in Jewish and Christian Perspective* (Augsburg Fortress Publishers, 2005)

In a joint way, Protestant and Catholic thinkers alike have in recent years publicly declared that the most surprising and marvelous thing about Mary is what she reveals about God. These revelations, these insights and perspectives, are not confined to ancient history. They are still being discovered today.

Yes, there is something about Mary of Nazareth that we intrinsically recognize as contemporary and true—and the only way to get in touch with it is by diving in and getting to know her.

That's exactly what we'll do in this book!

Many Marys, but Only One Mother Mary

As we set the stage for how we will discuss Mary in this book, there is one important fact that needs to be emphasized regarding her identity.

Over time, and as religious communities meditated on Mary and her significance to Christianity, believers began to christen the mother of Jesus with many names, such as Queen of Heaven and Blessed Virgin, or simply Mother of God.

Often, the names reflected an attribute or quality individuals associated with Mary, like Mother of Mercy or Queen of Peace. And always, Mary was claimed and made personal by specific communities of believers, becoming *Our* Lady, regardless of race, ethnicity, or nationality.

No matter how many names, however, there is only one Mother Mary. Much in the same way that I remain the same woman no matter what descriptive name or nickname is given to me—whether mom, daughter, Cuban, writer, Catholic, or shell collector!

You will hear Mary called many names associated with a place or a country, sometimes because she is said to have appeared to that particular town or nation—or simply because a certain group of believers called on Mary, the Heavenly Mother, to pray and to intercede for them and their needs.

Her First Portrait

The oldest "picture" we have of Mary is a fresco preserved from the beginning of the third century on the walls of the Priscilla Catacombs in Rome, Italy. The catacomb walls, which feature pictures of the good shepherd and depictions of Jesus' miracles from the Gospel stories, such as the healing of the paralytic, also have the scene called the *Virgin with the Child and the Prophet Balaam* (see the image that follows).

The oldest rendition of Mary, found in the Priscilla Catacombs in Rome.

(Public domain)

The painting features Mary seated on a throne and clad with a short-sleeved tunic and a covering on her head. Her body is slightly inclined in an attitude of motherly tenderness toward the child Jesus she holds in her arms.

Also within the Priscilla Catacombs, in an area called the Greek Chapel, another fresco on the ancient walls portrays the *Adoration of the Magi*. In this picture the Madonna is seated on a throne without back and she holds the infant in her arms. The kings, their heads uncovered, are clad in colorful cloaks as they approach the throne in profile, each bearing a gift.

Lord Knows

It is a popular myth that the catacombs, such as the Priscilla Catacombs, were hiding places for Christians during the persecutions, but this is not true. The catacombs were underground burial chambers in the first centuries A.D. Romans preferred cremation, but Christians preferred burial because of beliefs about the resurrection of the body. About ten of the known catacombs are Jewish or some unknown sect. The word catacomb means *the hollows*.

The Many Names of Mary

Whether we call her the Madonna, the Blessed Virgin, the Queen of Heaven, or one of her many other titles, Mary is first and foremost mother of Jesus. And everything we tell about her brings a clearer and more expansive understanding of him.

This Mary of Nazareth, the mother of the son of God, is not like anyone else, and yet as a woman and as a mother she is still a lot like us. Throughout this book, you will explore what all the names given to Mary really mean, why she has so many titles, and why they're relevant today.

Role Playing: Mother of Jesus of Nazareth

I think it's safe to say that everyone knows that Mary is the mother of Jesus. Yet what else we know of Mary from Scriptures and tradition is quite extensive. For example, why is her character so strategically placed in so many Gospel stories and moments?

For starters, there is never a time that Mary is mentioned or referred to in the Christian Scriptures where she is not telling us something about this son of hers named Jesus!

At the risk of stating the obvious, the Gospels and the other texts of what's commonly referred to as the New Testament are about Jesus, the Messiah, the son of God the Most High.

In a few Scripture passages Mary plays a central role. In others, she is merely present as these events unfold around her. In either case—and in all cases—she points us toward Jesus, telling us something about her son.

In the story commonly referred to as the Visitation (Luke 1:39–56), Mary goes to see her kinswoman Elizabeth, who is unexpectedly pregnant. When Mary enters the house and is greeted by Elizabeth, John the Baptist's mother, the baby inside Elizabeth leapt in her womb with joy.

Elizabeth, filled with the Holy Spirit, cried out in a loud voice, "Blessed are you, Mary, among all women and blest is the fruit of your womb!"

Elizabeth went on to say, "Who am I that the mother of my Lord should come to me?"

When Elizabeth calls Mary blessed she is announcing her importance as the woman chosen by God to carry his own son. And when Elizabeth goes on to say, "Blest is she who trusted that the Lord's words to her would be fulfilled," she is acknowledging Mary's critical "yes" in the story of salvation.

The Visitation is no casual story. It is a critical and important moment described by the Gospel writer Luke in much detail, and everything about the story testifies and points to an explanation, a declaration, about Jesus' identity.

Christians believe that Jesus is the long-awaited Jewish Messiah, the Savior of the world, and God's only son. In Chapter 5 we will discuss in more detail the significance of the incarnation in salvation history. But for now it's important to know that God worked in history through Mary's "yes," and Elizabeth's acknowledgment of that "yes."

In a very real way, this Mary story and others like it become the Gospel in a nutshell, bringing significance to overall themes and making declarations of faith regarding Jesus.

Mary always points us to her son. Of all the things we can learn and describe about Mary, nothing is as critical and important as her role as mother of Jesus.

In future chapters you will read about and survey all the biblical references to Mary, exploring how these stories reveal Mary to us. But above all, you will see what they reveal about her son. You will also read about other ancient sources and traditions that add and complete the picture of what we know about Mary of Nazareth.

Holy Mother
"Mary, my dearest mother, Give me your heart So beautiful, so pure, so Immaculate, so full of love And humility, that I may Receive Jesus as you did— And go in haste to give him To others" —Mother Teresa of Calcutta

What Are Our Sources?

There are quite a few ancient texts that were not included in the canon of the *Bible* that profess to present details about the life of Mary, including the names of her parents (Joachim and Anna) as well as other facts about her early life.

Sunday School

The English form of the Greek name *Biblia*, meaning *books*, the **Bible** is the name given in the fifth century to the entire collection of sacred books, or the "Library of Divine Revelation." Sometimes called the sacred Scriptures, the Bible is the classical name for both the Hebrew Bible of Judaism—as well as the combination of the Old Testament (Hebrew Scriptures) and New Testament of Christianity. The Bible has been nicknamed by many "the good book."

Perhaps the best known of these texts is the *Protevangelium Jacobi* (the first gospel of James), dating back to approximately 150 A.D.

Other sources provide details on Mary's life, such as a collection of fifth-century Ethiopian legends called *The Transitus Mariae*, and *The Golden Legend* by Jacobus de Voragine (around 1260 A.D.), which chronicles many legends about saints' lives that also include details about Mary's life.

As Marian scholars continually remind us, none of the details outlined in these sources are as trustworthy as those in the Bible. Yet it is important to recognize that these stories exist—and that these legends have influenced both the individuals and the community of believers, including the way the Christian church celebrates some of these events in the life of Jesus.

The Bible

No other source contributes to the portrait of Mary like the Gospel of Luke and the Acts of the Apostles, both attributed to Luke, the disciple of Jesus, as author.

It is in Luke that we find the details of Jesus' birth, the pregnancies of Mary and Elizabeth, and the description of the shepherds. Luke also gives us stories of the child Jesus through the presentation of Jesus in the temple, and of his journey to Jerusalem with Mary and Joseph when Jesus was 12 years old.

But in addition to Luke, other Scripture sources, and biblical scholarship, I will use oral traditions, stories, and artistic portrayals of Mary throughout the centuries to guide our understanding of what makes Mary unique.

To get a complete picture of Mary, we must dig beneath the surface of the various texts and try to get to the heart of this woman.

We will take that step by examining her qualities and learning how she lived her faith so that we can know her heart. It is critical to hear what believers and nonbelievers have said about her if we are to understand her importance. It is essential that we ponder the qualities that make Mary who she was and is if we are to incorporate her unique role in the Christian tradition.

Recent Texts

In addition to the Bible and other ancient texts, there are also more recent documents claiming to present details about Mary's life that are based on private revelation through various believers' mystical experiences.

Mystics have been around since before Christ, and there has been a strong mystic tradition in the Christian Church from the beginning. Mystics are people with a unique spiritual consciousness of the reality of God. Throughout history, some mystics have written down (for others) accounts of their prayer experience because of the revelations and insights about the Divine that they offer to the body of believers.

Although mystics usually experience and tell us about God in terms of character qualities, this "information" also includes facts or details.

Even contemporary mystics such as the visionaries in Medjugorje (one of the modern sites in Croatia where Mary is said to be appearing to a group of children) allege that they have received supernatural or divine revelations revealing specific details of Mary's life, including her birth date!

Like an evolving colorful mosaic, each story we know of Mary—whether through Biblical sources, oral tradition, or artistic renditions—portrays a woman of faith whose love for God and trust in his providence were the compass of her life.

Mary provokes us, prodding us to respond to the deepest question of our heart— "What is the purpose of life? Why am I here? Is there more to life than the suffering I see around me and the few fleeting moments of joy?"

Just as Mary heard the proclamation that God was to be born in human form and believed it, each person who has heard the story of Jesus in the past two millennia has had to make a choice: is Jesus who he says he is?

Mary can and does lead us as we undertake this journey.

The Least You Need to Know

◆ The Annunciation was the moment in which God's messenger told Mary that she would become mother to Jesus.

◆ The Christian church proclaimed Mary the Mother of God over 1570 years ago.

◆ Mary always points us to her son, Jesus.

◆ Mary's unique embodiment as both virgin and mother emphasizes her special place in Christian history.

Chapter 2

Setting the Stage

In This Chapter

- Finding Nazareth
- Jews in the Roman Empire
- How the Bible was put together
- The importance of oral tradition

It is quite remarkable that the three great monotheistic religions—Judaism, Christianity, and Islam—all emerged out of the region that we now know as Israel and the Palestinian territories. Smaller in square miles than the state of New Jersey, this Middle Eastern world is a paradox. Great proclamations of truth, justice, mercy, and love have been coupled with intense religious and ethnic hatred and fighting.

In the past 2,000 years, it has been a Roman province, a Crusader kingdom, and a part of the Ottoman Empire. It's precisely this amazing amalgamation of complicated history, and how evident it still is today, that impressed me the most on my first trip to the Middle East.

Whatever else can be said about that part of the world, however, we can add with confidence that its people have transformed and defined the course of human history. It's true! In getting to know Mary of Nazareth, therefore, it is important to first understand a little bit about her world.

Where in the World?

Nestled between the easternmost edge of the Mediterranean Sea and the country of Jordan, the northern half of Israel is a lush region with green valleys, forests, fertile farmland, and the lovely Sea of Galilee.

This is also serious Bible territory. It is here that Jewish scholars produced the *Talmud* and the *Kabbalah*. In Galilee (as it is still known today) Jesus grew up with Mary and Joseph and did most of his ministry.

Sunday School

The **Talmud** is a collection of ancient Rabbinic writings that is considered the basis of religious authority in Orthodox Judaism. The Talmud includes discussions on Jewish law, Jewish ethics and morality, customs, legends, and other stories. The **Kabbalah** (or Kabala, Kabalah, and other variations) is a body of mystical teachings, rabbinical in origin, which are based on a mysterious interpretation of the Hebrew Scriptures.

The Region of Galilee

The name Galilee, from the Hebrew word *Galil*, or "to roll," meant a circle or district. Not only is this Mary's native homeland, this is the region where Jesus began his ministry, performed many of his miracles, and found his disciples.

The Galilee region includes mountain ranges rising to a height of 4,000 feet in Upper Galilee, and to 1,800 feet in Lower Galilee. The land here is considered very fertile and productive, especially in the southern part, which has more valleys and plains.

Safed, a sacred Jewish city and modern-day artist colony, is the main city in the northern Galilean region. And Nazareth is its chief city in the south.

Jews from Galilee spoke a distinct dialect and had particular business, family, and religious customs that made them stand out to other Jews, and especially to people from Jerusalem.

According to historians, both Christianity and Judaism flourished in the Galilean region under the Roman Empire, as evidenced by the ruins of ancient synagogues, churches, and monasteries from that period, which were destroyed by Muslims in later centuries.

Lord Knows

The Roman Empire is a broad name given to the lengthy administration that succeeded the Roman Republic. At its greatest extent, the Empire included territories from Britain and Germany to North Africa and the Persian Gulf. After the year 395 A.D., it was divided into the Byzantine Empire and the Western Roman Empire. The last emperor of the West, Romulus Augustus, was ousted by the Goths in 476 A.D., but the Byzantine Empire survived for another 1,000 years.

Exactly Where Is Nazareth?

Mary was born and lived in the town of Nazareth, located geographically in the center of this region, almost exactly halfway between the Sea of Galilee (18 miles to the east) and the Mediterranean Sea (21 miles to the west) and 81 miles due north of Jerusalem.

In Nazareth, the angel appeared to Mary announcing Jesus. And it is here that Jesus lived with his mother until the age of thirty, when he began his years of public ministry and preaching.

The town of Nazareth is in the most southerly hills of the Lebanon range, just before it drops down to the Plain of Esdraelon. The town itself lies between hills in a hollow plateau about 1,200 feet above the level of the Mediterranean.

Because it has such a prominent place in the Christian tradition, it is ironic that Nazareth is not mentioned at all in the Hebrew Scriptures, although we know from various sources that the town was important enough in Mary and Jesus' time to have a synagogue.

Modern-day Nazareth has a population of over 52,000 residents. One of its main attractions is the Church of the Annunciation, which stands on the site traditionally believed to be where Mary lived during Gabriel's birth announcement to her. This particular church is the fifth structure to be built on this spot, and it incorporates fragments of some of the earlier buildings, including a fifth-century Byzantine church.

A *Very* Brief Historical Snapshot

The Roman Empire is the term conventionally used to describe the dominion that succeeded the Roman Republic during the time of Emperor Augustus, who ruled from 27 B.C. to 14 A.D.—which sets us exactly during Mary's life and the birth of Jesus.

At its greatest, the Roman Empire encompassed territories stretching from Britain and Germany to North Africa and the Persian Gulf. The traditional date used for naming the end of the empire is 476 A.D., when the last emperor of the Western Roman Empire was deposed.

Life in ancient Rome revolved around the city of Rome, home to monumental structures like the Coliseum, theaters, gymnasiums, as well as many taverns and public baths.

But the vast majority of the people in the empire never made it to Rome, experiencing instead the empire's power through regional procurators who were in many ways quite autonomous.

In the ancient Jewish world, the separate kingdoms of Israel and Judah lost their autonomy to the Roman Empire during the first century B.C. by becoming first a client kingdom, and then one of its provinces. From about the year 6 A.D., they were ruled by Roman procurators who were responsible for maintaining peace and collecting taxes.

The Roman Empire and the Jews

From the development of the arch in architecture to poetry and sculpture, the Roman Empire's influence on government, law, culture, art, and many other aspects of Western life remains undeniable.

Slaves and slavery were part of the social order. In the eyes of the Roman law, status mattered, and all people were not equal. Your status helped to define everything about what you could do, even how you dressed. In addition to slaves and free inhabitants, the Roman system also distinguished between citizens and noncitizens.

Within this very elaborate and prejudiced class system, the Jews and their differing religious beliefs were often unpopular. This meant that close-knit Jewish communities developed and thrived in most towns in order to enable Jews to maintain and subsist within their own religious laws and practices.

Mary and Joseph, as members of the Jewish culture and faith, lived under the rule of the Roman Empire.

Even though they found Jewish religious practices bizarre and alien, the ruling Romans only cared that Jews be peaceable, which meant that, in general, the Romans tried to ensure the Jews' freedom of worship.

Jews in the Roman Empire, therefore, were not persecuted for religious reasons. However, if there was ever a question of political unrest, among the Jews or other ethnic groups, the Romans did not hesitate to immediately extinguish the conflict or subdue the people involved.

From the biblical stories of Mary and Joseph's early years, we know that they were law-abiding Jewish citizens within the Roman Empire. They followed Jewish religious practices, and they obeyed the dictates of the Romans.

A good example of this takes place in the narrative of the birth of Jesus, when Joseph and a pregnant Mary travel from Nazareth in Galilee to the town of Bethlehem in Judea, to register as part of a census ordered by Caesar Augustus. (Luke 2:1–5)

Women in the Roman Empire

Within the class-structure of the Roman Empire, historians generally agree that the woman's place was basically indoors, taking care of the family and household.

A woman lived under the protection of the head of the household, usually her father or husband. She was not entitled to public office or to participate in political activities in general. Even when accompanied, travel for women was all but out of the question.

In the Roman culture, everything classified and categorized your class. Even the color and type of clothes you wore labeled your class—which made your status public for all to see.

Romans even differentiated in class and privilege between groups of families, or *gens*, that shared a common name and a belief in a shared mutual ancestor. And women often carried a female version of this *gens* or identification, which makes it extremely difficult for historians to disentangle the individual identity of women in documents that have been preserved.

The lack of individual identity for women in the Roman Empire stands in stark contrast to the way Jesus referred to and addressed many women in the Gospels.

References to women by name in ancient sources are scarce, making the specific written references to Mary and other women in Jesus' life quite noteworthy.

Jewish Women in Mary's Era

Collecting evidence about the life of women in the Roman Empire—and Jewish women, in particular—is a complicated process involving the discernment of often completely different kinds of information.

In other words, it's very difficult to make absolute statements to describe the life of Jewish women, like Mary (see the mosaic that follows).

An up-close look at Mary's face; a mosaic, from the Cathedral of Our Lady of Perpetual Help in Oklahoma City.

© *Anamaría Scaperlanda-Ruiz*

Traditionally the answer has been to point to certain texts, laws, or even art from that period and to derive a conclusion from them. But, at best, this combined information gives us a portrait of a hollow woman, emphasizing one particular cultural practice.

For example, some historians emphasize the evidence that women became the property of their fathers and husbands, an idea foreign to our Western mind.

Yet even this piece of evidence is not absolute.

Lord Knows

Much in the same way that Rome was the center of life—both in culture and government—in the Roman Empire, Jerusalem and its holy Temple were the center of Jewish faith and Jewish worship, primarily in the offering of sacrifices. Because to pronounce God's holy name is prohibited in Jewish law, the Hebrew name for the Temple, Beit HaMikdash, translates as *The Holy House*, a name given only to the Temple in Jerusalem.

There is documented evidence from early papyrus providing proof that Jewish women were involved in commerce in the first century, and that at least some women were able to act legally on behalf of themselves and their children. This is incredible!

A recent study of women in early Jewish synagogues even presents evidence that women held offices in local synagogues in their own right, an idea that is not generally known.

In addition to these examples, there are other factors to consider.

Perhaps the law (as defined by the men who composed it!) tells us about the way that these men think women *should* be, not the way they actually lived! What if the literature or speeches we have from that period celebrate the symbols of womanhood and not the real living women?

In terms of seeing Mary within this reality, however, the most important fact to remember is that Mary was not only a Jewish woman within the heavily classed Roman culture, she was a devout and dutiful Jew.

Mary followed Jewish practices, as well as obeyed Roman laws.

A Jewish Marriage

We know from historians and biblical scholars that in the Jewish culture, girls were considered marriageable somewhere around the age of 12, though obviously the actual age of the bride varied.

Mary's marriage to Joseph would have been arranged by parents, as was the Jewish custom.

What's perhaps most difficult for us to understand is that this matrimonial process consisted of two steps: a formal exchange of consent before witnesses, and the later taking of the bride to the groom's home.

Although one might use the term "marriage" to define the second step, in legal terms, it would be more appropriate to apply "marriage" to the first step, because it gave the man rights over the girl.

As has already been noted, the Gospels make it clear that Mary and Joseph followed Jewish law and were both devoted to their faith, observing the various aspects of the law. This is certainly true of their marriage.

And this is what makes the story of the annunciation such a scandal. We know from the language used that Mary and Joseph would have been in the first step of the marriage process, that is, bound to one another but not living together.

Mary's pregnancy at this stage would not have been tolerated in Jewish culture because it would have meant either sex between the couple before the proper time or sex with someone else—adultery, for which the penalty was death.

But in addition to being an upright Jew, Joseph was a merciful man, and this, too, is part of the wedding story. In spite of learning the news of Mary's pregnancy, Joseph chose not to exercise his right to hold Mary accountable in a public accusation—by stoning—within Jewish law. Instead, Joseph decided to divorce her, to break their marriage process, quietly.

Ultimately, however, the angel of the Lord appeared to Joseph in a dream and told him not to fear taking Mary as his wife, explaining that she had conceived this child through the Holy Spirit. The Lord also told Joseph that Mary would have a son and that they were to name him Jesus because he would be the savior of his (Jewish) people.

Stained glass image of the marriage ceremony of Mary and Joseph from the Cathedral of Our Lady of Perpetual Help in Oklahoma City.

© Anamaría Scaperlanda-Ruiz

A Word About the Bible

Speaking of history, let's back up for a minute and look at the process that brought together these stories and their texts to become the Bible, as we know it today.

The books of the Bible that are accepted as Holy Scripture are referred to as the *canon*, from the Greek word Kanon, for *measuring* or *rule*.

The early church set the canon of the New Testament at the Councils of Hippo (393 A.D.) and Carthage (397 A.D.), which also confirmed the texts in the Old Testament from the code of Hebrew Scriptures. The church believed then, and believes now, that the canon of Scripture was set under the guidance of the Holy Spirit.

Why the Different Number of Books?

This might seem like an obvious thing to say, but it is important to note that the Bible is not one single text, but a collection of books. As was previously noted, sometimes one speaks of what's written in the Bible by calling it the Sacred Scriptures, from the Latin *scriptura* ("writings").

The Hebrew Bible consists of 39 books written by many different writers, in different languages, over a span of several centuries before Christ.

In the Christian Bible, the 27 books of the New Testament, written originally in Greek, are all about Jesus, the Christ, the Messiah, and about his followers who were the early church. They were written approximately between 50 and 125 A.D.

Catholic Bibles contain seven more books than Protestant Bibles do, all from the Hebrew Scriptures: Tobit, Judith, Wisdom, Sirach, Baruch, and 1 and 2 Maccabees. Protestants call the books *Apocryphal* and consider them to be noncanonical; Catholics consider them to be inspired, labeling the books as *Deuterocanonical*.

Protestant Bibles match the present-day Jewish canon, and Catholic Bibles follow the Jewish canon called the *Septuagint*, used by the apostles and the early church.

The New Testament books begin with four Gospels—Matthew, Mark, Luke, John—and include the Acts of the Apostles, which records the early Christian church, as well as many epistles or letters. The order of the books does not represent the order in which the books were actually written.

The Noncanonical Texts

Many early Christian texts were proposed as additions to the New Testament but were rejected by the major canons.

Sometimes called apocryphal, these noncanonical texts have been considered fictional or of lesser value than the canonical works. They include Gospels, New Testament acts, and apocalyptic (or end of the world) writings.

Among this literature, there are a number of ancient texts that provide information specific to Mary. The *Protevangelium Jacobi*, or first gospel of James (c. 150), for example, examines Mary's early life and gives us details such as the names of Mary's parents, Joachim and Anna.

Unfolding Oral and Written History

After the death of Jesus, stories of his teachings spread by word of mouth from community to community.

A major moment in this unfolding history of Christianity was the conversion of Saul, who became the apostle Paul, and who authored many of the letters, or epistles, that became part of the Christian Bible.

In Chapter 9 of the Acts of the Apostles, we read about a violent man named Saul who for many years persecuted "the Lord's disciples," actively seeking to arrest and take to Jerusalem "anyone he might find, man or woman, living according to the new way" (Acts 9:2).

Yet after his conversion to Christianity, this same man took on a new name, Paul, and became a major missionary of the faith, preaching to Jews and non-Jews alike.

Much in the same way that we would use our country's efficient and well-developed interstate system to travel cross-country, Paul, a Roman citizen who was very familiar with the Roman system of roads, put it to good use!

Paul preached and wrote to the communities in the empire's great cities, Ephesus, Philippi, Corinth, Athens, and others, speaking to people in their homes and synagogues. He traveled some ten thousand miles across regions and countries ruled by the Roman Empire.

In a very real way, it is accurate to describe the Gospels as developing backwards. The oldest "preaching" about Jesus, as witnessed in the text of the Acts of the Apostles, concerned Jesus' death and his resurrection. This preaching became the account of the passion and death of Jesus, which eventually developed into the oldest consecutive written narrative about him.

As more people came to faith through this proclamation of Jesus' death and resurrection, the early Christians began to focus on the stories and words from Jesus that they had been told. These collections of sayings, parables, and miracles turned into logical, cohesive records of the ministry of Jesus.

A major historical shift took place when Roman emperor Nero, trying to divert attention away from himself, blamed the burning of the city of Rome on the strange new religious sect called the Christians.

This took place a mere thirty years after Jesus' crucifixion, while Jesus' followers were actively and progressively spreading the Jesus story throughout the Empire.

At this point, the Christians were viewed with great suspicion, and their practices, such as breaking bread together and love feasts, were seen as very strange by the Romans.

> ### Lord Knows
>
> The fifth book in the New Testament, the Acts of the Apostles is considered to be written by Luke, a skilled author who provides a historical account of the early years of the Christian church. Acts is a companion text to the Gospel of Luke. It records the history of the Jerusalem church and details the missionary and preaching activity of Peter and Paul.

So it wasn't very difficult for Nero to influence public opinion and convince the Romans that it was the bizarre Christians who had set Rome on fire.

Nero collected all the Christians, torturing and executing them in horrid public exhibitions.

Paradoxically, it was Nero's public persecution and execution of Christians that strengthened and drew together the community of Christian believers.

By the end of the second century, an official Christian creed was being written and adopted—not long after the Gospel of John was written.

In 313 A.D., Emperor Constantine accepted Christianity in an official act called the Edict of Milan. Christianity became the official religion of the Roman Empire at the Council of Nicaea in 325 A.D.

A Chronology: How the "New" Testament Was Written

The earliest New Testament documents are the epistles of Paul, written in each case to meet particular needs of various local Christian communities.

For example, the first letter of Paul to the community of Corinth, Greece (1 Corinthians in the New Testament), urges uniformity of belief and aims to correct some of the erroneous opinions that he heard were affecting the community.

Although all four Gospels record the words and deeds of Jesus, culminating in the story of his Passion and death, each Gospel is written in a distinct and personal style, and addresses different early communities. We will discuss in detail each Gospel in the next section of the book and how each one presents Mary's role in the Christian story.

> **Holy Mother**
>
> "Such was Mary that her life alone is a lesson for all … Let the virginity and the life of Mary be portrayed before us as in a picture from which as from a mirror is reflected the beauty of chastity and the loveliness of virtue."
>
> —Saint Ambrose (c. 340)

The dating of the New Testament books has been described as a roller-coaster ride, a rather appropriate metaphor.

Originally, the ancient view regarding the Bible was simply to say that each book was written by one of the apostles, or by a disciple of an apostle, shortly after the resurrection of Jesus. Scholars later contradicted this notion, saying that many of the books in the New Testament were written much later, in the second century.

But as Scripture scholarship and the study of language continue to advance, a good number of scholars are bringing the dates backward, closer to the ancient position!

Setting aside the veracity of all the specific years—which are only estimations, at best—there are several generalities that can be named.

The Gospel of Mark is believed to be the oldest of the four Gospels, written in the late 60s (though some say as early as the early 40s).

Most Scripture scholars agree that Matthew and Luke were next, written in the 80s (or as early as the 50s), and the last Gospel to be written was John, sometime in the 90s.

The Least You Need to Know

◆ Mary was born and lived in Nazareth, in the region of Galilee.

◆ As a Roman subject and a Jew, Mary obeyed Roman law and followed Jewish practices.

◆ Two major events in the spreading of the Christian message were the conversion of Paul and Nero's public persecution of believers.

◆ The story of Jesus was written down backward: first outlining his death and resurrection, then his preaching, and finally, his birth.

A Glimpse at the Mother of Jesus

In This Chapter

- ◆ Early Christian sources on Mary

- ◆ The facts we have reconstructed about her life

- ◆ Mary's genealogy and relatives

- ◆ Did Mary have other children?

Like getting to know a new classmate or office acquaintance, becoming familiar with Mary involves learning both her facts and her personal stories.

What we "know" of Mary of Nazareth is actually made up of a blend of many sources: the chronicles in the New Testament, other (nonbiblical) accounts dating back to the early Christian era, and tradition. This chapter provides an overview of these sources and what they tell us about Mary.

Anna and Joachim: Mary's Parents

All the information we have about Mary's parents, Joachim and Anna, come from non-canonical sources, such as the gospel of the Nativity of Mary, the gospel of Pseudo-Matthew and the *Protoevangelium*, or gospel of James (see the image that follows).

A stained glass image of Mary with Anna, her mother, from the Cathedral of Our Lady of Perpetual Help in Oklahoma City.

© Anamaría Scaperlanda-Ruiz

As we have already noted, although the first gospel of Saint James is not included in the canon of the Bible, this second century text was an important source of what came to be accepted tradition.

In other words, whether the content became an official part of the Bible or not, its stories and ideas influenced both the individual faith of Christians, as well as the general body of devotion of and knowledge about Mary through the centuries.

In addition to the gospel of James, several early Christian church historians, including, John Damascene, Germanus of Constantinople, and Gregory of Nyssa affirm the belief regarding the names of Mary's parents—both considered saints by the Catholic and Orthodox churches.

The gospel of James is also the chief source for the tradition that says that the earliest home of Joachim and Anna was located in Sephoris, a city about four miles northwest of Nazareth. Sephoris was the capital of the province of Galilee as well as an intellectual center of the Jewish religion. It remained an important city for the region until the end of the fourth century.

> **Lord Knows**
>
> The feast of Joachim and Anna is celebrated in the Roman Catholic Church on July 26. In some cultures, this is used as a feast to honor grandparents, reminding the grandparents of their responsibility to develop faith in the next generations—and reminding the young to treat grandparents with value and respect.

Tradition that was passed down through the centuries says that Joachim and Anna lived in Jerusalem when Mary was born. In commemoration, as early as the fifth century the Roman empress Eudocia built a church over the place where it was believed that they had lived.

Many of the oral traditions and legends, in fact, are confirmed and expanded on as archeologists discover and identify these ancient structures. By recreating the early constructions, the archaeological findings have identified what the people of that time period believed—and even shown us how they worshipped.

This is especially true in recreating early belief regarding Mary since so much of what we know about Mary has been passed down through oral and other traditions.

Genealogy

Learning about where we come from, both geographically and genealogically, is always important in helping us better understand who we are. Mary's genealogy is especially important because of what it tells us about her son.

As Saint Paul notes in his letter to the church community in Rome, Jesus Christ was "descended from David according to the flesh." (Romans 1:3) So it follows, then, that if Mary were not of Davidic descent, then her son Jesus, who was conceived by the Holy Spirit, could not be of the seed of David!

Lord Knows

King David was one of the most well-known kings of ancient Israel, and the most mentioned man in the Hebrew Bible! His 48-year-rule is recorded in the books of Samuel, Chronicles, and Kings. According to 2 Samuel (7:12–13), God was so pleased with David's life that he promised David his family lineage would go on forever. Jews believe that the Messiah will be a direct descendent of David, and Christians trace Jesus' lineage back to him.

Sunday School

Prophecies are revelations about events in the future, often about a particular period or about a certain group of people. A prophecy, however, is not merely a prediction, but one that is made by divine inspiration.

Many texts in the Hebrew Scriptures prophesize, or foretell, facts about the coming of the Messiah. One key factor in these *prophecies* is that the Messiah would be a descendent of King David.

In the first chapter of the Gospel of Luke we hear of Jesus' Davidic descent. As the story of the birth announcement progresses, the angel Gabriel says to Mary that her son will be called "Son of the Most High," and that the Lord God will give him "the throne of David his father."

Other Relatives

The most important of Mary's relatives must be the one we know the most about!

Again, from the first chapter of Luke, we know that Elizabeth was a "kinswoman" to Mary, although we don't know exactly what that relationship was. It has been a common interpretation that Elizabeth was Mary's cousin.

Elizabeth was a descendant of Aaron (Luke 1:5) and the wife of Zechariah, a priest of the priestly class of Abijah (Luke 1:5)—both of whom were "just in the eyes of God, blamelessly following all the commandments and ordinances of the Lord." (Luke 1:6)

Elizabeth's most important role, however, was as mother of John the Baptist, who preceded Jesus and "went about the entire region of Jordan proclaiming a baptism of repentance which led to the forgiveness of sins." (Luke 3:3)

Like countless prophets in the Hebrew Scriptures, John's role was to call all to repentance, and in so doing to prepare the way for Jesus and his message of salvation.

In the Gospels of Luke, Mark, and Matthew we also hear that John the Baptist baptized Jesus in the River Jordan, a moment when the skies opened up and a voice from heaven declared, "This is my beloved Son. My favor rests on him." (Matthew 3:17; Mark 1:11; and Luke 3:22)

In the Gospel of John, it is John the Baptist who testifies out loud, "This is God's chosen One." (1:34) John is also the one who sees Jesus walking by and literally points him out to the disciples, "Look! There is the Lamb of God!" (1:36)

An Ordinary Life

There are no pictures preserved for us to know what Mary looked like, physically. As early theologians pointed out from the beginning, by not having a real external image of Mary, we are freed to view Mary as she best speaks to us!

Holy Mother
"I love Mary so much, all my daughters are named Mary. Mary Alice, Mary Jo, Mary Jean." —Mary Joseph Zarrella (c. 1961), Tell City, Indiana

The mere fact that her story has survived over the past two thousand years testifies to a community of believers who recognized that Mary told them something important about Jesus, the central figure of their faith.

Mary's Place of Birth

When it comes to Mary and Jesus, the sources of information as well as their accuracy can, and have been, broadly debated by Biblical scholars for centuries.

As we have already discussed, some texts became part of the Biblical canon itself; other ancient texts were not included due to questions about their authenticity or accuracy. There are three completely different traditions, for example, about the place of birth of Mary of Nazareth.

The first tradition says that Mary was born in Bethlehem. The second tradition placed the birth in Sephoris. And the third and most probable tradition is that Mary was born in Jerusalem, where her parents are believed to have lived and died.

Again, the important thing to remember is this: from her ancestors to where she lived after *Pentecost*, everything that we know about Mary, whether notated in Scripture or passed down through tradition, was considered important because in some way it led Christian believers to a clearer understanding of who this Jesus was—and his role as the long-awaited Messiah.

> ### Sunday School
>
> The day of **Pentecost** is noted in the Christian church as the day on which the Holy Spirit descended upon the apostles, and on which, under Peter's preaching, many thousands were converted in Jerusalem (Acts 2). The Pentecost was an annual pilgrimage festival to Jerusalem, which found the disciples, including Mary, in one place (Acts 2:1). The Greek name for the Jewish feast of Pentecost means "fiftieth (day)," referring to the distance, in days, from the Passover.

What's in a Name

The name Mary is adapted from the Latin and Greek Maria, and from the Hebrew Mariam or Miriam, a most typical name for a Jewish woman of that time.

The name Miriam was not only characteristic in the Jewish tradition, it was also a popular name among Mary's Jewish contemporaries because of the first recorded Miriam—the sister of Moses and Aaron, whose story was told and well known from the Hebrew Scriptures.

As Jewish scholar David Flusser points out, this great significance of women in early Christianity is clearly to be seen in connection with the high regard Jesus himself afforded women. And the important position of women since Jesus throws additional clear light on the devotion of Mary in the early Christian church.

A Temple Virgin

According to at least two early noncanonical texts, Joachim and Anna presented the child Mary in the Temple when she was three years old, and at this time, Mary made a vow of virginity (see the image that follows).

Gregory of Nyssa (died c. 385) and Germanus of Constantinople (c. 715) go along with this testimony, although the feast of the presentation (commemorating the presentation of Mary to the Temple) is mentioned for the first time in a document from 1166.

From Constantinople and the Eastern church tradition, the feast was then introduced into the Western church, where it eventually appeared in several documents and became a feast of the whole church.

A stained glass image of the presentation of Mary in the Temple from the Cathedral of Our Lady of Perpetual Help in Oklahoma City.

© *Anamaría Scaperlanda-Ruiz*

Other Children

While agreeing about the fact that Mary was a virgin when she conceived Jesus by the power of the Holy Spirit, Christian traditions differ on the question of whether Mary had other children after Jesus, or whether she was perpetually a virgin.

What the Bible Says

There are about 10 references in the New Testament to "the brothers of Jesus" or to his "sisters."

Here are a few:

"He was still addressing the crowds when his mother and his brothers appeared outside to speak with him." (Matthew 12:46)

"His mother and his brothers arrived, and as they stood outside they sent word to him to come out. The crowd seated around him told him, 'Your mother and your brothers and sisters are outside asking for you.' He said in reply, 'Who are my mother and my brothers?' And gazing around him at those seated in the circle he continued, 'These are my mother and my brothers. Whoever does the will of God is brother and sister and mother to me.'" (Mark 3:31–35)

"His brothers came to be with him, but they could not reach him because of the crowd. He was told, 'Your mother and your brothers are standing outside and they wish to see you.' He told them in reply, 'My mother and my brothers are those who hear the word of God and act upon it.'" (Luke 8:19–21)

"After this he went down to Capernaum, along with his mother and brothers [and his disciples] but they stayed there only a few days." (John 2:12)

These stories might all sound straightforward, but in reality, the question of whether or not Mary had other children besides Jesus can't be totally settled by Scripture.

The differences in belief about Mary's virginity and whether she had other children besides Jesus involve different interpretations based on language and translations from the original text.

First of all, the word *brethren* or *brothers* is translated from the Greek *adelphos*, a term that is not restricted to the literal meaning we give it in English of a full or half brother. As Scripture scholars point out, *adelphos* was used to describe any number of kin or relatives, as well as other close relationships, including that of disciples.

The same is true for the word *adelphe* (sister) and the plural *adelphoi* (brothers).

To make it even more complex, neither Hebrew nor Aramaic—which was the language spoken by Jesus and his disciples—have a word equivalent to what we term cousins, so the word *brother* was applied to all close relations, including cousins as well as relatives by marriage.

How to Understand the Culture

Besides specifics to language and translations, it is important in examining this information to also try to understand the Jewish definition of family.

Two good cultural equivalents of the extended understanding of family in our modern culture would be the Hispanic and Asian cultures.

In the Hispanic world, for example, a reference to family would not have the immediate or nuclear family understanding that most non-Hispanic whites in the United States would assume.

As a Cuban-American, the term *my family* applies not only to my husband and children, but also to my parents, brother, grandparents, aunts, uncles, cousins. You get the picture. This was quite a different shift in thinking for my non-Hispanic Texan husband when we got married 24 years ago!

Much in the same way, for the Jews of Jesus' day there was no distinction between immediate and extended family, as we use those terms today. In fact, the Hebrew language had not even developed a word for *cousin*, because this relationship was thought of simply as another family member.

Finally, there are two Scripture references that provide important clues as to whether Jesus had brothers, at least in the American culture sense of that term.

First, James and Joseph, who are named as brothers of Jesus in Mathew 13:55, appear to be sons of another Mary (Matthew 27:56), a disciple of Christ whom Matthew calls "the other Mary."

And second, when Jesus is dying on the cross, there is a moment when he entrusts his mother to the care of his beloved disciple. (John 19:26) But as a member of a strong Jewish family, Jesus would have had no right to give Mary to the care of one of his disciples if, indeed, he had had brothers. Following Jewish custom, his brothers would have been entrusted with taking care of Mary after Jesus died.

Protestant Understanding

It might seem odd to some people today, but the first sixteenth-century Protestant *Reformers* took for granted and accepted Marian doctrines.

Lord Knows
The Reformation (and **reformers**) was a sixteenth-century religious movement throughout Western Europe that aimed at reforming and reorganizing specific doctrines and practices of the Christian church. Martin Luther started the main Reformation. The Reformation ended in division and the establishment of new religious institutions, such as Lutheranism, Anabaptists, and the Reformed churches. It also led to what is known as the Counter-Reformation within the Roman Catholic Church.

In fact, the original Protestant Reformers were in agreement over many ideas that we now consider divisive about Mary—including both her virginal conception *and* her perpetual virginity.

As it was for the early Christians, for these early reformers Mary's perpetual virginity personified her unique and honored role in the Christian faith.

Martin Luther defended Mary's virginity as part of the mystery of Christ. He noted, "It is an article of faith that Mary is Mother of the Lord and still a virgin … Christ, we believe, came forth from a womb left perfectly intact."

French reformer John Calvin was not as lavish as Martin Luther in his praise of Mary, but he never denied her perpetual virginity, and often referred to Mary as "Holy Virgin."

Still, the idea that Mary remained a virgin after Jesus is an alien one for contemporary Protestants, who continue to interpret the Gospels to conclude that Jesus had siblings.

Holy Mother

"It was given to her what belongs to no creature, that in the flesh she should bring forth the Son of God … I firmly believe that Mary, according to the words of the Gospel as a pure Virgin brought forth for us the Son of God and in childbirth and after childbirth remained a pure, intact Virgin. The more the honor and love of Christ increases among men, so much the esteem and honor given to Mary should grow."

—Ulrich Zwingli, founder of the Reformation in Switzerland

Prevailing Catholic View

The Roman Catholic and Orthodox traditions, on the other hand, state that Mary not only was a virgin when she conceived and gave birth to Jesus, but also that she remained a virgin after his birth.

This tradition dates back to the early years of the church and to the people's awareness that, as the vessel of God in this world, Mary was truly blessed and holy.

To call Mary *Ever Virgin*, in fact, is an ancient Christian tradition, officially recorded as early as 391 in the Synod of Milan, which put in plain words the ever-virgin theology.

In a spiritual sense, to believe in Mary's perpetual virginity is to recognize that Mary gave herself entirely to her Creator, in both body and soul, therefore belonging only to God. Much like religious women and men today who live a vow of celibacy, Mary's love was deliberately and completely focused on one thing—the perfect love that only God provides.

For early believers, it made sense that Mary's purity and virtuousness be recognized not only in relation to her great faith, but also with regard to her physical form because it was, after all, through her body that the God Most High entered the world!

This is not to say, however, that the Catholic Church sees Mary's virginity as merely symbolic in nature. Nothing would be further from the truth. The liturgy of the Catholic Church unequivocally celebrates Mary as the Ever Virgin.

The Least You Need to Know

- Early noncanonical Christian texts have influenced what we know and recognize about Mary.

- Mary was probably born in Jerusalem, where her parents Anna and Joachim lived.

- Mary's genealogy is important because of what it tells us about Jesus.

- Early Protestant Reformers agreed with current Catholic theology that Mary remained a virgin all of her life.

Part 2

Encountering Mary—As Mother

Mary of Nazareth was many things, but foremost of all, she was a mother. And not just any mother, she was the mother of Jesus the Christ, the long-awaited Jewish Messiah! In fact, from the very first reference to Mary of Nazareth in Scripture at the Annunciation until the last time that she is mentioned in the Christian Bible, Mary is referred to or recognized as the mother of Jesus. That's quite a significant description. But what does it tell us about the portrayal of Mary?

Any woman can testify to the fact that after you give birth, you are forever described as someone's mother! I imagine Mary liked it that way. In this part, we will visit in detail all the references to Mary found in Scripture—first in general, and then by focusing on each major story and how Mary lived it as a mother. Some of these stories will be very familiar; others will surprise you. We will hear and interpret the Annunciation by the angel Gabriel, the birth of Jesus, the presentation of Jesus in the Temple, Mary and Joseph's hasty get-away into Egypt, and the searching for a lost and runaway pre-teen Jesus!

Chapter and Verse

In This Chapter

- Where is Mary in Scripture?
- Prophecies from Hebrew Scripture
- Different authors, different points
- Peter, Paul, and Mary

Mary, the mother of Jesus, appears in all four Gospels, and it is this collection of writings that provides us with the most important witness to Mary found anywhere in Scripture.

Although Mary is mentioned in a good number of passages in the body of the Gospels, by far the vast majority of references to and about Mary take place at the very beginning and the very end of the Gospel narratives. This chapter will review all the passages in Scripture where Mary is mentioned.

Mary in Scripture

The mother of Jesus is referred to only 19 times in all of the New Testament, but this infrequency is disproportionate to her importance in the Christian story.

Mary is most often mentioned in the Gospels of Luke and Matthew, the only two to record the story of the birth of Jesus. It is no surprise, then, that the majority of the biblical references to Mary focus directly on her role as mother of Jesus.

What Scripture tells us about Mary begins with genealogy, if only to emphasize, of course, the fact that Jesus himself was of Davidic descent and the fulfillment of the Hebrew Scriptures.

Lord Knows

Much has been written about the "construction" of the genealogy of Jesus in Matthew's Gospel. But the genealogy is not meant to be historical, or comprehensive, but rather, to teach a lesson. The genealogy incorporates history from Hebrew Scriptures as an invitation to Christians to get to know Jesus by getting to know his "family." In essence, it says, read the Hebrew Scriptures!

Overview of the Scripture References

As you read in previous chapters, Mary's parents are known to us only through non-canonical writings, such as the gospel of Saint James. The New Testament does not mention Joachim and Anna at all, although we do know that Mary lived in Nazareth, a city in Galilee, at the time of the Annunciation. (Luke 1:26)

The two birth narratives (Matthew and Luke) are packed with details about Mary, as each writer skillfully unfolds different pieces of the story. There is so much, in fact, that we are going to break down the pre-birth and birth narratives in more detail in the next chapter.

After the birth story, the Gospels tell us that Mary and Joseph took Jesus to Jerusalem so that he could be presented to the Lord "according to the law of Moses," offering a temple sacrifice of a pair of turtledoves. (Luke 2:22–24)

We also hear that when Jesus was a baby, Mary and Joseph were forced to flee to Egypt for safety, after being warned by the angel of the Lord that Herod wanted to kill Jesus. Herod was clearly threatened and fearful of the news of a Jewish Messiah. (Matthew 2:13–16)

After Herod's death, however, Mary, Joseph, and Jesus returned to Nazareth (Matthew 2:23), where Scripture tells us the family lived until Jesus began his public ministry at the age of 30.

Mosaic of Mary and Jesus from the Cathedral of Our Lady of Perpetual Help in Oklahoma City.

© Anamaría Scaperlanda-Ruiz

In Nazareth, "the child grew in size and strength, filled with wisdom, and the grace of God was upon him." (Luke 3:40)

The only story we have of Mary as the mother of a growing child takes place when Jesus was a pre-teenager. To celebrate the feast of the *Passover* the year that Jesus was 12 years old, the family traveled to Jerusalem, as was their custom every year. (Luke 2:40–51)

But this time, as the parents returned to Nazareth at the end of the feast, Jesus stayed behind. (Luke 3:43) Again, we will discuss this frightening parental event with more detail in Chapter 8.

We hear nothing about the life of Mary between this story and the wedding feast at Cana (John 2:1–12), where an adult Jesus turned water into wine, performing his first miracle—at Mary's request!

There are several Gospel references that tell us that Mary was present during Jesus' three years of adult ministry, as he journeyed from town to town preaching and performing miracles.

> ### Sunday School
>
> The term **Passover** comes from the Hebrew Bible, and it is first mentioned in the Book of Exodus. Passover, also known as *Pesach* or *Pesah*, is a Holy Day observed by several religions, beginning on the evening of the fourteenth day of the Jewish month of Nissan and lasting for seven days. It commemorates the exodus and freedom of the Israelites from Egypt.

Yet Mary's unique and powerful presence is made known once again in the crucifixion story, where she stood at the foot of the cross (John 19:25) and remained faithful to her son until the end of his life.

The final mention of Mary in Scripture takes place in the book of the Acts of the Apostles, where she is listed among the community gathered in Jerusalem between the time of Jesus' ascension to heaven and Pentecost.

When the day of Pentecost came and "found them gathered in one place," it is assumed that *them* is the group previously mentioned in Acts 1:13–14, which included "women in their company, and Mary the mother of Jesus." (Acts 1:14)

The number of references for Mary in Scripture might seem like too few for the mother of Jesus. But in reality they are more than enough to portray the devotion of a mother who not only gave birth to the Messiah, but who actively participated in his life and ministry—and accompanied his disciples even after Jesus' death.

In spite of hardship and persecution, in spite of not fully comprehending the mystery of God made man, the depiction of Mary in Scripture shows us a woman of courage who trusted God's design for her life.

Different Audiences

Each Gospel narrative, like a well-crafted article, emphasizes different themes and ideas regarding Jesus, based on the audience for which it was written.

> **Sunday School**
>
> A **rabbi** is a person trained in Jewish law, ritual, and tradition, and ordained as chief religious official of a synagogue. A rabbi is also considered a scholar who is qualified to interpret Jewish law. Calling someone *rabbi*, however, was also equivalent to *my master*, a Hebrew title of respect for a teacher or spiritual leader. Jesus' followers sometimes called Him rabbi.

The birth narratives in Matthew and Luke are good examples of this difference in purpose. And it explains why different aspects of Mary are emphasized in each Gospel.

For Luke, Jesus came to reconcile the chosen people of God, the Jews, with their creator. But Jesus' message as told to Luke was not political or majestic, as many Jews anticipated. From the beginning, Luke presents us with a completely new way of thinking.

The news of the birth of the Messiah in Luke's story is first proclaimed publicly, not to the *rabbis* or to the ruling class, but to simple, humble shepherds working in the fields!

When the angel of the Lord appeared to them he said, "Tonight, in the city of David, the Messiah has been born. You will find the infant in a manger, wrapped in swaddling clothes. And so the shepherds went in haste, and found Mary and Joseph and the baby lying in a manger." (Luke 2:15–17)

What is more, Luke emphasizes, after they saw the baby, the shepherds understood what had been told to them concerning this child! For Luke, this is the Gospel message, the good news, proclaimed in a nutshell.

It is to the poor, the unimportant, and the ordinary people in the Jewish community that Jesus came, not the high ups, the comfortable, or the important. What is more important, Luke predicts, is that when they hear and see Jesus, these people of humble origins will understand.

Matthew, as we've mentioned, incorporates a genealogy in his narrative, which would be important to the Jews listening to his account.

Matthew also includes in his birth story astrologers from the east guided by a star as they traveled to Bethlehem (Matthew 2:1) to see the newborn king of the Jews.

By including non-Jews in the birth narrative, Matthew emphasizes from the beginning of his Gospel account that the Messiah Jesus came not only for the Jews, but for *all* of humanity!

The star led the astrologers to the place where the child was, Matthew tells us, and entering the house they found the child with Mary, his mother.

Lord Knows

"We Three Kings ..." begins the famous Christmas carol. In reality, we don't know much about "the astrologers from the east" who came to worship Jesus. We don't know how many there were, or that they were kings, or even that they were men! Only that they were familiar enough with the sky to recognize this star as a supernatural phenomenon. Whoever they were, they presented Mary's baby with "gold, frankincense, and myrrh," signs of homage, even to a newborn king.

"They prostrated themselves and did him homage. Then they opened their coffers and presented him with gifts of gold, frankincense, and myrrh." (Matthew 2:9–11) This symbolically shows us that even non-Jews can and do recognize in Mary's son the king of kings.

Prophecies About Mary

There are many passages in the Hebrew Scriptures that Christian biblical scholars single out as prophecies referring to Mary.

Here I will present only two as examples of how Christians regard Mary as part of the fulfillment of God's promise of salvation for his people.

In the culmination of the story of Adam and Eve's ejection from the garden of paradise, God said to the serpent who tempted them, "I will put enmity between you and the woman, and between your offspring and hers. He will strike at your head, while you strike at his heel." (Genesis 3:15)

Because it says, "I will place hostility between you and the woman," the prophecy promises a woman to be victorious over the devil, at least through her offspring.

Christians named this passage as the first promise of a redeemer for mankind—and the woman's offspring as Jesus Christ, the Messiah.

The prophecy in Micah 5:1–2 predicts the place of birth of the Messiah, noting, "But you, Bethlehem-Ephrathah too small to be among the clans of Judah; From you shall come forth for me one who is to be ruler in Israel; Whose origin is from of old, from ancient times. Therefore the Lord will give them up, until the time when she who is to give birth has borne. And the rest of his brethren shall return to the children of Israel."

This is, in fact, the prophecy that the chief priests named for Herod when the astrologers came to him seeking the newborn king of the Jews.

According to this prophecy, the Messiah must be born in Bethlehem, an insignificant town in Judea. Although a descendant of King David, his family will be unknown until the time of the Messiah's birth.

The Mary in Luke

The most intimate and detailed depiction of Mary in the New Testament is found in the Gospel of Luke, where she is given a lot of attention.

Sunday School
The **incarnation** is the belief that the Son of God was conceived in the womb of Mary of Nazareth, and that Jesus is, therefore, true God and true man.

We will discuss later both her beautiful Magnificat of praise (Luke 1:46–55) and the significant encounter that Mary has with Simeon and Anna at the parents' presentation of Jesus in the temple. (Luke 2:25–40) Both scenes are unique to Luke's Gospel.

Luke illustrates in detail for us the now familiar announcement of the angel Gabriel. We've already discussed the Annunciation, and we will come back to some of its themes in the next chapter as we discuss the *incarnation* and the nativity stories.

An ethnic portrayal of a prayerful, pregnant Mary, from the Cathedral in Port-au-Prince, Haiti.

© *María Ruiz Scaperlanda*

One of Luke's main themes throughout the Gospel text is already presented in no uncertain terms as part of the Annunciation—and it is intricately connected to his understanding of Mary. It has to do with the words that the angel Gabriel declared to Mary: "nothing is impossible with God." (Luke 1:37)

This message about God's capabilities is one of Luke's most powerful themes, and it is directly related to his vision of Mary as the model of discipleship. Only someone who is living a committed life of prayer can believe and live this mystery, this reality, that nothing is impossible for God.

Holy Mother

"Mary is in love. She is experiencing the greatest of all human emotions. While carrying within herself the Great High Priest, Mary is already living her own call to priesthood: a call to gather the people of God together in a community of love."
—Patricia McCarthy, *The Scent of Jasmine: Reflections for Peace in Everyday Life* (Liturgical Press, 1995)

Luke is also the only writer to record the episode of the boy Jesus in the temple, again giving us a glimpse into Mary as mother. (Luke 2:51)

But for Luke, Mary is always both mother and disciple. The Mary presented in the Gospel of Luke is one who clearly was the first to receive the news of God's salvation. She was also the first to assent to God's plan, and to proclaim the mysterious reality of a God made human.

The Mary in Matthew

Mary is first mentioned by name in the Gospel of Matthew, as part of Jesus' genealogy: "Jacob was the father of Joseph, the husband of Mary. It was of her that Jesus who is called the Messiah was born." (Matthew 1:16)

Mary is not simply the mother of a child born of royal ancestry, but the mother of the child who is the fulfillment of the royal line of David, and therefore, the long-awaited Messiah!

This presentation of Mary within Jesus' genealogy is a teaching tool used by Matthew to set up his main theme about Mary. For Matthew, Mary's main role is to show how her son Jesus fulfills the prophecies of the Hebrew Scriptures.

Although nothing is said of Joseph prior to the Annunciation, we find in Matthew Joseph's side of the pre-nativity story. It is also in Matthew that we get a glimpse of Jesus' relationship to his earthly father, as the son of the carpenter.

Among all the stories for the years of Jesus' public ministry, Matthew mentions Mary only twice, but in both instances he emphasizes Mary's presence as mother in Jesus' life.

In one scene Mary comes to the place where Jesus is, seeking to speak to Jesus. (Matthew 12:47) In the next chapter, her name is mentioned only in reference to him: "Isn't Mary known to be his mother?" (Matthew 13:55)

But this shouldn't surprise us too much. After all, Matthew seems to be into naming these family relations, and in particular, into seeing women's roles in this personal story.

When the Hebrew Scriptures note a single line of descent, it normally doesn't include women in its list of names. But Matthew includes not one or two, but *four* women in his genealogy of Jesus: Tamar, Rahab, Ruth, and the wife of Uriah (Bathsheba). Why?

Rahab and Ruth, and possibly Tamar and Bathsheba, are non-Israelite women who in spite of being foreigners play an important enough role in Israelite history to be mentioned by name in the Hebrew Scriptures. Both Rahab and Ruth are recorded in Scripture as having professed faith in the God of Israel.

The other two women are central characters in stories about Hebrew heroes. Tamar's scandalous story about her sexual encounter with Judah (Genesis 38) is what keeps in motion the Davidic line. And it was the scandalous sexual union of King David with Bathsheba, wife of Uriah (2 Samuel 11–12), that gave birth to Solomon.

There are many interpretations as to why Matthew listed Jesus' genealogy this way. But my favorite explanation is by Princeton professor Katherine Doob Sakenfeld, who believes that what the four women have in common is not readily visible to the eye.

According to Sakenfeld, like Mary, none of their personal stories fit the way things are "supposed" to be, at least by human standards. Clearly, though, they were the work of God.

The Mary in John

John wrote no birth or infancy stories, and he never even addresses Mary by name.

The first mention of Mary in the Gospel of John is at the story of the wedding at Cana.

John does not call her by name, but simply refers to Mary as "Jesus' mother." And Jesus, in return, addresses her as "woman," a standard form of address that—contrary to what we may assume—implied no rudeness in that setting and culture. It was, in fact, considered entirely courteous, and even a term of honor in Jesus' day, as scholars of the original language note.

In this simple story best known because it became the place for Jesus' first recorded public miracle, it is his mother who notices that there is a need and who asks Jesus to help out, saying simply, "They have no more wine" (John 2:3) for the celebration.

Lord Knows

The Bible clearly condemns drunkenness, but it never prohibits drinking wine in moderation. From the New Testament we know that Jesus himself drank wine, at least often enough to be accused of being a "drunkard" by his critics. (Luke 7:34) Even his first recorded miracle at Cana was to turn water into wine (John 2:1–11)—and not just average wine, but good enough for the waiter in charge to note, "People usually serve the choice wine first ... what you have done is to keep the choice wine until now." (John 2:10)

This is the Mary in John's Gospel—confident, honest, with an obviously intimate and personal relationship with her son. We might not have details from John about the many years that Jesus and Mary lived together, but through this story we can imagine, and we can even appropriately assume that this would not be Mary's first time to make a request of Jesus.

The relationship portrayed here between Mary and Jesus is close and friendly. They were obviously comfortable with each other.

We will look at this story in greater detail in Chapter 9, as well as to its parallel, the crucifixion story, in Chapter 10. In both of these stories from the Gospel of John, Mary is referred to as "the mother of Jesus," and she is addressed by Jesus as "woman."

The Mary in Mark and Paul's Writings

The Gospel of Mark never mentions Joseph, describing Jesus only as "the son of Mary" (Mark 6:3). And it includes only two small stories about Mary, both of which refer to Mary, as opposed to being about or inclusive of Mary.

In the first one, Mark says that Mary and Jesus' brothers were standing outside where Jesus was teaching, prompting the lesson from Jesus that "whoever does the will of God is brother and sister and mother to me." (Mark 3:35)

In the second story, Jesus is in the temple teaching when the local people in Nazareth dismiss him by saying, "Is this not the carpenter, the son of Mary ...?" (Mark 6:3)

This is, however, the first time Mary's name is given chronologically.

Mark's Mary is at best marginal. There simply is not much noted by him about the mother of Jesus, and nothing about Jesus' father.

Because Mark was the first Gospel to be written, it makes sense that his apparent inattentiveness to details about Mary is simply because the Gospel writer was interested in presenting other, more pressing and urgent details about Jesus.

For Mark, the message of Jesus revolves around two titles: "Christ" and "Son of God." All the themes of his narrative are built around these two concepts.

Although Paul doesn't mention Mary by name in any of his letters, he does make references to her. For example, in his letter to the Galatians, Paul writes: "but when the designated time had come, God sent forth his Son born of a woman, born under the law to deliver from the law those who were subjected to it, so we might receive our status as adopted sons. (Galatians 4:4–5)

Like Mark, Paul's concern is always to make specific theological points regarding Jesus' identity. In the case of Galatians, for example, he is merely describing the mystery of the Incarnation, the doctrine that the Son of God was conceived in the womb of Mary and that Jesus is true God and true man.

Mary in Other Second-Century Sources

As we have already mentioned, there are quite a number of ancient texts that have not only survived since the beginning of Christianity, but which have, to a large extent, supplemented the canon of the New Testament and shaped Christian tradition. This is especially true regarding what is accepted and thought about Mary of Nazareth.

Although we know from the Pentecost passage in the Acts of the Apostles that Mary was present on the day the community received the Holy Spirit, we don't have any further specific mention of her in the New Testament.

What we know of her post-Pentecostal life, in fact, all comes from tradition.

One of the most influential, perhaps *the* most influential, ancient text on Mary that is not a part of the New Testament is the *Protevangelium* or gospel of James.

The author of this text claims to be no less than the apostle James, although the manuscript is attributed to the second century.

The gospel of James is entirely focused on Mary: her birth, her youth, her pregnancy. The gospel opens with the miraculous conception of Mary by an elderly Joachim and Anna, who had been childless all of their marriage. Like Luke and Matthew, the text of the Gospel of James describes the Annunciation, but it ends with Mary's delivery of the baby Jesus.

To state the obvious, this text is highly focused on Mary, and not on Jesus.

Holy Mother
Hail, Holy Queen, Mother of Mercy, our Life, our Sweetness, and our Hope. To Thee do we cry, poor banished children of Eve. To Thee do we send up our sighs mourning and weeping in this valley of tears. Turn then, most gracious Advocate, Thine Eyes of Mercy toward us, and after this our exile show us the Blessed Fruit of thy Womb, Jesus. O clement, O loving, O sweet Virgin Mary. Pray for us O Holy Mother of God That we may be made worthy of the promises of Christ.
—Also known as the *Salve Regina*, ancient prayer of the Christian church (c. 1000), author unknown

It is ironic, however, that the gospel of James is so little known by Christians, especially because it is specifically from this one text that we derive many of the "details" that have become part of Marian tradition: the names of her parents, Joachim and Anna, the description of Joseph as an elderly widower, the birth of Jesus in a manger, and the virginity of Mary before and after Jesus' birth.

The gospel of James is a great example of how some texts—as old as the New Testament—that did not become a part of Holy Scriptures still managed to influence Christian tradition in a major way.

The Least You Need to Know

- Mary is mentioned 19 times in the New Testament.
- Matthew and Luke are the only Gospels that tell Jesus' birth story.
- For Luke, Mary is both mother and disciple.
- Paul never uses the name of Mary when referring to the mother of Jesus.

The Incarnation and Nativity Stories

In This Chapter

- ◆ Looking at the incarnation
- ◆ Going to Bethlehem
- ◆ Shepherds, angels, and astrologers
- ◆ Mary's essential role

It's been said before: it only takes a single moment to completely transform our lives, changing our reality and our understanding of life forever. One phone call. An accident. A baby being born. This is not being overly dramatic; it's realizing the unpredictability of our life.

Mary had many such moments in her life. In this chapter, we will look specifically at two stories that not only transformed Mary's life forever, but that also altered the course of human history: the Annunciation and the birth of Jesus.

The story of the Annunciation is found only in Luke's Gospel. And the nativity or birth of Jesus appears in the Gospels of Matthew and Luke.

Live! From Nazareth

Once upon a time, an angel named Gabriel was sent to a small village named Nazareth, a town in Galilee, to give a message to a young Jewish woman named Mary.

Mary, who was a virgin, was pledged in marriage to Joseph, a righteous man and a descendant of the house of David.

Lord Knows

Nazareth was in Jesus' time, and remains today, a small city located in the lower Galilee region, not far from the Sea of Galilee. It is Mary's hometown, and the town where Jesus grew up. "[Mary and Joseph] returned to Galilee and their own town of Nazareth. The child grew in size and strength, filled with wisdom, and the grace of God was upon him." (Luke 2:39–40)

The angel appeared to Mary and said, "Be glad, Mary! The Lord Most High is with you, and he has blessed you and set you apart from all other women." (Luke 1:28)

Mary was frightened by the angel's sudden appearance, but above all she was deeply troubled by his words, wondering what this heavenly being could really mean by those words.

But the angel gently smiled and waited, before continuing, "Don't be afraid, Mary. God is so very pleased with you! That's why you will become pregnant with a son, and you will give him the name Jesus. Your child will be like no other. He will rule over the world and be called the son of the Most High!" (Luke 1:30–32)

Mary was speechless. She grabbed for the chair next to her and sat down.

The angel waited.

At last, the young woman took a deep breath and whispered, "How can this happen? I am still a virgin ...." (Luke 1:34)

Her words trailed into a silent pause. Gabriel waited, and then reached out for her hand.

"Mary, you know that God can do anything .... You will conceive by the power of the Holy Spirit, not by man. It will be the Spirit of God who will dwell in you, and this holy child will be the Son of God!" (Luke 1:35, 37)

Stained glass image of the moment of Gabriel's announcement to Mary from the Cathedral of Our Lady of Perpetual Help in Oklahoma City.

© *Anamaría Scaperlanda-Ruiz*

After that, as if letting Mary in on a holy secret, Gabriel added, "There are amazing things happening for your cousin Elizabeth! Everyone thought that she was too old, but she is already six months pregnant!" He paused. "Nothing is impossible with God. Nothing." (Luke 1:36–37)

Something within her leaped for joy. She looked into Gabriel's eyes.

"I do believe. May it happen to me as you say. I am, now and always, my Lord's servant." (Luke 1:38)

And with that, the angel Gabriel left her.

Incarnation

The incarnation is the doctrine or belief that the Son of God was conceived in the womb of Mary and that Jesus is, therefore, true God and true man.

In other words, the incarnation is the name we give to the result of the annunciation! It begins with the reality that Mary conceived a child by the power of the Holy Spirit—and that this child was the son of God.

And the end result of that event is her son Jesus, both divine and human, and perfectly both.

The word *incarnation* comes from the Latin *incarnates* or *incarnare*, which means "to make flesh."

Lord Knows
Christians do not believe that Jesus is part God and part man, but rather fully human and fully divine—perfect in divinity and perfect in humanity.

It was what the beginning of the Gospel of John describes when it says: "In the beginning was the Word; The Word was in God's presence, and the Word was God .... The Word became flesh and made his dwelling among us." (John 1:1, 14)

The Jerusalem Bible translation puts it this way, "The Word was with God and the Word was God .... The Word was made flesh, he lived among us."

Sunday School
According to the dictionary, a **mystery** is anything that baffles understanding and that cannot be explained. We also refer to a *mystery* when we speak of a religious truth that is ultimately incomprehensible to reason— and that is knowable finally only through divine revelation.

God chose to come into the world in the form of a baby? What a scandalous proposition!

The incarnation does not say merely that God took on human form, or that a man became God. Instead, it proclaims that in this act of the incarnation, God was conceived and birthed in Mary's womb, thus becoming simultaneously fully human and fully divine.

Not one or the other, but both at the same time. This is the *mystery* and the reality of the incarnation.

A Godly Command: Fear Not!

A few years ago I read a totally nontheological but very human (and funny) portrayal of the whole Gabriel scene in which a quite reluctant Mary argues and debates with the angel before finally consenting to his announcement.

One doesn't read anything quite that provoking in the Gospel of Luke, but I have no problem imagining the possibility.

Gabriel's news must have sounded rather outrageous and distressing to a single, celibate, engaged young woman.

First an angel of the Lord appears and tells her that she's special to God. He lets her know that she will become pregnant without having sex, by the power of the Holy Spirit—and that her child will be the son of God.

Can you imagine all that had to be racing through Mary's mind?

Her "How can this be?" to Gabriel was full of emotion, full of all the questions that were surely racing for attention within her. And, yes, it surely must have included the kind of fear that comes with shock, like the feeling of being dumped into a cold ocean and gasping for breath.

The word *fear* appears in the Bible anywhere from 180 to 501 times, depending on your translation. And the command "Fear not" is mentioned specifically as often as 170 times!

There's a reason for that. Fear is one of our most basic instincts. It is meant to keep us safe, to help us wisely discern a situation, to protect us from impending danger. Yet fear also paralyzes. It keeps us from seeing the big picture of possibility in front of us because we begin to obsess about the threat of danger. It is no wonder, then, that the commands to "fear not," "do not be frightened," or "do not fear" are repeated over and over by angels, by prophets, and often by Jesus himself.

Something made Mary stop, catch her breath, and be able to focus on the good in the news that the angel came to tell her. Mary recovered her breath as soon as she was able to hear the truth, the assurance, the godly safety, that was present in Gabriel's final words: "nothing is impossible with God."

It's not because there was no longer reason to fear, but rather, that Mary's focus was no longer on the fear. Her focus became the power of God being in control, especially of all she could not understand.

Honest Questioning

A therapist friend once told me that our feelings (and sharing our feelings) are the most honest part of who we are. It's where God is. Perhaps that's why I love Mary's questions and the blunt way she talks to Jesus.

Holy Mother
"Honesty is the first chapter in the book of wisdom." —Thomas Jefferson

You can appreciate and be grateful for Mary's ability and desire to be honest with herself, and to be honest with those around her.

I see this clearly in Mary's capacity to ask questions when things simply didn't make sense to her—and to say what she's thinking, even if it might not seem appropriate. Here are some examples:

When the angel's message didn't seem sensible, Mary asked, "How can this be?" (Luke 1:34)

When a 12-year-old Jesus basically runs away from home, from his parents, because he wanted to stay in Jerusalem talking in the temple, it is Mary who asks him, "Son, why have you done this to us?" (Luke 2:48)

When Mary realizes that the wine ran out at the wedding celebration that she and Jesus were attending, she told Jesus, "They have no more wine." And in spite of his obvious reluctance to do anything about it, Mary simply instructs the waiters to "Do whatever he tells you." (John 2:3–4)

Even confronted with what she clearly recognized as divine intervention (an angel speaking to her!), Mary was real and honest. She shared her anxiousness and worry with her son. She told her adult child about something she thought he should take care of, and he obeyed.

This is a mom that I can appreciate and relate to!

But what I admire the most is Mary's willingness to be honest with herself, and to share those feelings in a sincere and genuine way. Her attitude of openness to God's will in her life is clearly and intricately connected to her honesty and her truthfulness, what Jesus later describes as the "pure of heart." Mary models what it means to honor oneself and those around one with honesty.

This beautiful quality is clearly seen in her responses at the Annunciation, and it is at the heart of the nativity story.

The Main Event

The details of Jesus' birth are split between two Gospels. As we pointed out in the previous chapter, only the Gospels of Matthew and Luke include the nativity story in their texts. And they each incorporate different aspects and details of the account.

But what emerges from combining them is a lovely and moving story about a faithful and prayerful woman.

Going to Bethlehem

During the time that Mary was pregnant, and after she and Joseph were together in marriage, Roman Emperor Caesar Augustus ordered a census of the whole empire.

The census required that everyone go to register in their hometown, which for Joseph was Bethlehem, King David's town. This detail is important because it once again emphasizes Jesus' Davidic lineage.

So Joseph and a very pregnant Mary, his espoused wife, traveled to Bethlehem to register.

The text does not say why "there was no room for them in the place where travelers lodged" (Luke 2:7), but more than likely it was due to the heavy traveling taking place because of the required census.

The Gospels also don't specify how long Joseph and Mary were in Bethlehem before Jesus was born, but because we know that they were still lodging in the place where Mary "laid him in a manger" (Luke 2:7) at the time of the birth, it is safe to assume that Jesus was born not too long after their arrival.

Only the Gospel of Luke makes it a point to tell us these details preceding the birth.

Jesus' Birth

Ironically, we don't know much more detail than that about Mary's actual delivery!

What emerges from the story is the picture now familiar to us at Christmas time: Mary, Joseph, and the baby Jesus surrounded by animals.

Luke says that, "While they were there [in Bethlehem for the census] … she gave birth to her first-born son and wrapped him in swaddling cloths and laid him in a *manger*, because there was no room for them in the inn." (Luke 2:6–7)

By Luke's mention that there was no room in the place where travelers normally lodged—and the note about Mary placing the newborn baby in a manger—we can assume that Mary and Joseph spent that particular night giving birth and sleeping with the animals.

A baby lying in a manger in a barn is not the portrait most people would picture for the birth of the son of God!

Sunday School
A **manger** is what we call the container (usually in a barn or stable) that holds the food for cattle or horses.

The Other Characters

From those brief remarks regarding the birth in each Gospel, the action jumps to some of the other characters associated with the nativity story. Their stories are told in fairly specific detail.

There are shepherds specifically sent to find Mary and the baby. There are angels, a multitude of them. And there are astrologers from the east who have a run-in with King Herod in Jerusalem.

Why Shepherds?

Even for modern readers, it is hard to miss the echo of King David's humble shepherd beginnings in Luke's story—and in the choice of people who are selected to hear the news of David's successor. We don't have to know a lot about the culture in Jesus' time or about the life of a shepherd to get the message.

Shepherds living in the fields, taking turns keeping watch over their flock (Luke 2:8) are going to be stinky, tired, and dirty. They are most likely uneducated, simple, and poor. They are not only simple and ordinary, but also the lowly and the forgotten in any culture or time. It is to these people that the angel of the Lord appeared!

They were afraid (Luke 2:9). Who wouldn't be afraid? Yet the angel assured them that they had nothing to fear from this announcement, and in fact, this news is one of joy. "In David's city a savior has been born to *you*," the angel emphasized. "Go find him. You will recognize him when you see him in a manger, wrapped in swaddling clothes." (Luke 2:10–12)

Suddenly there was not one angel, but a multitude of angels, praising God and saying, "Glory to God in high heaven, and peace on earth to those on whom his favor rests." (Luke 2:14)

One of the most beautiful moments of the birth story took place next.

After the angels left them, the shepherds decided to go immediately and find this baby, so they went "in haste," they rushed, to Bethlehem where they found Mary and Joseph, and the baby lying in the manger, the container that holds food for the animals.

Picture Mary, with a newborn child lying in a simple box, still feeling the unexplainable mixture of rush and exhaustion that follows giving birth. And a group of dirty, excited, smiling shepherds appears, telling her that they, too, saw an angel, who told them to come and worship their savior—her child.

And Mary "treasured all these things and reflected on them in her heart." (Luke 2:19) She could not have known what it all meant, how she could really mother the Messiah. But she was open to the unknown, and to all the possibilities in store for her.

The text tells us that "once they saw, [the shepherds] understood what had been told them concerning this child." (Luke 2:17) They understood that God was right there. They understood that God's message of salvation was also for them, the simple and the ordinary. And they understood the joy of this amazing proclamation.

And that is why the shepherds returned, "glorifying and praising God for all they had heard and seen." (Luke 2:20)

A Word About Angels

Luke is quite comfortable with the concept of angels as messengers of the Lord, and he's not shy about recording some of these moments in his Gospel.

Holy Mother
"'Thy will be done on Earth as it is in heaven.' The divine and blessed angels of God do the will of God, as David says when he sings, 'Bless the Lord, all you his angels, you that are mighty in strength, doing the things he wills.' In effect, then, in so praying, you say, 'As your will is done in the angels, Master, so also let it be done on Earth in me.'" —Cyril of Jerusalem (c. 350)

Within the first two chapters of the text, in fact, there are several heavenly messengers at work.

- It was an angel who appeared to Zechariah, Elizabeth's husband, to tell him that she would give birth to a child whom he would name John.

- We know the name of the angel, Gabriel, who announced to Mary her pregnancy, and the identity of her son.

- An angel of the Lord appeared to the shepherds in the fields.

Angels would have been familiar to the Jews in Jesus' day because the Hebrew Scriptures often speak of angels. They appeared to Abraham, for example, before going to Sodom to find ten honest men. There was an angel at the gates of Eden as Adam and Eve were cast out. And Jacob both wrestled an angel and saw angels in his dreams. (See Genesis 8:24; 19:1; 32:24)

We know that angels are spiritual beings with intellect and will but no physical form. We simply don't know what they look like. Nothing in the Bible tells us that they have wings.

But in order to relate to humans, angels do sometimes take on the appearance of human beings, and at those times they might appear male or female.

On Magi, Kings, and Wise Men

We already talked in the last chapter about the significant role played by the "astrologers from the east" in Matthew's Gospel. But let's look at how the story unfolded.

Sometime after Jesus' birth (we don't know how long after), during the reign of King Herod the great, a group of astrologers from the east arrived in Jerusalem. Some Bible translations simply call them "wise men."

Because these men would have recognized the star in the sky as a supernatural event of great spiritual significance, they went to King Herod first to ask where they could find the newborn king of the Jews.

In later Christian tradition, these wise men became known as kings, and their three gifts they offered baby Jesus became the basis for their number. Eventually, they were named Caspar, Balthasar, and Melchior in the Western church; Caspar is traditionally thought to be dark skinned.

The fact that the wise men saw "his star," indicates that they recognized this child as the Messiah, which is exactly what scared and disturbed Herod.

Herod immediately gathered all the chief priests and scribes in Jerusalem and asked them where prophecy said that the Messiah was to be born.

They, of course, quoted to him the prophecy from the Hebrew Scriptures (Micah 5:1) naming Bethlehem in Judah, information that Herod passed on to the wise men— but not before finding out from them "the exact time of the star's appearance." (Matthew 2:7) This told Herod the approximate age of the newborn king.

Herod also instructed them to come back to him with information about the child, supposedly so that he could "go and offer him homage, too." (Matthew 2:8) But of course, they never did. The astrologers were told in a dream not to return to Herod, returning to the east—probably Persia, East Syria, or Arabia—by a different route.

Stained glass image of the three wise men at the birth of Jesus, from the Cathedral of Our Lady of Perpetual Help in Oklahoma City.

© Anamaría Scaperlanda-Ruiz

Without Mary, There Is No Birth Story

After leaving Herod, these wise men from the east "were overjoyed at seeing the star" (Matthew 2:10) and once again followed it all the way to Bethlehem and to the place where the child was.

On entering Mary and Joseph's house, they "found the child with Mary his mother." (Matthew 2:11) The text tells us that upon seeing the child with Mary, the wise men prostrated themselves, lying face down to the ground to pay him homage.

Mary is not an observer in this story. She is a part of it. She is there, with Jesus, as these men come to humbly acknowledge his kingship.

This young Jewish mother is not only central to the story of the birth of the Messiah, she is fundamental to it. Without Mary, there simply is no birth story.

Amazing Grace

The angel Gabriel declared Mary full of grace (Luke 1:28). We sing about grace and we say grace, as in a prayer before meals. But how can we define it? The word itself comes from the Latin *gratia* or *gratus*, meaning "pleasing."

On the one hand, grace might be as difficult to describe as it is to capture a snowflake or hold a grain of sand. Yet most of us can recognize it in those moments when God's presence is completely unexplainable—and the most real.

Grace is what makes us holy and reminds us that we are connected to the transcendent, the eternal, and the divine. It can also be a sort of supernatural push or encouragement when we need it the most.

Mary was, indeed, full of grace. Because she received and carried the son of God in her womb, she was a unique vessel of grace. But Mary also chose to be open to grace by her attitude, her posture, and her responses.

Mary's Prayerful Attitude

Twice in the second chapter, Saint Luke tells us that when confronted with what would be confounding circumstances for any mother, Mary brought both the situation and her feelings to prayer.

◆ When strangers came to see her newborn child, telling tales of a multitude of angels singing and about an angel of the Lord announcing the Messiah's birth, Mary listened. She "treasured all these things and reflected on them in her heart." (Luke 2:19)

◆ After finding their lost son in the Jerusalem temple and becoming confused by his explanation and his actions, Mary listened. She "kept all these things in her memory," or as another translation notes, she "stored up all these things in her heart." (Luke 2:51)

We will look at the story of Jesus in the temple later with more detail. But in examining this and any other stories involving Mary, it is essential to be mindful of her prayerful attitude.

Mary could have had many reactions to the amazing and perplexing events that took place in her life. But she chose an attitude of prayer and reflection as her basis, her foundation.

Holy Mother

"... As with all children, my child is meant to wander away from me, to places where I will be unable to protect her [him]. I admire her principles and her tenacity, but I worry about the risks she will incur in their expression. So, like Mary, I pray for the patience to be able to let go. To be able to "reflect on things" and "hold them in my heart." But more than anything I pray for a heart that is strong enough to bear them."

—Martha Manning, *Chasing Grace: Reflections of a Catholic Girl, Grown Up* (HarperSanFrancisco, 1997)

A prayerful attitude is one that acknowledges God's presence whether it is obvious or hidden from our eyes and perception. Mary consistently and deliberately took into her heart's prayer all that she did not see or understand.

The Least You Need to Know

- Jesus was born in Bethlehem, fulfilling the Messiah's prophecy.

- The incarnation is the belief that Mary's child was both fully human and fully divine.

- Mary is fundamental to the Messiah's birth story.

- Mary's prayerful attitude guided every aspect of her life.

Chapter 6

Presenting Jesus

In This Chapter

- ◆ According to Jewish law
- ◆ Present Jesus to whom?
- ◆ Anna and Simeon
- ◆ Living with prophecy

Immediately following the birth story, the Gospel of Luke is the only of the four Gospels that presents two events that witness how Mary and Joseph obeyed Jewish law.

On the eighth day, the newborn baby is circumcised, following the law for purification, and given the name of Jesus, the name that the angel told Mary before he was conceived. And when Jesus was somewhere around a month old, following Jewish custom, Mary and Joseph presented him to the Lord at the Temple in Jerusalem.

This chapter will describe what happened when Mary and Joseph presented Jesus in the Temple.

Mary and Joseph Bring Jesus to the Temple

It must have been an exciting, joyous journey from Nazareth to Jerusalem for Mary and Joseph. They had so much to be grateful for!

Stained glass image of the Holy Family from the Cathedral of Our Lady of Perpetual Help in Oklahoma City.

© Anamaría Scaperlanda-Ruiz

The presentation of Jesus to the Lord was not only about obeying the law, although that was clearly important to them. It was about publicly acknowledging God's goodness in their life in the form of this newborn baby son named Jesus.

As the Gospel of Luke tells us, when it was time, and according to the Law of Moses, the couple brought him up to Jerusalem so that he could be presented to the Lord at the Temple.

They had no reason to expect that anything out of the ordinary would happen to them, not on that day! And yet, it did. Not one, but *two* people, both elders at the Temple, came up to them when they recognized Jesus as the Messiah.

According to Jewish Law

The law for consecration of the first-born male is found in Exodus 13:1–2: "The Lord spoke to Moses and said, 'Consecrate to me every first-born that opens the womb among the Israelites, both man and beast, for it belongs to me.'"

> ### Lord Knows
>
> In the Bible, Moses was the Hebrew prophet and lawgiver who led the Israelites out of Egypt and across the Red Sea on a journey known as the Exodus. Moses was also the prophet who received the Ten Commandments from God on Mount Sinai. Check out Charlton Heston as Moses in the 1956 movie *The Ten Commandments* (a classic!)—or read the book of Exodus in the Hebrew Scriptures to learn more about him.

Luke described the presentation of Jesus this way, "For it is written in the law of the Lord. 'Every first-born male shall be consecrated to the Lord.' They came to offer in sacrifice 'a pair of turtledoves or two young pigeons,' in accord with the dictate of the law of the Lord." (Luke 2:22–24)

As we know from the Hebrew Scriptures and other ancient documents, rights of succession (and family responsibility) in ancient Israel were given to the first-born son. That first-born son was considered holy, and as such, he belonged to God, as the Exodus passage pointed out.

The Importance of Jerusalem

As a dedicated and devout Jewish couple, Mary and Joseph not only wanted to obey the Law of Moses, they were also eager to participate in this Jewish ritual of thanksgiving and praise.

Imagine the joyful attitude as they traveled to Jerusalem to present their son to God, to consecrate him to the One who gave Jesus to them. It would have taken Mary and Joseph several days to make the 81-mile journey south from Nazareth to Jerusalem. But it was important to do the ritual presentation at the Temple in the holy city of Jerusalem.

As I've said before, Jerusalem was the center of life for the Hebrew people—and the Jerusalem Temple played a central part in the life of the Jewish people.

The Temple was considered God's own house in the midst of his people, and as such, it was the holiest place. In addition to being the center of worship, the temple was also a visual and public symbol of God's choice of the Israelites as his very own people.

I Second That Emotion

Mary and Joseph probably were one of many couples who brought their first-born son to the Temple that day to offer a sacrifice and to present him to the Lord.

Their focus as they walked into the Temple was to "perform for him the customary ritual of the law" (Luke 2:27), but as they completed the ritual, their act became anything but anonymous.

First, an elder named Simeon walked up to them with a look of recognition so powerful that Mary allowed him to take Jesus in his arms, lifting Jesus up to heaven as he blessed God for the child.

Then a few moments later, an elderly woman named Anna entered the scene. As soon as she saw the child Jesus, she, too, began to give thanks and praise to God.

Simeon and Anna were people of deep prayer whose lives were dedicated to professing their faith by "worshipping day and night in *fasting* and prayer" (Luke 2:37) at the Temple. Although Simeon was not a priest in the temple, both he and Anna embodied the heart of Temple worship: the service of God.

Sunday School

Technically, of course, **fasting** means to eat very little or abstain from certain foods. But fasting is also a religious discipline, and can be both a public and a private practice. Although it has also been used as an expression of mourning, as a spiritual rite, fasting can be understood as a humbling of oneself before God, as well as a discipline for opening the self to God in prayer.

Simeon Recognizes Jesus

Just imagine the scene. Mary and Joseph, like other Jewish parents who had come to the Temple that morning, were carefully paying attention to the rituals and the worship of the day. Their focus, without a doubt, was on their first-born son. Yet as they completed their ritual, a man who acted like he knew them, walked up to them and motioned to hold their son.

If Mary handed Simeon her baby, Simeon's face unquestionably must have professed love and trust.

Simeon is described by Luke as a just and pious man who had been given a revelation by the Holy Spirit about the Messiah. Simeon would not die, he was told, until he had seen the Messiah of the Lord with his own eyes.

Simeon believed, and he waited.

On that particular, ordinary day, the Holy Spirit inspired Simeon to go to the Temple, to be there at that specific moment in time. When Simeon walked in and saw Mary and her child, he immediately recognized Jesus as the long-awaited Jewish Messiah.

Taking Jesus into his arms, Simeon, whose name means *God has heard*, began to bless God out loud with words that have become a prayer still said every night by monks around the world.

> "Now, Master, you can dismiss your servant in peace; you have fulfilled your word. For my eyes have witnessed your saving deed displayed for all the peoples to see: A revealing light to the Gentiles, the glory of your people Israel." (Luke 2:29–32)

Then Simeon walked to Mary and Joseph and blessed them. As he handed Mary her newborn son, Simeon looked Mary in the eye and said words that no mother would ever want to hear.

"This child of yours will have great influence, but he will not be accepted. He will be opposed by many in Israel, especially those with power." (Luke 2:34)

Simeon paused, touching Mary's hand as he added sorrowfully, "and you, you yourself will experience great pain. Your heart will feel pierced by a sword, *so that the thoughts of many hearts may be laid bare*." (Luke 2:35)

While they were still standing silently, deeply stunned by the prophetic words of Simeon, Anna came in.

Anna's Presence

Unlike Simeon, we never hear Anna say even one word.

We know she is the daughter of Phanuel of the tribe of Asher, because Luke thought it was important to tell us this detail.

We also know that Anna is an elderly woman, 84 years old, who "had seen many days." (Luke 2:36) And we know that her life consisted of prayer, fasting, and worshipping day and night "constantly" in the Temple. (Luke 2:37)

This is how the Gospel of Luke described what happened after Simeon's prophecy: "Coming on the scene at this moment, [Anna] gave thanks to God and talked about the child to all who looked forward to the deliverance of Jerusalem" (Luke 2:38).

Anna's life was about waiting. We are never told that she had been promised the privilege of seeing the Anointed Lord. But like Simeon, Anna had dedicated her life to waiting in prayer for the arrival of the Messiah.

Anna, whose name means "grace" or "favor," lived a life of silent witness—and God blessed her faithfulness by allowing her to arrive at that place in the Temple, at that precise moment, so that, like Simeon, she could see Mary holding the Messiah!

And Anna not only recognized Jesus as the Messiah, but she responded by immediately giving thanks to God and proclaiming the good news of his presence to anyone who would hear.

A Few Surprises: Prophecies

Even before Anna appeared on the scene, it was clear that Joseph and Mary were taken aback by the events at the temple. It was quite unbelievable, the way the elder named Simeon simply walked up and asked for their child, offering a prayer in thanksgiving for seeing Jesus.

Luke simply says that the parents were "marveling" at what was being said about their son, Jesus. The Jerusalem Bible translation says they "stood there wondering." (Luke 2:33)

I think a more accurate, or at least more specific, description would likely be that Mary and Joseph were simply stunned, even shocked, by Simeon's spontaneous prayerful ritual.

But before they could even react, before they could say even a word or response to each other, Simeon spoke again. This time, his words were a prophecy about Jesus—and about Mary.

Stained glass image from the Cathedral of Our Lady of Perpetual Help in Oklahoma City.

© *Anamaría Scaperlanda-Ruiz*

Prophecies are revelations of divine will. The Hebrew Scriptures are full of prophets and prophecies, often about events that would come about in a particular period or to a certain group of people. Often, prophecies involve events that will take place in the future. But they are much more than a forecast of what's to come. A prophecy is a prediction that is made by divine inspiration.

I imagine that Mary was more than a little hesitant in the face of the constant surprises that came her way. From angelic announcements to unexpected guests dropping in at the birth of her son, her life was one startling event after another.

But this was different.

As a devoted and prayerful Jewish woman, Mary undoubtedly recognized that Simeon's words, as surprising as they obviously were, were also a prophetic vision about her son, and about her life.

Living in the Present

I imagine Mary standing in the Temple, feeling too stunned to speak, instinctively cradling her newborn son close to her chest.

One might be tempted to label Simeon's prophecy as simply a prediction of bad news. But I think it was much more than that.

What Simeon did was to name the truth that he felt and heard and recognized in his heart about this child, this Messiah that he had waited all his life to see.

Like a grandfather whose concern leads him to name out loud the worries that he has out of love for one of his grandchildren, Simeon had a vision. And he felt a need to share it with Mary out of love for Jesus, and compassion for Mary.

Still, how does one respond to that kind of news? To an announcement that is both so enormous and so personal?

It is no coincidence that Anna came into the scene "just at that moment," to not only see the Messiah with her own eyes, but to embrace, both literally and figuratively, a stunned and shaken new mother.

After Simeon's words, Anna came to Mary with her own silent prophecy. She would suffer, yes. But she would never stand alone in her suffering.

Anna's presence at that particular moment was itself a prophecy—a promise—to Mary.

The Scripture passage doesn't tell us any details about how Mary reacted to Simeon. No explanation about what was going on inside. Only that a prophetess named Anna came just at that moment.

And without words, without any further ritual or clarification, Anna made her own prophecy to Mary.

By her presence, Anna reminded Mary of the peace that comes from living in the present moment, especially when one is aware of the promise of pain and suffering that is to come.

As Good As It Gets

Most of us who've seen the movie will never be able to forget the scene where Jack Nicholson's character in *As Good As It Gets* walks through a therapist's waiting room and casually drops the reality bomb: What if this is as good as it gets?

Holy Mother
"One day I came to the chapel and Mother [Teresa of Calcutta] motioned to me to come over by her. It was wonderful to be kneeling there next to her in prayer. There is an indescribable sense of peace in her presence. After Mass, she looked me in the eyes and said, 'I will teach you something. If ever you feel distressed during your day—call upon our Lady—just say this simple prayer: Mary, Mother of Jesus, please be a mother to me now.' I must admit—this prayer has never failed me"—Photographer Michael Collopy in "Works of Love Are Works of Peace: Mother Teresa of Calcutta and the Missionaries of Charity" (*Catholic Insight*, October, 1997).

Finding a way to live daily life as it is, and learning to find the blessing in what you get, that's the challenge that Mary faced after leaving the temple on the day of the presentation.

Mary and Joseph began that morning in Jerusalem with one idea of what the day would be like, and without warning, everything changed.

We are never told how long it took Mary to find her voice again after listening to Simeon's prophecy. Nor do we hear just how difficult it must have been for her and Joseph to find the strength to stand up and walk out of the temple that day. We know only that "when the pair had fulfilled all the prescriptions of the law of the Lord, they returned to Galilee and their own town of Nazareth." (Luke 2:39) Yet how fitting, and how much like real life, is the ending of that scene.

Yes, Mary undoubtedly felt myriad emotions after encountering two prophets at the temple that day. One promised her suffering. The other promised her presence. And both reminded her that life is never what we think it's going to be.

Mary of Nazareth never apologized to anyone for depending upon and trusting her Creator. She simply lived each moment, as good as it gets, and she let God demonstrate, through her, what God can do.

Pondering and Mothering

Some of us get a few years to learn the significant lessons that Mary was offered in just her first few months of being a mother!

This seems like a very poetic way of saying that Mary could not immediately comprehend the significance of God's action in Jesus, even as a baby. How could she?

These are staggering events and prophecies even for the most risky soul. Yet what makes Mary's stance bold and courageous is the fact that she took in all the news, all the events, all the prophecies, all the predictions, all the feelings and the wonderings—and she let them reside in her heart.

Like any mother gazing into the face of her beautiful baby, Mary had to be bewildered by the vast number of possibilities—the dance of the "could-bes"!

She trusted God. She gave herself and her son completely to her Creator. But that didn't prevent her from feeling loss and worry and fear and anxiety over her son's growing up.

Mary's pondering in her mothering is a beautiful model of her journey of faith.

Mary allowed the events, no matter how troubling or unpredictable, to roll around in her head until she grasped their meaning. She didn't need to get it, not right away. It was okay to be confused and to not understand!

But above all, Mary allowed her honest and pure heart to feel whatever feeling it was that stood before her. Pain. Joy. Anxiety. Protectiveness. Peace. Awe. Even uncertainty and questioning.

It is this openness of her heart that Simeon predicted would sometimes pierce her, like a sword cutting into the very center of her being.

And it is this openness of her heart that disarms us even now when we hear her story. Perhaps this is what Simeon meant when he also prophesied that the thoughts of many hearts might be laid bare?

Mary's pondering in her mothering was no less than her being completely real with God, in everything. And the result was, we are told, "the child grew in size and strength, filled with wisdom, and the grace of God was upon him." (Luke 2:40)

The Least You Need to Know

- Mary and Joseph took Jesus to the Temple to present him to the Lord, according to Jewish law.

- The Temple of Jerusalem was considered God's own house in the midst of his people.

- Simeon and Anna were prophets who predicted Mary's suffering and who promised her God's presence.

- Mary trusted God wholeheartedly with whatever situation she was facing in her life.

Chapter 7

Mary and Joseph's Flight into Egypt as Refugees

In This Chapter

- Following a dream
- Herod's massacre
- Refugees into Egypt
- Returning to Nazareth

We don't know how old Jesus was when the wise men from the east came to see him. We only know that their visit took place during the reign of King Herod, and that the Gospel of Matthew describes the wise men entering the house and finding "the child" (not the baby) with Mary his mother. (Matthew 2:11)

That means that Jesus was not necessarily a newborn, but he was young, probably under two years old. It was right after the wise men left them that Joseph was warned about Jesus being in mortal danger. He was instructed by God to take the family out of the country, immediately.

In this chapter we will look at what crisis made Joseph and Mary leave their homeland in the middle of the night and take refuge in the land of Egypt.

Leaving in Haste

Like modern-day *refugees* departing under threat of their lives, Mary and Joseph took only their beloved son and a few of their essential things with them as they left their home in a hurry for Egypt.

There was no time for elaborate plans or long worries. Joseph was warned, and they had to leave immediately—that very night—for an alien place and an unknown future.

Sunday School
A **refugee** is someone who has left his or her native country and who is unable to return to it because of persecution or fear of persecution.

We know that it was not the first time that the angel of the Lord appeared to Joseph in a dream, because that was also the way that the Lord chose to communicate with Joseph about Mary's pregnancy.

But this dream was different. Even the language used to describe the story tells us of its urgency and the importance of its message.

Suddenly, an angel of the Lord appeared in a dream to Joseph with a *command!* (Matthew 2:13)

Lord Knows
This might sound funny, but ironically, the birth of Jesus did not actually take place in the year 0, which is when the calendar shifted from the years marked as B.C. (for *Before Christ* or *Before the Common Era*) and the years A.D. (for *Anno Domini* or *after Christ*). Historically, King Herod died in 4 B.C., and scholars assign 7 or 6 B.C. as the actual date for the birth of Jesus.

A Leap of Faith

"Get up, Joseph. Right now." Joseph plainly heard the words, instantly sitting up in bed. "Take the child and his mother to Egypt. It is not safe for them to be here. Herod is jealous of your child and he wants to kill him. Do not return to your country until I tell you that it is safe." (Matthew 2:13–14

Imagine waking up after having heard such a troubling and disturbing message! Adrenaline must have immediately pumped through his veins as he mechanically began to gather their things, all the while attempting to think through in his mind what they were going to do.

In his desire to protect and shelter his family, no doubt Joseph waited until he could breathe calmly before waking Mary and bundling up the child Jesus for the journey. He wanted to be strong. He had to be strong.

Joseph had learned to trust his dreams and visions a long time ago. It was one of the most powerful ways that God had communicated with him, and he was thankful for that.

But he didn't remember ever receiving a message like this one, with such a burning rush and threat of danger. There was no time to think things through or to consider how to make a decision. He had to act immediately.

He stopped in the middle of the dark room, put down the bag, closed his eyes, and took a deep breath, asking God for the courage to take this immense leap of faith.

When he woke Mary, he reminded her that God had been faithful in showing them his presence every step of their journey together—and that surely he would do it in a special way as they undertook this fragile and immense step in the journey.

Mary and Joseph packed only the things they considered indispensable, and they left that very night for Egypt, a country neither of them had ever been to, or ever dreamt of going to!

Foreigners in an Alien Land

What a mixture of emotions must have been going through Mary that night. She still could not believe that they had walked out of their home, leaving behind many things that they could not carry with them, but that had sentimental value.

Egypt. She didn't know much about Egypt, except that it was a long journey and a difficult one to make any time, let alone traveling on your own, without a caravan.

How would they eat? Where would they rest? How safe was it? And how would they live after they got there? Would they be accepted? Where could Joseph work?

Her head was struggling with her heart for attention, throwing out many questions that Mary simply did not have answers for.

All Mary knew was that they were making an immense trade—all that was familiar and everything that they knew for a foreign country, a foreign culture, a different language, and an unknown future, in a land that had once enslaved her people.

As the 37 million refugees in our world today would understand, this was not a journey of choice. Undoubtedly, Mary would do anything to keep her beloved son safe. She would and she could endure anything for his sake. What mother wouldn't?

Stained glass image of the Holy Family's flight into Egypt from the Cathedral of Our Lady of Perpetual Help in Oklahoma City.

© *Anamaría Scaperlanda-Ruiz*

But knowing that this journey was something they had to do did not prevent Mary from experiencing huge waves of emotion. Dread. Apprehension. Worry. Exhaustion. Fear. Loneliness. Terror. Vulnerability.

What a long and difficult journey that must have been for Mary, even as she clutched her Jesus tight in her arms, longing to keep him safe from harm.

Herod's Massacre

As soon as Herod realized that the astrologers from the east were not going to come back to him with news about Jesus or how to find the newborn king of the Jews, he felt deceived and "became furious." (Matthew 2:16)

Whether he became insane in his fury or simply was mad, what Herod chose to do next was a horrible act of evil.

Based on the date that he had been given by the astrologers as the onset of the appearance of the star, Herod calculated the approximate age of the child Jesus.

To be certain that he'd find Jesus and kill him, Herod ordered his men to massacre "all the boys two years old and under in Bethlehem and its environs." (Matthew 2:16)

Without telling him about these details, this was the threat that the angel of the Lord warned Joseph about, and the reason for the family's urgent departure from their home.

Quiet Obedience

We might associate the word *obedience* with discipline or with following regulations, but to obey, quite literally, means to give ear or to listen. The word *obey* comes from the Latin word *obedire*, which combines *ob* or "to," with *audire* or "listen, hear."

Obedience was always Mary's posture in her life.

Consistently and repeatedly, Mary listened. She heard with her heart the hopes and the dreams that the Lord had for her and her life. She listened to what was hardest to hear. And she gave her consent. Mary understood that it was not enough to listen. Obedience always requires a yes, a go-ahead that must be as personal as it has to be honest.

> **Holy Mother**
>
> "Only after the last judgment will Mary get any rest: from now until then, she is much too busy with her children."
>
> —French preacher Jean-Marie Baptist Vianney, also known as Cure d'Ars (d. 1859)

When told about the conception of her child through an act of the Holy Spirit, Mary said yes. When she was surprised by shepherds and wise men who had come to honor her baby, Mary consented to their presence. When told of a prophecy about her son that warned her of piercing suffering, Mary humbly and silently accepted. And even when sent away from her home without explanation to an alien land and culture for an unforeseen amount of time, Mary listened and obeyed.

Holy Dreams and Discernments

Most ancient religions acknowledge dreams as a possible venue through which the spiritual speaks to people. But rational Western society has a difficult time accepting that something so personal and so intangible can have much worth!

Dreams played an important role in the Hebrew Scriptures, often in relation to receiving a message from a messenger of the Lord. Many of the great Hebrew figures recognized God's voice in their dreams, with Abraham being the first person whose dreams were recorded.

One of the best-known characters in Hebrew Scriptures to be associated with dreams was Joseph, the son of Jacob and Rachel.

When he was about seventeen years old, Joseph encountered the jealous hatred of his brothers. Their anger only increased when Joseph shared with them his dreams, and his brothers "hated him so much that they would not even greet him." (Genesis 37:4)

Finally, one day Joseph's brothers plotted together and sold Joseph into slavery out of pure jealousy. The merchants who bought Joseph brought him into Egypt, where eventually he became known for his ability to interpret dreams—even for Pharaoh.

Pharaoh was so pleased with Joseph's wisdom in interpreting his dreams and with his counsel that he set up Joseph as overseer over all the land of Egypt. (Genesis 41:43)

Joseph explained his gift of dreams: "Surely, interpretations come from God. Please tell the dreams to me." (Genesis 40:8)

In the New Testament Scriptures, Mary's Joseph has four dreams in a row, recorded within just a few short verses of each other.

Like her husband, Joseph, Mary understood that God gives direction to those who are open to him—in the manner that is best suited for each person.

Mary always trusted Joseph's dreams, and embraced them as messages for the whole family.

Echoes of Hebrew Stories

The flight of Mary, Joseph, and Jesus into Egypt is technically a reversal from the Hebrew Exodus story, where Moses led the Israelites *out* of Egypt and freed them from slavery in order to journey to Sinai (Exodus 25:37) and the Promised Land.

But it is also a direct quotation from Hosea's passage in the Hebrew Scriptures, "out of Egypt I called my son" (11:1), a reference that Matthew and his listeners would have understood as Israel's experience of salvation.

Out of Egypt, out of the bondage of slavery, God called his people Israel.

Lord Knows
The Israelites held the name of God in such high reverence that they never said the name of God or Yahweh, but instead used *Adonai* (meaning "the Lord"). The first Christians also followed this, considering the name of Jesus to have the highest veneration. "So that at Jesus' name every knee must bend in the heavens, on the earth, and under the earth, and every tongue proclaim to the glory of God the Father: Jesus Christ is Lord!" (Philippians 2:10–11)

The Moral of the Story

The flight into Egypt is a story about trust in divine providence. Not only did Joseph listen with an obedient heart to the message that the Lord sent him—but his wife Mary relied on Joseph's ability to listen, embracing this truth for the well-being of their whole family.

It is this joint wisdom that protected them, all of them. But in a special way, it is this collective act of trustful faith that protected their son Jesus from death, literally, at the hands of Herod's wrath.

Wisdom vs. Knowledge

In this story, especially when combined with Simeon's prophecy mentioned in Chapter 6 (during the ritual presentation of Jesus at the Temple in the holy city of Jerusalem), Mary models a beautiful understanding of what it means to be a wife, and to trust God as a couple.

We know that Mary stood at the temple, stunned by Simeon's prophecy for her and for her son. In that particular moment, the message, all of the messages, were for Mary. It was to her, specifically, that Simeon turned after blessing her and Joseph.

But it was as a couple that they responded. As the verse that immediately follows tells us, when "the *pair* had fulfilled all the prescriptions of the law of the Lord, *they* returned to Galilee." (Luke 2:39)

In the next chronological story, this time in the Gospel of Matthew, it is Joseph who receives the main message. It is Joseph who is warned about the family. But it is the couple that responded to the message!

To have knowledge is simply to gather or receive specific information about something— like hearing a prophecy, or being told a message in a dream.

But Mary and Joseph had wisdom, which is the ability to discern or judge what is true, what is right. And they lived out this wisdom by trusting each other as a couple.

Wisdom comes from awareness, an understanding regarding the information that is received. It also requires good judgment, an action that takes steps and affirms a position.

Mary and Joseph took this action as a duo, not as single individuals each listening to God. And in their sharing, they lived out the wisdom that best graced their entire family.

Trusting What She Could Not See

As in so many other instances in Mary's adult life, the flight into Egypt required a complete trust in a goodness and a bounty that she could not see, at least, not with human eyes.

Where did Mary find the strength to face a monumental event like fleeing her home for an unknown country? The answer is in her heart. It *is* her heart.

It is there that Mary "went" when things did not make sense. It is her heart where Mary took her questions, her fears, her awe, and her wonderings. And it is in the stillness of her heart that she found the peace to trust the future, the present, the past, and all she could not see, to the God Most High to whom she had dedicated her entire being.

Holy Mother

"[Jesus] became man by the Virgin so that the course which was taken by disobedience in the beginning through the agency of the serpent might be also the very course by which it would be put down. Eve, a virgin and undefiled, conceived the word of the serpent and bore disobedience and death. But the Virgin Mary received faith and joy when the angel Gabriel announced to her the glad tidings that the Spirit of the Lord would come upon her and the power of the Most High would overshadow her, for which reason the Holy One being born of her is the Son of God. And she replied 'Be it done unto me according to your word' [Luke 1:38]."

—Justin Martyr, in *Dialogue with Trypho the Jew*, Chapter 100 (155 A.D.)

The Return to Nazareth

Matthew tells us that Mary and Joseph settled in Egypt, where they lived as refugees for an unnamed number of years, "but [until] after Herod's death." (Matthew 2:19)

When it was safe, an angel of the Lord appeared to Joseph in a dream telling him to "take the child and his mother, and set out for the land of Israel" because those who wanted to kill Jesus were now dead. (Matthew 2:19)

So Joseph obeyed.

Because he had been warned in a dream that Herod's son had succeeded him as king in Judea, Joseph led the family instead to the region of Galilee, choosing to settle in Mary's hometown of Nazareth.

Since Joseph was a carpenter, Nazareth offered him abundant work in neighboring Sephoris, a city that was being rebuilt as capital of the region at that time.

The Child and His Mother

As a Cuban-American refugee whose family left the island before I had reached the age of two, I feel a special kinship with this powerful story.

The story of Mary and Joseph's flight into Egypt is a sort of national anthem for refugee families around the globe who understand all too well the mixture of emotions and the indescribable situations faced by those who are forced to leave their country.

As my own mother so passionately did, I have no problem envisioning how committed Mary would have been in teaching Jesus about his home.

There is a very high level of ardor and dedication felt by refugee parents regarding the knowledge that their children have about the place and the people of their native culture.

Because leaving their home country is something they were forced to do, they don't know if their own children will ever see, smell, touch, or experience the place where they were born. And so the parents feel it is up to them to make sure their children "get it."

This would have been true for Mary as she educated her son Jesus in Egypt, not knowing how long or if they would ever return to their beloved Israel. Not only because she was a devout Jew, but also because she was a refugee mother living in an alien land, Mary must have felt the same tremendous responsibility to pass on the story of their flight.

Telling why they left, and what fleeing their country meant to them, is very significant to refugee parents.

Finally, and most importantly, Mary must have wanted with her whole heart and being to profess and to share with Jesus what their refugee story meant to her, specifically in terms of what it proclaimed about God.

It's not enough to merely know the factual details of the story. As a refugee mother, it would have been vital for Mary to want her son to understand the *why* of their story.

In other words, Mary would have wanted, above all, for Jesus to know in his heart, not just his mind, that God's providence had brought them there, to that foreign land. And that it was God's providence that would continue to carry them wherever their journey would take them next.

The Least You Need to Know

- Joseph was told by God in a dream to flee with Mary and Jesus into Egypt.

- They became refugees living in Egypt.

- In an effort to kill Jesus, Herod massacred all the boys under the age of two in the Bethlehem region.

- The family lived in Egypt until Joseph was told in another dream that it was safe to return to Israel.

Chapter 8

Searching for Jesus at the Temple

In This Chapter

- Another Jerusalem excursion
- Losing Jesus for three days
- Where else, in the Temple
- His Father's business

After the presentation of Jesus at the Temple and the flight into Egypt, there is a huge jump in years as far as what's recorded in the Gospels about the family life of Jesus and Mary.

The next story we have is narrated in the Gospel of Luke, which took place when Jesus was 12 years old, and it is the topic of this chapter.

Hide and Seek

Going to Jerusalem every year for the feast of Passover was a family tradition for Mary and Joseph.

Along with hundreds of other Jews from the region, the couple walked the long 81-mile hike from Nazareth to the holy city with their friends and family every year. It was not only ritual, it was a pleasant experience that the family would have looked forward to. In this particular year, however, everything changed.

After the celebration of the feast was over, as the couple headed home from Jerusalem to Nazareth with their traveling group, Jesus remained behind in the city—unbeknownst to his parents!

How Could They Lose Jesus?

Any parent can testify that nothing in the world is more terrifying than the possibility of "losing" your child.

The summer that my youngest daughter, Michelle, turned 12, I agreed to let her and her best friend meander on their own through Westminster Abbey in London. After all, I told myself, they were old enough to know how to act in that kind of setting, and I would not be far if they needed me.

When they were fifteen minutes late meeting me at the exit door where we agreed to meet, I was worried, and a bit annoyed. When they were thirty minutes late, I began asking the guards at that exit if they had seen her, describing the two girls and what they were wearing. When an hour had gone by, my fear had turned to anxious panic.

It's indescribable, really, that mix of emotions that a parent experiences in that kind of situation. But it's not difficult for any parent to imagine.

Mary and Joseph would have been traveling in a large crowd, where children walk with friends and parents mingle as they travel, unconcerned about their child's safety because of the number of other adults helping to keep an eye on all the kids.

It's not difficult to conceive how Mary and Joseph could travel an entire day without becoming concerned about Jesus' whereabouts.

There were lots of adults traveling with them. These were relatives and friends who did this at least once every year and who knew each other well. Jesus was not a little child, but a confident and strong 12-year-old boy. And he had made this journey to Jerusalem many times with his parents and their group.

At the end of the day, however, when Mary and Joseph touched base with each other and realized that neither of them had seen Jesus all day, I can imagine the fear and anxiety with which they must have searched their caravan.

Have you seen Jesus? Who was the last person to see him? Where were we when you saw him? How long ago was that?

Besides dread and anxiety, there is immediate massive guilt. How could I lose my own child? What kind of parent would do that? Every minute that goes by when your child is missing feels like an hour.

Mary and Joseph must have felt terrible anguish when they finally came to the conclusion that Jesus was not with their group—and that the only thing they could do was to trace their steps back to Jerusalem.

The Other Side: Where Did Jesus Go?

I find it much harder to imagine the other side of the story.

What in the world was Jesus thinking? How could he start walking home with his parents' group, and then suddenly decide to stay back in Jerusalem—without telling his parents?

There's no doubt that as a refugee child living in Egypt for years, Jesus would have grown up hearing the story of his family's flight from home. The idea that his parents would do anything for his safety and well-being would be clearly impressed in his heart.

Holy Mother

"For his incarnation, God chose birth from a human mother. From the moment that she knows that she will bear a son, she is totally in the service of this mission: Concentrated expectation, devoted service, listening to every word and sign, sharing in His work in faithful perseverance until His death and beyond."

—Edith Stein (d. 1942 A.D.), *An Edith Stein Daybook: To Live at the Hand of the Lord* translated by Susanne Batzdorff (Templegate, 1994)

How could he just walk away? He must have known that this would alarm and frighten his parents like nothing else in the world could.

The Gospel of Luke only tells us that "the child Jesus remained behind unknown to his parents," and that "thinking he was in the party, [Mary and Joseph] continued their journey for a day, looking for him among their relatives and acquaintances." (Luke 2:43–44)

I Don't Get That: Consent Without Understanding

It took Mary and Joseph *three whole days* to finally find Jesus. Surely they started walking back to Jerusalem without delay at the end of their caravan search that first day, walking through the night without wasting time or even resting.

But even when they arrived back in the city, they must have spent hours that next morning asking anyone and everyone in Jerusalem whether they had seen their son.

What a frantic process! Tracing back their steps to all the places they had been during the Passover feast, pleading with everyone to think and recall: Have you seen a boy about this height, with dark hair, light eyes, broad shoulders. He was wearing … please, try to remember!

Finally, someone must have told them that they had seen a boy with those features at the Temple, and in spite of their exhaustion, Mary and Joseph raced to the sanctuary.

"[T]hey came upon him in the Temple sitting in the midst of the teachers, listening to them and asking them questions. All who heard him were amazed at his intelligence and his answers." (Luke 2:46–47)

When I finally found my daughter Michelle, it was obvious that she and her friend had both been crying, evidently as frightened as I had been by our separation. In between sobs, I learned that the girls thought we had agreed to meet back at the entrance of the Abbey—while I thought we had agreed to meet at the exit door. It's an understandable miscommunication.

I seized Michelle in my arms and embraced her tighter than I ever had. Neither of us wanted to let go. I felt thankful and joyous. I was angry. I was tremendously relieved. I felt confused.

In addition to the myriad emotions that Mary must have felt standing there watching Jesus, finally seeing her son with her own eyes, she, too, must have been confused.

It is obvious by the way that Luke describes the event in the Gospel that Jesus did not "get" it. He didn't run up and hug his parents. He didn't seem or act overjoyed at being found. In fact, he didn't even act concerned, or aware that there had been a problem! Jesus did not act at all like a child who had been lost.

When his parents saw Jesus, Luke tells us, they were "astonished," a word that also means amazed, dumbfounded, incredulous, overwhelmed, surprised, speechless, shocked.

Yes, that seems like a more accurate description!

Playing Mom

The next moment in the story belongs to Mary.

She stared at her son, assessing his demeanor and his expression, and no doubt judging his attitude.

Right there, in front of all the rabbis and the teachers of the Temple, Mary decided that what she had to say would not wait any longer.

Lord Knows

The Seder Meal traditionally associated with the feast of Passover takes place on the first night of Passover. From a Hebrew root word meaning "order," the seder is a special family meal filled with ritual. Aimed at remembering the significance of the Passover, the seder includes a specific set of information that must be covered in a specific order.

Mary looked at Jesus and asked him how he could do this to them. Couldn't he see how worried and anxious they had been? For the past three days they didn't know where he was and they'd been searching, literally, everywhere for him …. They asked him why had he done this. (Luke 2:48)

The mother who is addressing these words to her 12-year-old son is not afraid to say what she's thinking, even in public. Even as a woman speaking in the Temple in front of all the rabbis!

She is a mother who's not inhibited—to show her emotions or to share them with her child. She was upset and worried. She had even felt panicked. She was heartbroken and grieved. She was exhausted, physically and emotionally, after the three days spent searching for her beloved son.

On top of it all, Mary was still shocked by having to face and to deal with a situation so completely out of character for Jesus. Her son had evidently never done anything remotely similar to this before.

Even standing in that multitude of emotions, Mary is being wholly honest and direct, and she is obviously expecting the same kind of response from her son. Which makes Jesus' reply to his mother all the more puzzling to her.

Stained glass image of Mary and the child Jesus from the Cathedral of Our Lady of Perpetual Help in Oklahoma City.

© *Anamaría Scaperlanda-Ruiz*

What Was His Father's Business?

Without seeming at all anxious or overly concerned about everything Mary had just said to him, or about the fact that she said it in front of everyone at the Temple, Jesus calmly replied: "Why did you search for me? Did you not know I had to be in my Father's house?" or as the Jerusalem Bible translation puts it, "Did you not know that I must be busy with my Father's affairs?" (Luke 2:49)

We don't have a record of what Mary said next. I picture one of those silent moments in which words are simply not needed. Mary's face must have said it all—confusion, grief, sadness, love, concern.

And Jesus' reply must have been just as heartfelt, full of compassion. Perhaps he simply walked up and hugged her, one of those embraces that transcend time and that fill us with love deep in the bones.

Mary and Joseph's Faithfulness

Mary and Joseph, Luke tells us, "did not grasp what he said to them." (Luke 2:50) They did not understand what Jesus meant by being busy with his Father's business or why he had to be in his Father's house, supposedly the Temple.

How could they be expected to know?

Suddenly, in a moment's breath, what Mary and Joseph were facing as parents was no longer about a lost child, but a son coming of age as the Messiah of his people.

It was one of those pivotal moments in life that happens when we least expect it, and perhaps precisely because we don't expect it. But in an instant, everything changed.

They knew that something happened. Something was clearly different. But, no, they did not understand. They could not grasp what Jesus was truly saying to them.

Nor did they need to, at least in terms of knowing what to do next.

They were still Jesus' parents. And he was still a 12-year-old child.

So Jesus "went down with them then, and came to Nazareth, and was obedient to them." (Luke 2:51) For Mary and Joseph, being obedient to their own vocation as parents as best they could was all that mattered. And that was all they needed to know and act on right then and there.

An Unfinished Symphony

As Mary knew in her heart after so many transforming events in her life, there is no such thing as a complete moment.

No event is completely one thing or another, not even monumental moments like the birth of a child. When Jesus was born, Mary experienced a bliss and contentment that she had never known before. She also experienced physical pain, and bewilderment when strangers came to worship her child.

There is no such thing as clear-cut pure joy. Mary knew that the most happy events, like the presentation of her child in the Temple, became a reminder of the painful and difficult calling that her son was destined to live, and the suffering she would endure.

Even the most ordinary events in her life reminded Mary of the reality that sadness and joy are always kissing, or as contemporary writer Karl Rahner describes it, "here, in this life, all symphonies remain unfinished."

Seeking Holiness

Mary of Nazareth understood this tension, perhaps like no one else ever will. And she also lived out this feeling of incompleteness of life by making peace with it.

> ### Lord Knows
>
> Mary's name is often connected with the word *holy,* a term of respect associated with something sacred, as in regarded worthy of worship or veneration. But the term "holy" is probably adopted as a conversion for the Latin word *sanctus.* Its primary meaning related to becoming (or being preserved) whole.

If she didn't comprehend the meaning of the events, Mary didn't have to pretend that she did. If she was frustrated and confused by her son's behavior, even when she could see how comfortable Jesus acted in front of the Temple teachers, Mary told Jesus what she was thinking and feeling.

She didn't have to make believe or to overcome her feelings, or even change what made sense to her. She simply accepted it, lived it, and was honest about it all.

After we are told that Jesus "went down with them then, and came to Nazareth, and was obedient to them," Luke the Gospel writer once again brings us back to Mary. (Luke 2:51)

His mother Mary "meanwhile kept all these things in memory," storing them in her heart. (Luke 2:51) As she did before, Mary brought all these experiences into her heart—what she felt and what she learned, what she grasped and what she didn't understand.

And in her heart, she considered. She contemplated. She wondered. Above all, she allowed God to bring to her his awareness through that memory, in his time, and in his own way.

And the Child Grew in Wisdom

This story of losing and finding Jesus in the Temple is the final narrative we have of Mary's parenting of a young child. Yet already, before the texts jump ahead to Jesus as an adult, there was a moment of transition in Mary's mothering and in her relationship with Jesus that took place here. After all, this is the story where Jesus—at the age of 12—speaks his first recorded words.

After the Temple event, Jesus went back and lived under Mary and Joseph's authority. As Luke noted, Jesus, for his part, "progressed steadily in wisdom and age and grace before God and men." (Luke 2:52)

But the change had already happened. The shift had taken place. And something inside Mary recognized it. That's why she had no verbal response to Jesus' words about his Father's business, regardless of her lack of understanding—or the feelings still present within her after searching for him for three days.

Something inside Mary knew that things were different, whether she could name the change or not. Yet in spite of this, Mary the mother of Jesus knew there was only one thing she could do. She had to go home and do her part in raising this amazing child.

The Least You Need to Know

- ◆ Mary and Joseph celebrated the Passover in Jerusalem every year as a family.

- ◆ When Jesus was 12, he didn't tell his parents he wasn't joining them on the family caravan returning home to Nazareth. Mary and Joseph searched for three days before finding him in the Temple back in Jerusalem.

- ◆ His response to Mary about being in the Temple in Jerusalem doing his Father's work was the first time that Jesus' words are recorded in the Gospels.

Part 3

Encountering Mary—As Disciple

Disciple. There's a word we don't use every day, at least not in reference to and description of our daily living! But for a Christian, being a disciple and living the principles of discipleship are at the heart of the faith. The word *disciple* actually comes from the Latin word *discere*, or "to learn." And for most of us, learning what this means is a lifelong journey.

Mary the mother of Jesus was the first person to acknowledge and embrace the reality that Jesus was the Son of God, and so we call her the first disciple. In this part, we will look at three major events occurring in Jesus' adult life, examining Mary's role as disciple: the miracle of the wedding at Cana; the death and crucifixion of Jesus; and the arrival of the Holy Spirit to the early Christian community at Pentecost, after Jesus' ascension into heaven.

Chapter **9**

The Wedding Feast at Cana

In This Chapter

- Mother of Jesus
- John: one of a kind
- The first miracle
- Do what he tells you

At the words *wedding feast*, it's not difficult to imagine a fun, joyous, and engaging wedding gala with lots of guests and abundant food and wine. A true celebration!

That was the setting for Jesus' first miracle recorded in the Gospels—the wedding at Cana in which Mary was a major character.

The mother of Jesus appears in two major moments in the Gospel of John: the wedding at Cana, and the crucifixion. John is the only Gospel in which the wedding at Cana story appears.

In this chapter we will look at the significance of Mary's role in the story of the wedding at Cana.

The First Miracle

There was a wedding at Cana in Galilee, and the mother of Jesus was there. Jesus and his disciples also had been invited. (John 2:1) So begins the story of the first miracle performed by Jesus: turning water into wine at a wedding feast.

It sounds like a big shindig, one of those events where everyone in town is invited, including Mary and Jesus and his disciples. There were tons of guests, lots of food, music, and plenty of wine.

Holy Mother

"[T]he Lord said to his Mother, 'Let your heart rejoice and be glad, for every favor and every gift has been given to you from my Father in heaven and from me and from the Holy Spirit. Every soul that calls upon your name shall not be ashamed, but shall find mercy and comfort and support and confidence, both in the world that now is and in that which is to come, in the presence of my Father in the heavens.'"

—John the Theologian, *The Falling Asleep of Mary* (400 A.D.)

But at a certain point in the celebration, the wine ran out, and Mary—who is referred to here not by name but as the mother of Jesus—went to her son and said, "They have no more wine."

At first we wonder what the point of her statement is, or if anything will happen, because Jesus' response to Mary is so abrupt. He said, "Woman, how does this concern of yours involve me? My hour has not yet come." (John 2:4)

But Mary's reply is simply to turn and say to those who were waiting on tables, "Do whatever he tells you," obviously assuming that Jesus would take some action.

Which of course, he does. Jesus tells the waiters to fill the six stone water jars at hand with water—and then he turned the water into wine. At fifteen to twenty-five gallons per jar, this was a lot of wine!

We never see Jesus touch the jars or do anything special with the water. He doesn't say a blessing or even utter specific words out loud that show that something had happened—it just does.

As John described it, after the waiters filled the water jars to the brim, Jesus ordered them to "draw some out and take it to the waiter in charge" for inspection. (John 2:8)

When this master of ceremonies tasted the water made wine, he called the groom over and said to him, "People usually serve the choice wine first; then when the guests have been drinking a while, a lesser vintage. What you have done is keep the choice wine until now." (John 2:9–10)

John ends the wedding at Cana story by pointing out that this was the first of the signs revealing Jesus' glory, and it was because of it that "his disciples believed in him." (John 2:11)

The Making of a Wedding Feast

In Jewish tradition, wine was a visible sign of God's loving gifts to human beings, as well as a sign of wisdom used in Jewish rites of purification.

Weddings in Palestine took three days, with the feasts lasting as long as a week. Weddings were elaborate events that included processions, speeches, religious blessings, and a wedding banquet feast.

So to run out of wine unexpectedly was a big, big deal!

What Does It All Mean?

My husband and I know what it's like to get married on a tight budget. Both of us were recent college graduates on our way to graduate school at the time of our wedding—and many of the wedding things that most couples take for granted were given to us as gifts by loving friends. Our cake. My wedding dress. The musicians at the wedding. Even the reception plans!

By the mere fact that Mary was so aware of what was going on at the celebration, and the fact that the waiters listened to her instructions regarding Jesus, it seems likely that Mary was somehow connected with the people getting married.

She could have been a relative, or a very good friend helping the couple and their families to have the best celebration possible.

It could be that when she became aware that there was a problem, Mary felt compassion for the newlyweds and didn't want them to be embarrassed; their happiness mattered to her.

Or maybe running out of wine wasn't as embarrassing as it was merely a tough situation. Who wants to be told that they are out of wine in the middle of a feast?

We are not really informed about what Mary was thinking, only that she was one of the first people to notice that the hosts had run out of wine, and so Mary went to tell Jesus.

Jesus' reply is interesting, at best. Full of hesitation, he asks Mary, "Woman, how does this concern of yours involve me?" (John 2:4)

The manner and language in which he says this, however, and the fact that he addresses his mother as "woman," might sound rude and harsh to the modern ear.

But the phrase and the term are Hebrew expressions that literally translate as, "what is this to me and to you?" or basically, "what does this problem have to do with me?"

A key to the story is the next statement Jesus makes: "My hour has not yet come," (John 2:4) or in other words, it's not time to begin this work yet!

But Jesus' reply does not change Mary's concern. She simply and immediately instructs the waiters to "do whatever he tells you," assuming that Jesus would ultimately respond to her, and the waiters appear willing to take her instructions.

Stained glass image of the wedding miracle at Cana from the Cathedral of Our Lady of Perpetual Help in Oklahoma City.

© Anamaría Scaperlanda-Ruiz

It is interesting that neither the groom nor the headwaiter knew the miracle had taken place; only the waiters were aware of the water turned to wine. But so were Jesus' disciples, who seemed to be the important audience for this story.

The wedding at Cana story ends with a dual announcement: this was the first of Jesus' "signs," and it was through this sign that his disciples believed in him.

Lord Knows

The word *hour* in the Cana story refers to the moment when God determined that it was time for Jesus to begin the work of salvation. The reason that Jesus was opposed to his mother's request in Cana was because his "hour" had not yet come. (John 2:4)

All of Jesus' life was directed to the great final "hour" when he gave his life on the cross, which then became the moment of redemption.

The Gospel of John Stands Alone

The Gospel of John was the last of the Gospels to be written. It is also the only one written in a lyrical and symbolic style.

This Gospel is completely different in technique and theology from the other three Gospels, known as the *Synoptic Gospels* because they share similar stories and the same chronology of events.

By contrast, the Gospel of John presents a whole different set of accounts and sayings of Jesus. And even the stories that it does have in common with the other Gospels are set in different parts of its Gospel narrative!

Sunday School

The **Synoptic Gospels** is the term used for the first three Gospels of the New Testament (Matthew, Mark, and Luke), which share content, style, and order of events—and which differ largely from John. The word Synoptic comes from the Greek *sunoptikos*, from *sunopsis*, meaning general view or seeing the whole together.

"In the Beginning"

From the opening phrase, John consciously echoes the beginning of the Bible and the book of Genesis.

Genesis begins with the story of creation, and the statement, "In the beginning, when God created the heavens and the earth," (Genesis 1:1) the earth was nothing but a dark and formless wasteland.

John opens his Gospel by telling us that "in the beginning was the Word" (John 1:1)—Jesus—and the Word was in God's presence, and the Word was God. Through Jesus, John notes, all things came into being, and found life and light, and the light shines on in darkness.

Just as God created the world in Genesis 1, John 1 presents the Word (Jesus), who was there at the beginning and yet brings creation to a new beginning, a new way of life.

The Uniqueness of the Gospel of John

John's language is elegant and sophisticated. In this Gospel Jesus frequently uses terms that have both literal and deeper metaphorical meanings. Jesus, for example, described himself as "living water" and "the bread of life," telling those who follow him that they will be "awaken[ed]" and experience "new birth."

As is true with the two Mary scenes, there are stories in John that appear in no other Gospel (like Jesus washing his disciples' feet). And none of the scenes in which Mary appears in the other Gospels turn up in the Gospel of John.

There are no parables in the Gospel of John. And when Jesus speaks, it is in long speeches full of intricate symbolism.

John's purpose for writing is more theological than historical, and he doesn't apologize for it. As he describes in his own words at the end of his Gospel: "These [events] have been recorded to help you believe that Jesus is the Messiah, the Son of God, so that through his faith you may have life in his name." (John 20:30)

Because his aim is not to write a complete biography of Jesus, John notes that there are "still many other things that Jesus did," (John 21:25) but that he has selected only the material he deems necessary for conveying his message that Jesus Christ is the Son of God made man.

The Cana story is a great example of John's style and symbolic presentation. For example, it is no coincidence that there are six stone water jars for the Jewish rites of purification because six is the allegorical number of imperfection in the Hebrew Scripture.

This means that the jars and the number of jars have been interpreted to symbolize human nature, which is transformed into something entirely new by Jesus (the water transformed into wine).

"Woman" as Name

After she is mentioned in the first sentence of the story and she sets the action in motion, we don't hear anything else about or from Mary in the wedding at Cana story.

An interesting aside to this story is the fact that the waiters actually obeyed Mary's (a woman's!) command to do what Jesus told them.

Perhaps it was just the way Mary acted, with such authority, but all we know is that she spoke—and they listened, as did Jesus.

As we discussed in an earlier chapter, Jesus addresses Mary as "woman" both times in the Gospel of John. We will parallel some aspects of this story with the second Mary appearance in the next chapter, at the crucifixion.

Addressing the women he encountered as "woman" is Jesus' normal form of address, and it is considered entirely courteous. Still, there is no precedent in Hebrew or Greek for a son to address his mother that way, so we can assume this to mean that there must be a special significance in how John used it here.

We can rule out rudeness another way. Because Jesus once again addressed Mary as "woman" at the foot of the cross as he is dying, the term was obviously not meant as a lack of affection for his mother.

Ultimately this unusual address draws attention *to* Mary, it does not take it away from her. And as we will see, it is the crucifixion that will make clear why, for John, Mary is both a true believer and truly "mother."

The Signs and the Hour

John's special symbolic language seems to return again and again to two specific terms—the "signs" (of Jesus) and "the hour."

The entire plot of the Gospel of John, in fact, is directed toward what he calls "the hour": Jesus' crucifixion and glorification.

And this is the language that Jesus uses at the wedding feast to remind his mother that it is not time for the mission he was sent here to accomplish, that "the hour" had not yet come!

After he performs the miracle, John points out that the turning of water into wine is the first of his signs, the first public demonstration of Jesus' power, and in effect, the beginning of the journey toward "the hour."

Performing Signs

The Cana story ends with the declaration that this was the first of Jesus' signs, the first time that Jesus revealed his glory in public.

It is no coincidence that Mary was not only present at this major event in her son's life, but that she encouraged it to happen when and how it did.

And it is no coincidence that she is presented as "woman" once again at the end of John's narrative, at the end of his Gospel, when in fact all of Jesus' signs and his glory have been fulfilled in his death and crucifixion. (See John 19:25–27)

Like bookends at the beginning and the end to his text, the two stories featuring Mary highlight for John Mary's role as "the mother of Jesus," and the first disciple, the first to believe him as Messiah.

The Command in This Story

Although many consider the dialogue between Jesus and Mary very awkward in this scene, for many reasons, I do love how Mary speaks.

Not only does Mary go up to her son with expectation and certainty, but also by doing so she effectively declares her belief and certainty that Jesus was the Messiah.

Mary's request implies faith in Jesus. There is no hesitation. She is completely sure of his abilities, and that's how Mary approaches her son.

Mary also lives out this confidence in the language she uses to tell the waiters what to do. Her instructions, "Do whatever he tells you," (John 2:5) leave no room for discussion! And they are her final recorded spoken words in Scripture.

The Bigger Picture

This command to "do whatever he tells you" is also symbolic of how Mary's life always points to Jesus, to the Christ.

To do whatever he tells you is how Mary models for us the way that she lived her own life, in faithful obedience and with complete certainty in the power of God to act at any given point.

Mary is mentioned in the first line of this story as the "mother of Jesus," a title that John uses for Mary up to nine times in his Gospel. And it is in this role that her conversation with Jesus is to be understood and that her actions are to be interpreted.

Mary was the instigator, the mastermind, if you will, of the beginning of Jesus' public ministry in this Gospel.

How do we interpret further what that means? Well, that awareness will continue to unfold for another millennium!

Mary in the Public Life of Jesus

The miracle at Cana takes place right after the call and invitation of the first disciples, and right before Jesus goes to Jerusalem and cleanses the Temple.

The call of the disciples is the term we use for how Jesus invited the first disciples to join him. The stories vary from Gospel to Gospel, but the message is always the same. The men heard an invitation to "come and follow" Jesus—and they said yes.

The cleansing of the Temple is the story of Jesus going to Jerusalem and being distressed by the selling and trading taking place at the Temple. In the Gospel of John, Jesus cleansed the Temple by turning over tables and expelling even the animals being sold (which were necessary for Jewish purification rites).

By placing the wedding at Cana in front of these two stories, John sets the event within the period in Jesus' life that we call the public ministry years (as opposed to all the years that we know nothing about).

> **Lord Knows**
>
> These are the seven "signs" or miracles that are told in the Gospel of John:
> 1. Turning water into wine at Cana (John 2:1–12)
> 2. The healing of the nobleman's son (John 4:46–54)
> 3. The healing of the paralyzed man (John 5:1–15)
> 4. The feeding of the five thousand (John 6:1–15)
> 5. The storm on the lake and Jesus walking on the Sea of Galilee (John 6:16–24)
> 6. The healing of the blind man (John 9:1–17)
> 7. The raising of Lazarus from the dead (John 11:1–44)

It seems unlikely that it is a coincidence, then, that the mother of Jesus appears at the beginning of this ministry in John. Mary is the first believer of the Messiah whose petition leads to Jesus' first miracle!

Mary believed *before* there was a sign. And Jesus' disciples, by contrast, believed in him after Jesus revealed his glory by performing this first of his signs. (John 2:11)

Mary is mentioned briefly again immediately following the verses on the wedding at Cana. "After this he went down to Capernaum, along with his mother and brothers [and his disciples] but they stayed there only a few days." (John 2:12)

Except for this fleeting mention, however, there is no other reference to Mary in the Gospel of John during the years of Jesus' public ministry.

But when Mary does appear again it is at the foot of the cross, where Jesus entrusts his mother to the care of the "beloved disciple" who for John is nothing less than the ultimate model of Christian faith.

Unforgettable Jesus

It is interesting to note that there are no proclaimed miracles in the Gospel of John.

Let me rephrase that. There *are* seven miracles in John—but instead of being presented as miracles, John introduces them as signs that point to a deeper and multi-layered theological understanding.

John's first part of the Gospel, in fact, is traditionally called the Book of Signs, which is made up of seven signs (miracles), some of which are worked into highly effective dramatic scenes. The signs in the Gospel of John are then followed by discourses from Jesus that explain their significance.

This Book of Signs aims at making Jesus unforgettable, and it begins with the story of John the Baptist (John 1:19) and concludes right before the story of Jesus' passion and death. (John 12:50)

The second half of the Gospel of John is called the Book of Glory, which tells the story of Jesus' passion and resurrection.

The Many Points of Cana

Perhaps the most important aspect of looking at the story of the wedding feast at Cana from a Marian point of view is what it portrays about the character and faith of the mother of Jesus.

The woman who speaks to her son in this story speaks her opinion with confidence. She is not only sure of herself, she's sure of her relationship with her son—and she's certain of her son's role as Messiah for his people.

Mary asked her son to take care of a need—and her son acceded to her request. But the point is that Mary asked for a sign, a miracle, that she knew Jesus as the Son of God could, and would, do!

And in so doing, Mary acted in deliberate faith, sure of her belief in Jesus as the Christ, the anointed Messiah.

Holy Mother
"I think I will hold on to Mary for the rest of my life. She still seems so young to me, just a girl who finds herself in the center of a plot that stretches beyond this time and place.
I watch her walk away. Her back is straight, and she grasps Joseph's arm … I watch them leave, and I cry. I cannot move, even when Mary glances back and smiles. She knows that on another day I will appear on her pathway again. I know it too. Because now I have an interest in this baby. In the middle of my own life, far from this time and place, I have pinned my hopes upon the Christ child. And I will walk with him many times before my own journey is through."
—Vinita Hampton Wright, *The Winter Seeking: a novella* (WaterBrook Press, 2003)

Why We Want to Remember

The wedding feast at Cana might be an unusual account in its style and its dialogue. Like anything else we examine that took place two thousand years ago, there is a lot to take into account regarding the meaning and the intent of the story.

But like any family story that is passed on from one generation to the next—and that continually shifts and grows with each new telling!—the main points of the story are truly the heart of the matter.

This is Jesus' first miracle.

He performed this public sign because his mother requested it. The event took place at the beginning of Jesus' public ministry, and his mother Mary was a central character in the story. By her request, and by the manner in which she made it, Mary truly witnessed her faith in her son, her certainty in his mission as the Messiah. And the last words recorded by Mary are: "Do whatever he tells you," a command that we will look at more closely later on in the book.

From Cana, we have to wait to see Mary again until the story of Jesus' passion and death, where we finally find her at the foot of the cross.

The Least You Need to Know

- ◆ Mary speaks her last words in Scripture at the wedding at Cana.
- ◆ Cana was the first sign by Jesus, his first miracle, and his mother requested it.
- ◆ By Mary's request, Jesus turned water into wine at a wedding feast.
- ◆ The next time Mary appears in the Gospel of John is at Jesus' crucifixion.

Mary at the Foot of the Cross

In This Chapter

◆ Mary at the cross

◆ A Roman crucifixion

◆ Presence as discipleship

◆ There is your mother

Michelangelo's *Pietà* might be the most recognized and famous artistic rendition of Mary and Jesus, an astonishing white marble sculpture portraying the suffering agony of a mother looking down at her lifeless son on her lap.

Although this particular moment in the crucifixion story, where Mary is holding Jesus as he's taken down from the cross, is not described in Scripture, it is implied by the narrative of the passion and death of Jesus as told in each of the four Gospels. This is the focus of our chapter.

A Mother's Love

Before talking about the Scripture passage describing Mary at the foot of the cross, or getting into her heart and mind during the death of her son, let's take a moment to briefly outline the story of how Jesus died.

This crucifixion event, and all the moments that led to it beginning with his arrest, is what's traditionally referred to as "the passion" of Jesus.

Lord Knows

Michelangelo Buonarroti, who also painted the famous fresco ceiling of the Sistine Chapel, created the *Pietà* before he was thirty years old. The moving image depicts Jesus' limp body resting heavily in Mary's arms, his right pierced hand hanging toward the front. Mary's head is bowed, and her right arm wrapped around her son's back. The *Pietà* is a life-size marble sculpture in St. Peter's Basilica in Rome, where it has been since the eighteenth century.

As I have said before, it was the cross, the resurrection, and the time that the disciples had with a resurrected Jesus that became the first narratives written down by the Gospel writers.

After the 1995 bombing of the Murrah building in Oklahoma City, the phrase "we will never forget" became the motto, the message that Oklahomans wanted to preserve. From car bumper stickers to billboards, the message has remained. We will never forget their deaths. We will never forget their lives. We will never forget or take for granted the gift of life.

For Christians, to remember the cross was the heart of the story of Jesus, the main point, and so it makes sense that when witnessing to others about the new life that the Messiah promised, they began by remembering how he died and that he resurrected.

Nicolas Coustou's Pietà, *also known as the* Virgin of Compassion, *in the choir of the Notre Dame Cathedral in Paris.*

© *María Ruiz Scaperlanda*

The Passion Narratives

All four Gospels describe in great detail the moments, the people, and the emotions that led up to and that brought Jesus of Nazareth to be crucified by the Romans.

There are many details in each Gospel about the passion narrative, and to cover them is not my purpose. Here's a general account of the events that took place the night Jesus died.

On the evening of the first day of the Jewish *Feast of the Unleavened Bread*, after Jesus celebrated the Passover supper with his disciples, he went with them to a place called Gethsemane to pray.

At some point during the night, an armed group of people was sent by the chief priests and elders to arrest Jesus. The group was led by one of Jesus' disciples, Judas Iscariot, who had agreed to help the chief priests arrest and kill Jesus for the price of thirty pieces of silver.

Jesus was first brought before the high priest, Caiaphas, and the scribes and elders—known as the Sanhedrin—who had already convened. These high leaders of the Jewish faith were afraid of the message Jesus proclaimed—that he was, indeed, the Son of God, the Messiah.

What were they going to do with an itinerant rabbi with large followings? After all, on more than one occasion, more than 5,000 people followed, listening to him speak. He preached to the poor and oppressed. He ate at the homes of tax collectors, cured lepers on the Sabbath, and like all prophets, he was a sign of contradiction and, therefore, a threat to the status quo, the comfortable—the Sadducees and Pharisees.

And it was fear that led them to plot to get rid of him.

Yet because Jewish law forbade them from carrying out a sentence of death, they tied Jesus up and took him to the Roman procurator, Pontius Pilate.

Pilate was afraid of Jesus, but he was even more afraid of an insurrection by the Jews. So he tried to get out of it by having Jesus beaten and tortured. He even attempted to trade Jesus' life for the release of a convicted murderer. But a rowdy and fierce crowd had gathered demanding Jesus' death.

As part of the torture, the procurator's soldiers stripped off Jesus' clothes and wrapped him in a purple military cloak. They placed a crown of thorns on his head and mocked him, spitting and hitting him as they said, "All hail, king of the Jews."

Finally, Pilate sent Jesus off to be crucified at a site called Golgotha (a name which means Skull Place). After they crucified him, they divided his garments among them, but they threw dice to see who would get his tunic. Then they placed a sign above his head that read, "This is Jesus, King of the Jews." (Matthew 27:37)

Lord Knows

Pontius Pilate was the governor of the small Roman province of Judea from 26 A.D. to 36 A.D. According to ancient historian Tacitus, he was also the procurator of that province. There are not many historical details about Pilate besides what's named in the Gospels, but tradition has it that his wife's name was Claudia Procula, and she is a canonized saint in Orthodox Christianity because in the Gospel accounts she urged Pilate to have nothing to do with Jesus. The belief that Pilate's wife became a Christian goes back to the second century, and may be found in the writings of historian Origen.

Two others were crucified with Jesus, one on his right and one on his left. It was about nine in the morning when they crucified him. (Mark 15:25)

From noon onward, there was darkness over the land. At midafternoon, Jesus cried out, "My God, my God, why have you forsaken me?" (Matthew 27:46) The curtain in the sanctuary was torn in two, and Jesus said in a loud cry, "'Father into your hands, I commend my spirit.' After he said this, he expired." (Luke 23:46)

When evening came, a wealthy man from Arimathea named Joseph, one of Jesus' disciples, asked Pilate for permission to take down Jesus' body. Joseph wrapped the body in fresh linen and laid it in his own new tomb. "Then he rolled a huge stone across the entrance of the tomb and went away. But Mary Magdalene and the other Mary remained sitting there, facing the tomb." (Matthew 28:60–61)

Near the Cross, There Stood Mary

The only time Mary's presence is directly acknowledged in the passion narratives in the Gospels is standing at the foot of her son's cross. "Near the cross of Jesus there stood his mother, his mother's sister, Mary the wife of Clopas, and Mary Magdalene." (John 19:25)

But it is difficult, and indeed impossible, to not imagine Mary on that day known as Good Friday when the central drama of Christianity unfolded when her son Jesus was crucified.

Scripture does not have to cover the other details of Mary's life because we know, as the early Christians would have known, that the mother of Jesus had to be there!

Somewhere inside her, Mary's heart must have occasionally wondered when it was going to happen—even without knowing what the end would be like. Yet the shock of hearing that day that her son had been arrested and taken to the high priests for questioning must have crashed through her body like that split second of sheer panic you feel after being in a car accident.

Mary followed and worked her way through the crowd at every place they took Jesus that night. She had to be there. And she made a point of standing and being somewhere that would allow Jesus to see her. How important it must have been to her to make sure that her suffering son knew he wasn't alone!

Street sign of the Via Dolorosa *(the Way of the Cross), noting the path that Jesus walked through the streets of Jerusalem.*

© *María Ruiz Scaperlanda*

Mary yelled in horror as dreadful lies were told about him and accusations were invented in order to make sure that Jesus' sentence would be death. She wept. She reached out and embraced her companions. And over and over she begged God for the help, the strength, to get through every moment of that horrendous night.

Without doubt, no one can fully imagine Mary's torment as she watched her son publicly accused, cursed, lied about, and tortured by scourging. What terror Mary must have felt hearing the crowd shout, "Away with him! Crucify him!" It was too much for any mother to endure.

The Gospel of Luke notes that "a great crowd followed him, including women who beat their breasts and lamented over him" (Luke 23:27)—surely Mary his mother would have been there, too.

What revulsion Mary must have felt at seeing her firstborn son being pushed like a criminal by the Roman soldiers and forced to carry the piece of wood on which he would be crucified. Did she find a way to face Jesus? Did she look for his eyes to assure him of her presence? Was she able to whisper words of comfort for him to hear above the hateful screams of the crowd?

Who knows how long it must have taken Jesus to reach the hill, the Place of the Skull, where the Romans typically crucified criminals outside the city of Jerusalem.

The agony of watching her son's suffering as he carried the heavy wood through the city's streets must have felt like a second lifetime to Mary.

Because public crucifixions in general, and this one in particular, would have drawn a large crowd, it is likely that Mary had to fight her way through the mob of curious onlookers. And at the site, she probably had to work her way closer by convincing the belligerent soldiers assigned to do that kind of morbid duty to let her go and remain by her suffering son.

The profound anguish that Mary must have felt as she watched her son's hands and feet being nailed on a piece of wood is simply unimaginable. Her heart must have wanted to do anything to stop the pain she saw and felt in her son's mangled and bloody body.

Holy Mother

Lord Jesus,
we gather in spirit at the foot of the Cross
with your Mother and the disciple whom
you loved.
We ask your pardon for our sins
which are the cause of your death.
We thank you for remembering us
in that hour of salvation
and for giving us Mary as our Mother.
Holy Virgin,
take us under your protection
and open us to the action of the Holy
Spirit.
Saint John,
obtain for us the grace of taking Mary
into our life, as you did,
and of assisting her in her mission. Amen.
May the Father and the Son
and the Holy Spirit
be glorified in all places
through the Immaculate virgin Mary.

—*The Three O'clock Prayer* (said around the world every day at 3 P.M. by members of the Society of Mary)

I have no doubt she wished she could trade places with him. With each labored gasp by Jesus, Mary, too, must have struggled to seize a breath.

Mary of Nazareth, who had trusted the spirit of God to lead her throughout her life, now courageously clung to that same inner spirit to carry her through this indescribably ghastly event.

John tells us that near the cross of Jesus stood his mother. Yet it is extraordinary that after everything she endured in those agonizing hours, Mary could still stand!

Only the strength that Mary counted on from God the Most High could allow her the ability to be that present to her son, in spite of the anguish and exhaustion that she, too, must have felt.

I am reminded here of the exhaustion of childbirth, but this time, it was the slow and painful labor of watching your child die.

Nowhere Else but Here

Like a mother who is waiting to hear from surgeons after her son was critically injured in a car accident, Mary's vigil by the cross must have felt absolutely endless. But Mary wasn't in the waiting room. Like pouring salt on an open wound, every moment she stood by the cross enlarged her suffering and torment.

To make matters worse, she had to endure listening to bystanders taunt and insult Jesus. Yet she heard her son respond: "Father, forgive them; they do not know what they are doing." (Luke 23:34) Did Mary know that forgiveness has the power to heal? Was she able to forgive?

When one of the criminals hanging with him mocked him saying, "Aren't you the Messiah? Then save yourself and us," Mary heard the other criminal rebuke him saying, "Have you no fear of God, seeing you are under the same sentence? We deserve it, after all. We are only paying the price for what we've done, but this man has done nothing wrong." (Luke 23:41)

In spite of the pain, in spite of the anguish, Mary must have wept in thanksgiving hearing her son's compassionate response to the repentant criminal, "I assure you; this day you will be with me in paradise." (Luke 23:43)

And Mary watched in awe as darkness fell over the whole land and lasted until Jesus died. Because the Gospels say midafternoon, three o'clock has traditionally been considered the hour of Jesus' death.

What We Know of Crucifixions

The practice of crucifixion was used by the Romans only on despised enemies and dreadful criminals, as it was considered a dishonorable and humiliating death.

It was not uncommon for scourging to precede the crucifixion, to force the accused to lose large amounts of blood and to endure added suffering.

First-century Jewish historian Josephus described stories of Romans crucifying people in odd positions simply for the sake of amusement. To add to the humiliation in the Roman crucifixions, the victim was most likely naked while he was forced to carry the large piece of wood that would become part of his cross.

At the site, the victim was nailed to the wood using long iron spikes, probably through the wrist or just above the wrist, since the flesh of the hands cannot support a person's body weight.

Sometimes it only took hours, but often the victim took days to die, usually from suffocation. It was not unusual for the soldiers to break the prisoner's legs to accelerate the death.

Clearly, the goal was not just to kill the condemned but also to bring shame on him. That's why the body was not removed from the cross but left for vultures to eat it rather than allow for proper burial, adding to the person's dishonor.

Modeling Discipleship

Mary of Nazareth, who once had the power to affect the course of history by her yes or no to the angel Gabriel, became powerless to stop the torture and death of her son. All she had was the ability to say yes or no to God in the face of these events.

When I first watched Mel Gibson's movie *The Passion of the Christ*, I was struck most of all by the powerful portrayal of Mary in that 2004 film. There were many scenes that touched my heart, but two ideas presented in the movie are essential in understanding Mary.

First of all, the greatest gift Mary gave Jesus throughout the passion events was her presence. When all other disciples had left and even denied Jesus, Mary remained.

Lord Knows

Sometimes the words "apostles" and "disciples" are used interchangeably. But they are not the same. A disciple is someone who embraces and follows the teachings of another, so anyone who followed Jesus then or now is a disciple. The apostles is the name given to the original twelve men chosen by Jesus, sometimes simply called "the twelve." They are Andrew, James, John, Simon whom he named Peter, Philip, Bartholomew, Thomas, Matthew, James the son of Alphaeus, Simon who was called a Zealot, Judas the son of James, and Judas Iscariot (who betrayed Jesus) (see Luke 6:14–16). After the resurrection, the first group gathered elected Matthias to take Judas's place. (See Mark 3:16–19)

This is powerfully portrayed in the movie when Jesus falls for a second time as he's carrying the heavy wooden cross through the crowded streets, and Mary runs to Jesus to look in his eyes and tenderly touch his face. But above all, Mary wants him to see her face and hear her verify lovingly, "I am here!"

Mary the mother and Mary the disciple were faithful to Jesus, even unto death.

As a mother of four children who are each two years apart, I have had many years of teenagers and young adults "hanging out" in what's come to be known as the "Scap house." To these children, many of whom eat, sleep, and pray daily in our home, I have become "Mama Scap."

I thought of this as I heard John, Peter, and Mary Magdalene, all address Mary as "Mother" in *The Passion of the Christ*. Because she was a daily and obvious part of their lives, Mary truly was mother to them! And it is this reality that Jesus acknowledges on the cross before his death.

The Mother of All Faithful

There are two specifics about Mary that are made clear in the Gospel passion accounts. Mary stood near the cross as her son was dying. And from the cross before he died, Jesus commended his mother to one of his disciples.

Seeing his mother standing there by the cross with the disciple he loved, Jesus turned to Mary and said, "'Woman, there is your son.' In turn he said to the disciple, 'There is your mother'. From that hour onward, the disciple took her into his care." (John 19:26–27)

As he did in the story of the wedding at Cana, in the final moments of his life, Jesus addressed his mother as "woman." This time, however, it was to entrust Mary and the beloved disciple to each other.

Christian tradition has long interpreted this moment as much more than literally assigning one of his disciples to take care of his mother.

Jesus' words to Mary, "there is your son," are symbolic of Mary's motherhood to all Christian believers, not only this particular disciple or even the immediate group of disciples.

Jesus' gesture from the cross was an acknowledgment of what had already been in place with his disciples. Mary was already "Mother" to them, and now Jesus was giving his mother to the whole body of believers—across time and space.

You Shall Be Pierced by a Sword

At the crucifixion, the "hour" of his mission that Jesus spoke about in Cana, had now come.

But there are clear echoes in the passion account of another Gospel story—the prophesy by Simeon at the presentation of a young Jesus in the Temple. (Luke 2:34–35)

Surely Mary never forgot Simeon's haunting words that she "shall be pierced with a sword."

What Mary experienced watching her son Jesus die pierced and cut through her heart. It was, literally, a heartache—one that ripped a mother's insides to pieces.

And yet Mary stood. She remained. She was there at the cross by her son, until that final moment when Jesus said, "Now it is finished." And he bowed his head, "and delivered over his spirit." (John 19:30)

In Gibson's portrayal of the passion, there is a moment when Mary looks up at her son and passionately says, "Flesh of my flesh. Heart of my heart. My son, let me die with you."

No, this moment is not recorded in any written account of Jesus' passion and death—but it comes across entirely possible, and the portrayal enhances the tradition and the knowledge we have of Mary.

By choosing to remain at the cross, in spite of her own suffering, Mary consciously postponed her own distress and grieving in order to be present to her dying son.

And by doing so, she was able to declare to Jesus her mother's love by her presence, without words, in spite of her own broken heart.

Can You Drink the Cup?

For early Christians, the story of the passion and death of Jesus was the central and most important aspect of their faith. This one event, which was followed by Christ's resurrection, encompassed their entire understanding of salvation history.

Jesus, son of Mary, came to bring life out of death and light out of darkness. And he invited all who wanted to know this life to follow him. But to do so, they also had to be willing to drink the same cup that Jesus did. To do so is to know eternal life.

Because Christians have been trying to understand this mystery and embrace this promise for the past two thousand years, there have been many traditions that have come into being to help believers remember the passion. Sometimes these prayer traditions are referred to as *devotions*.

> **Sunday School**
>
> A **devotion** is an act of religious observance or prayer, especially when private, but it can also be a public observance. Sometimes *devotions* is used as a synonym for *prayers*, as in my children say their daily devotions before bedtime.

The Way of the Cross

One of the most powerful devotions or traditions created to help Christians remember the final hours of Jesus is called the Stations of the Cross or the Way of the Cross (in Latin, *Via Crucis* or *Via Dolorosa*).

The stations themselves are, literally, fourteen specific moments during the passion narrative. Most Anglican and Roman Catholic churches have "stations" somewhere in the church structure or grounds—meaning pictures depicting each scene or moment that is named. See the image of the Way of the Cross that follows.

Although they vary in number and even scene, the traditional fourteen stations are as follows:

1. Jesus is sentenced to death.

2. Jesus is given the cross to carry.

3. Jesus falls for the first time.

Portrait marking the Third Station of the actual Way of the Cross (Via Dolorosa) *in Jerusalem.*

© *María Ruiz Scaperlanda*

4. Jesus meets Mary on the way.

5. A man named Simon the Cyrene helps Jesus carry his cross.

6. A woman named Veronica wipes Jesus' face.

7. Jesus falls for the second time.

8. Jesus talks to the women of Jerusalem.

9. Jesus falls for the third time.

10. Jesus is nailed to the cross

11. Jesus dies.

12. Mary stands near the cross.

13. Jesus is taken down from the cross and laid in the arms of his mother.

14. Jesus is laid in the tomb.

As you can see, there are three scenes from the Stations of the Cross that acknowledge Mary's presence during the crucifixion story: on the way to being crucified; standing at the foot of the cross; and holding the body of her dead son—the scene so masterfully captured by Michelangelo's *Pietà*.

The tradition of the Way of the Cross developed as a tool to reflect and prayerfully walk "the way" that Jesus walked, his way of the cross.

The earliest roots of this prayer tradition are traced to the early Christians at Jerusalem who visited and honored the exact places of Christ's passion.

Some traditions affirm that Mary herself visited regularly these holy places of her son's passion. Over the centuries, Christians continued to visit these places to honor and remember the story of Jesus' suffering.

When it became impossible to go to Jerusalem to visit the actual places because of persecutions of Christians, a practice developed in which images were created to visually "visit" the place—and this eventually grew into a defined set of fourteen stations or moments in the passion.

Although the specifics varied over the centuries and from country to country, there is a written account in the fifteenth century that lists fourteen stations.

Mary's Sorrows

In the early 1200s, three hundred years before the Protestant Reformation, a prayer practice spread throughout Italy and Europe for meditating on Christ's passion by praying on "the seven sorrows of Mary." They are as follows:

1. The prophecy of Simeon.

2. The flight into Egypt.

3. The loss of the child Jesus in the Temple.

4. Mary meets Jesus carrying the cross.

5. Mary stands beneath the cross of Jesus.

6. Mary receives the dead body of Jesus.

7. Jesus is laid in the tomb.

This devotion of Mary's sorrows, practiced originally by a religious community called the Servite Order, encouraged the believer to meditate on seven sorrowful episodes in the life of the Virgin Mary.

The object of this devotion is to understand the spiritual suffering of the mother of God and her compassion with the suffering of her son.

This practice became popular because Christians hundreds of years ago recognized in Mary a model of what Jesus meant when he said, if anyone wishes "to come after me, he must deny his very self, take up his cross, and begin to follow in my footsteps." (Matthew 16:24)

Of the traditional seven sorrows, three of them are assumed because of Mary's presence at her son's passion and death: Mary meets Jesus as he's carrying the cross; Mary receives the body of Jesus after it's taken down from the cross; and Mary is present as Jesus is placed in the tomb.

One with Us

Why has Mary's suffering been so important to remember in the Christian tradition?

There is no suffering Mary endured that cannot be paralleled in contemporary (or ancient) human suffering:

- Being single and pregnant
- Fleeing your country as a refugee
- Losing your child and/or having a child run away from home
- Being told terrible news
- Watching someone you love suffer
- Worst of all, enduring the death of your innocent child

Holy Mother

"In dangers, in doubts, in difficulties, think of Mary, call upon Mary. Let not her name depart from your lips, never suffer it to leave your heart. And that you may more surely obtain the assistance of her prayer, neglect not to walk in her footsteps. With her for guide, you shall never go astray; while invoking her, you shall never lose heart; so long as she is in your mind, you are safe from deception; while she holds your hand, you cannot fall; under her protection you have nothing to fear; if she walks before you, you shall not grow weary; if she shows you favor, you shall reach the goal."

—St. Bernard of Clairvaux (d. 1153)

In the passion story alone, Mary witnessed the most horrid events as she watched her son be humiliated, tortured, and finally nailed to a cross until death.

Still, it's just not enough to say that we relate to Mary because Mary is human like us, so she understood suffering and heartache. If all she did was tolerate and survive her suffering, Mary's stories, as dramatic as they are, would sound no better than a bad country song!

The Importance of Mary's Suffering

Mary's suffering was not merely about survival.

Every story we have about Mary, even one as heartbreaking as standing by her son as he died on a cross, points to a woman who trusted in the goodness of God, in spite of what she could not see.

Surely she must have doubted if she would be able to remain standing at the foot of that cross. There were many moments when she had to feel completely incapable of facing the pain staring at her in the face.

But it was Mary's ability to turn to God, especially at all those difficult and painful moments in her life that allowed her to stand in fortitude.

Mary's suffering was what theologians call "redemptive" because it did not remain in the death and darkness, but instead brought about life and salvation.

How was this possible?

Not because of anything Mary did actually, except for one major thing: her openness to God's hand in her suffering.

Paul explained it this way in his letter to the Colossians (the church community in Colossae): "Even now I find my joy in the suffering I endure for you. In my own flesh I fill up what is lacking in the sufferings of Christ for the sake of his body, the church." (Colossians 1:24)

Every time Mary opened her heart to God in the middle of the pain, in the midst of the uncertainty, she allowed God's redemptive hand to change it, to transform it, to make it better. She became open to the possibility that life could come out of the inconceivable and the ridiculous, and, yes, even from the horrendous.

The Least You Need to Know

- All four Gospels—Matthew, Mark, Luke, and John—have a narrative of the passion and death of Jesus.

- Only the Gospel of John specifies that Mary was at the foot of the cross.

- Roman crucifixions were beastly and dehumanizing proceedings.

- Jesus commended his mother to his beloved disciple, and symbolically, to all who follow Jesus.

- Mary's suffering was redemptive because she trusted in life and salvation in the midst of her agonizing pain.

11

For the Last Time

In This Chapter

- ◆ Mary in the New Testament
- ◆ Present at Pentecost
- ◆ The lady of the Apocalypse
- ◆ Mary's assumption to heaven

Mary of Nazareth has been portrayed and described in innumerable paintings, sculptures, and pieces of literature over the course of the past two thousands years. The greatest of cathedrals and the simplest of street shrines have been dedicated to her. (See the image of Mary on the following page.) Poets and composers continue to invoke her, and her name has been whispered by believers seeking her help, guidance, and protection from the beginning of Christianity.

Because the final mentions of the mother of Jesus in the New Testament are brief, as we will discuss in this chapter, it makes her devotion from the earliest of Christianity all the more powerful. This devotion to the mother of Jesus clearly belonged to and was birthed from those early believers.

Acts 1: Scripture's Final Mention of Mary

It is a simple statement. She doesn't speak a word, at least not any that are recorded! But her presence is recorded both by her first name and by her prevailing role as the mother of Jesus.

A street sculpture of a cross with Jesus on one side and Mary on the other, from Finisterre, Spain.

© *María Ruiz Scaperlanda*

Lord Knows

Baptism is a religious ceremony marked by the symbolic use of water poured over a person to signify the person's purification—and belonging into the community of believers.

Describing the moments following Jesus' final instructions to his disciples and his ascension into heaven, the first chapter of Acts tells us that the group returned to Jerusalem from the mount called Olivet, outside the city.

Once in Jerusalem, "together they devoted themselves to constant prayer. There were some women in their company, and Mary the mother of Jesus, and his brothers." (Acts 1:14)

This, and the day of Pentecost which immediately followed, are the final events recorded in the New Testament that recorded Mary's presence.

Gathered and Waiting

The book of Acts begins with the story of Jesus' ascension into heaven, the moment when the apostles stood and watched as Jesus "was lifted up before their eyes in a cloud which took him from their sight." (Acts 1:9)

This community of believers, which at that point numbered about a hundred and twenty, surely must have felt a mix of emotions as they waited for the Holy Spirit, which Jesus specifically promised before his ascension.

Were they anxious? Worried? Fearful? Excited?

Probably a mix of all of these emotions!

Here they were, witnesses to Jesus' death and resurrection, their lives changed forever—and still without an understanding of what their life would now be like.

After Jesus returned to his Father in heaven, he told them that they were somehow supposed to be his "witnesses in Jerusalem, throughout Judea and Samaria, yes, even to the ends of the earth." (Acts 1:8)

But first, Jesus guaranteed them, they would receive the Holy Spirit.

Pentecost (Shavuot)

In the Jewish tradition, Shavuot, also known as the Festival of Weeks and Pentecost, is the second most important feast (with Passover being the first). Agriculturally it marks the harvest of the first fruits. Historically, it commemorates God giving the Torah to Moses at Mount Sinai.

Pentecost was the closing festival of the harvest and of the Paschal season, falling on the fiftieth day after Passover.

As with Passover, Jews from all parts and countries came home to Jerusalem to celebrate the feast.

When the day of Pentecost came, it found the community of followers of Jesus, including Mary, still gathered together in one place.

Suddenly the group heard a loud noise of strong rushing wind that swept all through the house where they were seated.

And in a description that echoes the burning bush that displayed the presence of God for Moses on Mount Sinai, tongues of fire came to rest on each of the disciples that had gathered there to pray.

Sunday School

John the Baptist baptized to prepare the way for Jesus. But Jesus asked his disciples to baptize believers "in the name of the Father and of the Son and of the Holy Spirit," proclaiming belief in the Trinity. (Matthew 28:19)

The **Trinity** is the central doctrine of the Christian faith. It declares that there are three distinct persons in one God, God the Father, God the Son (Jesus), and God the Holy Spirit.

Belief in a Triune God (the Holy Trinity) is a fundamental belief shared by all Christian denominations and expressed in all Christian creeds.

Each of them was filled with the Holy Spirit, and they began to speak in foreign tongues proclaiming the marvels of God as the Spirit prompted them.

Come Holy Ghost

Pentecost was without a doubt one of those moments in life that instantaneously changes everything.

Not only were these disciples of Jesus transformed forever by what they witnessed about Jesus' life. But they were now filled with the Holy Spirit and challenged to proclaim this Jesus to anyone and everyone who was willing to hear!

What is this Holy Spirit?

The Holy Spirit (sometimes called the Holy Ghost) is the third "person" of the Trinity. It is distinct from the other two persons, but coequal and coeternal with them.

Let me try to explain the Holy Spirit, by beginning with the Trinity.

Holy Trinity is nothing less than the central doctrine of the Christian faith. It declares that there are three distinct persons—God the Father, God the Son (Jesus), and God the Holy Spirit—in one God. Not three gods, but three *persons* in *one God*.

While it's ultimately a mystery that can't be rationally understood, the Trinity is a fundamental belief shared by all Christian denominations and expressed in all of the Christian *creeds*. Its foundation is found in Matthew 28:18–20, when a resurrected Jesus commanded his apostles to "go, therefore, and make disciples of all the nations. Baptize them in the name of the Father, and of the Son, and of the Holy Spirit."

This exact language is used to this day by all Christian faiths at baptism.

The Holy Spirit is often described as the giver of life or the spirit of God. It's what guides and sheds light on our faith and our understanding.

Spreading the News

But before we get too caught up in trying to give language to theological doctrines, let's go back to the day of Pentecost.

I think the dramatic scene that followed the descent of the Holy Spirit on the disciples provides a good visual for understanding the Holy Spirit.

In the second chapter of Acts, Luke describes how so many people had heard and were attracted by the sound of the loud wind, that a large crowd gathered outside the place where the disciples were gathered.

On seeing the crowd, the disciples began to speak and to praise God, and each person gathered there who was listening to them heard the message spoken in his or her own language.

In other words, even though the listening crowd included Jews, Cretans, and Arabs from many nations and regions who had come to Jerusalem for the feast of Pentecost, every person heard the words spoken by the disciples in his or her very own language.

The crowd was amazed, confused, and dumbfounded, and made a point of calling attention to the fact that all these speakers were Galileans! How could they know all these different languages?

Peter, who led the group, was the first to speak up about the life, death, and resurrection of Jesus the Nazorean. He explained to the crowd, "This is the Jesus God has raised up, and we are his witnesses. Exalted at God's right hand, he first received the promised Holy Spirit from the Father, then poured this Spirit out on us. This is what you now see and hear." (Acts 2:32–33)

What It All Meant

Imagine what must have been going through Mary's mind as she watched this incredible event unfold. What was she feeling?

Mary had always known that her son Jesus, a Nazorean like her, was not only a prophet from God; he was the Son of God, who had come to save and redeem the world.

But she must have been overwhelmed with thanksgiving and awe at what she had just witnessed. The spirit of God had descended on all of them!

These same disciples who lived through the anguish and suffering of watching their Lord Jesus die on a cross, whose hearts had been ripped open like hers by that horrid death—they were now able to proclaim and witness about his resurrection and the promise of life eternal.

Sometimes there are no words to describe emotions, but clearly Mary must have been filled to the brim with gratefulness that she, too, was a part of it. That she was allowed to witness the beginning, the igniting, of the new life that her son Jesus came to proclaim.

The event of Pentecost is remarkable not only because of the witnessing that took place as the Holy Spirit filled the disciples with God's presence and wisdom, but also because this moment marked the beginning of the Christian community's missionary life.

According to Acts, the day of Pentecost culminated with the baptism of some three thousand new Christians. (Acts 2:41) And the community devoted themselves "to the apostles' instruction and the communal life, to the breaking of bread and prayers. A reverent fear overtook them all, for many wonders and signs were performed by the apostles … Day by day the Lord added to their number those who were being saved." (Acts 2:42–43, 47)

It's important to keep in mind as we discuss the preaching carried out by those first believers, that the first disciples who followed Jesus were not learned or educated men. They were not rabbis or doctors of the law. They were simple folk, by and large (a fishermen, a tax collector, and so on) who had been called by their Master to spread the Gospel of his life.

The Book of Acts

Here are just a couple of notes on the Acts of the Apostles.

The book of Acts is a historical account of the early years of the Christian church, a record of the history of the Jerusalem church. It also describes the spread of

Christianity to other regions by telling stories of those early preachers, recording their words, their deeds, and even their deaths, much as the Gospels do for the life of Jesus.

You could say that Acts is meant to be a "life story" (or Gospel!) of the early Church.

The book of Acts is traditionally considered the companion and sequel to the Gospel of Luke. Both texts are addressed to Theophilus, and are written by the same author.

Lord Knows

"Mary the Dawn, Christ the perfect Day:
Mary the Gate, Christ the heavenly Way.
Mary the Root, Christ the mystic Vine:
Mary the Grape, Christ the sacred Wine.
Mary the Corn—sheaf, Christ the living Bread:
Mary the Rose—tree, Christ the Rose blood—red.
Mary the Fount, Christ the cleansing Flood:
Mary the Chalice, Christ the saving Blood.
Mary the Temple, Christ the temple's Lord:
Mary the Shrine, Christ its God adored.
Mary the Beacon, Christ the Heaven's Rest:
Mary the Mirror, Christ the Vision blest."

—Ancient prayer, anonymous

In both style and context, there is no other book like Acts within or outside the New Testament. It provides a unique picture into the life of the ancient church, but above all it shows us the mind-set and outlook of the early Christian believers.

The four Gospels focus on Jesus, his words, his life, and his ministry. The letters and *epistles* that make up the rest of the New Testament address specific Christians or Christian communities about particular areas of concern for that person or community. Acts, by contrast, provides a glimpse into the daily life and struggles of the early Christian community.

Sunday School

An **epistle** is a letter or a formal writing directed or sent to a person or group of persons. The letters from Paul and the apostles to Christian communities which make up the New Testament are often referred to as *epistles*.

Bringing the House Down

We know that Mary was a part of this growing Christian community described in the book of Acts, but there are no direct references to her by name beyond the Gospels and the beginning of Acts.

The book of the Acts of the Apostles really focuses on two main apostles: Peter, who gives many of the discourses and directs the action in the first twelve chapters, and Paul, whose conversion and missionary work is described in detail beginning in chapter thirteen.

It was the preaching and leadership of both men that powerfully and deliberately directed the spread of the early Christian community as it began to define them as "Church," and as a distinct faith, rather than another sect of Judaism.

A Note About Geography

Although Palestine, and specifically the region of Galilee, was the setting for the ministry of Jesus and some of his earliest disciples, most of the work of the early Christian church took place outside the region.

Setting aside the four Gospels, in fact, the remainder of the New Testament mentions places and communities outside of Palestine, such as the city of Antioch in Syria, Alexandria, Egypt, and Rome.

Paul's letters testify to this reality, addressing groups of Christians all over Asia Minor (modern-day Turkey), Greece, or other church communities around the Mediterranean Sea.

Saul of Tarsus

The great apostle Paul, as we mentioned before, was originally named Saul of Tarsus. Paul is described in the book of Acts as a Hellenized Jew and a Roman citizen from Tarsus, in present-day Turkey.

He was also a great persecutor of Christians prior to his conversion. Paul is not only a key figure in the spread and adoption of Christianity, his teaching was also fundamental in defining Christianity as a religion inspired and birthed by the spirit of God.

Paul wrote epistles to Christian communities everywhere, which became a major portion of the New Testament.

The names attached to the Pauline Epistles—Paul's Letter to the Romans and Paul's Letter to the Corinthians, for example—define the specific Christian community or group of individuals to whom they were addressed.

Lord Knows

Theophilus is the name to which both the Gospel of Luke and the Acts of the Apostles are addressed, so his life must have coincided with the writing of Luke and Acts, somewhere in the first century. There is one tradition that says that Theophilus was a Jew of Alexandria, and another that he was a converted Roman official. But there is yet another tradition that asserts that he was not a specific person but believers in general, because *theophilus* means literally "lover of God."

Peter, Paul, and Mary

Both in his letters and in what is recorded in Acts, Paul's interest in Mary seems to be most concerned with emphasizing the true idea of the Incarnation, desiring to teach a true understanding of the mystery of Jesus' coexisting divinity and humanity.

The only direct reference to Mary in the epistles is found in Galatians 4:4. The letter, written by Paul to a community of Christians in the area of Asia Minor, notes that "when the designated time had come, God sent forth his Son born of a woman, born under the law."

In the letter Paul wrote to the church in Rome, Paul's only reference to Jesus' birth is that Jesus "was descended from David according to the flesh" (Romans 1:3), again, to call attention to the fact that he was not only the Son of God, but also human.

Peter, on the other hand, is focused from the beginning on proclaiming the life of Jesus that he himself witnessed. And he does so by continually pointing to the cross and to Jesus' resurrection as he invites the Jews to be baptized and receive the gift of the Holy Spirit.

As Peter declares in his first discourse on the day of Pentecost, "let the whole house of Israel know beyond any doubt that God has made both Lord and Messiah this Jesus whom you crucified." (Acts 2:36)

Early Christian Preachers

After Paul and Peter had died and other Christians had taken charge of spreading the Gospel, Mary of Nazareth is mentioned by many of the early Christian writers.

For example, Irenaeus (b. approximately in 150 A.D.), who was a priest and became a *bishop* of the church in Lyons, calls Mary the church's most eminent advocate.

> ### Sunday School
>
> **Bishop** is from the Greek word meaning "overseer." As the early church became conscious of the necessity of organizing, the apostles first appointed deacons. Later, imitating the order in synagogues, they appointed presbyters, sometimes called bishops in the Gentile churches. Only James can claim to be regarded as a bishop (of Jerusalem) in the later sense of the term. In the modern church, a bishop has spiritual and administrative authority over a group of priests or ministers and the churches in a certain region. They are considered the successors of the apostles by divine institution.

Ignatius of Antioch, born in Syria around the year 50 A.D., wrote several epistles to the church at Ephesus with one of his topics being to urge that the church connect the mysteries of Jesus' life more closely with those of Mary's life.

For these early Christian leaders, the model of Mary's life was already an obvious source of inspiration and guidance for a believer growing in the Christian faith.

Other Places, Other Stories

Mary must have been an immense source of encouragement for this early Christian community that first gathered in Jerusalem to receive the Holy Spirit, and that then quickly grew as more and more people were baptized in the name of God the Father, Jesus the Son, and the Holy Spirit.

Imagine, knowing that the mother of this Messiah whose name you have just taken on by faith is still living among you!

In reality, what the New Testament did not provide in terms of data information on Mary, the human imagination and devotion did. It didn't take long before places associated with Mary and her life with Jesus were visited, becoming sacred spots where Christians gathered to pray.

What We Know from Other References

According to the book of Acts, during the periods of persecution, Jewish Christians left Jerusalem. Mary would have been among these refugees. But we can only conjure assumptions about what this meant as far as where she lived.

In addition, tradition places Mary living at least temporarily near the city of Ephesus, in Asia Minor, where documents say that the apostle John lived and died.

But historians say that it is more probable (based on the archeology, tradition, and assumptions from early sources) that even if Mary left, she returned and permanently resided in the city of Jerusalem, or near it.

Early Christian art featuring moments in the life of Mary also provides us with clues about her life and her importance to the early believers.

It was very common for graves of the early Christians to picture the saints, those who had died, often martyred for their faith, and Mary was among the most popular images.

Besides the representation of Mary found in the catacombs of Priscilla in Rome (which date back to the beginning of the second century), there are also pictures of Mary and the adoration of the wise men that are found in the cemeteries of Domitilla and Calixtus from the third century.

Mary was also painted in the fourth century in the cemetery of Saints Peter and Marcellinus. In one picture she appears with her head uncovered, and in another one she has her arms half extended in supplication, with the infant Jesus standing before her.

Because the earliest picture of Mary dates to the beginning of the second century and is found in the city of Rome, this tells us that a mere fifty years or so after the death of the apostle John (around 100 A.D.), the tradition of honoring and venerating Mary the mother of Jesus had already expanded from Jerusalem all the way to the Church community in Rome!

Cemetery art showing Mary, the mother of Jesus, and Mary Magdalene both at the foot of the cross, from Salzburg, Austria.

© María Ruiz Scaperlanda

The Lady in the Book of Revelation

The book of Revelation (also known as the Apocalypse) is unique within the New Testament, which in general is otherwise made up of historical narrative.

But Revelation, which was written sometime after 90 A.D., is an apocalypse, meaning a drama and prophecy regarding the end of the world.

One particular prophecy found in the book of Revelation has long been connected to Mary.

Although it's a little long, I think it's important to examine the passage as it stands, without trying to interpret it. It reads like this:

> A great sign appeared in the sky, a woman clothed with the sun, with the moon under her feet, and on her head a crown of twelve stars. Because she was with child, she wailed aloud in pain as she labored to give birth. Then another sign appeared in the sky: it was a huge dragon, flaming red, with seven heads and ten horns; on his heads were seven diadems. His tail swept a third of the stars from the sky and hurled them down to the earth. Then the dragon stood before the woman about to give birth, ready to devour her child when it should be born. She gave birth to a son—a boy destined to shepherd all the nations with an iron rod. Her child was caught up to God and to his throne. The woman herself fled into the desert, where a special place had been prepared for her by God; there she was taken care of for twelve hundred and sixty days. (Revelation 12:1–6)

Although the whole passage is traditionally understood as applying to the body of the church, these particular verses do specifically refer to a mother whose son was destined to rule all the nations. And this has been assumed to be and interpreted as referring to Jesus and his mother Mary.

Lord Knows

The name of Mary became very popular among Christians toward the end of the fourth century. Historians point to this phenomenon as another sign of the reverence and respect that the early church had for the Mother of God.

Scripture can operate on more than one level and have multiple meanings; it doesn't have to be an either/or, but it can be a both/and!

Nevertheless, the book of Revelation is not an easy text to grasp, let alone understand. It's a highly symbolic book, which presents very dramatic and often violent images to present the struggle between the Christian church and the powers of evil.

Ultimately, however, the book concludes with a message of hope for all believers, the final and everlasting triumph of the Lord Jesus Christ.

Why Acts Matters

The book of Acts is assumed to have been written by the evangelist Luke sometime around the years 85–90 A.D. Although the book is meant to describe the spread of Christianity and the founding of Christian communities in the early years of the faith, its main thrust is not the details of history as much as the reality of God in the history!

The text includes several personal discourses or presentations on the Christian faith by Peter and Paul, and it emphasizes the missionary vocation of the Christian faith.

Over and over, the preaching of the apostles presented in the book of Acts give testimony to what they had witnessed about Jesus—and it invited all believers to do the same.

Still the One

Because so much evidence points to Mary being remembered by the early church—from art and paintings in cemeteries to churches and children being named after her—it is proper to assume that the early Christians venerated Mary in a special way as the mother of Jesus Christ, the Messiah of God.

Just as Scripture makes no reference to Jesus appearing to his mother after his resurrection, it must have been a little disconcerting for early Christians that nothing else was written down telling the Church about the life of Mary.

But that is why it is so important to honor tradition and the oral stories that have been passed on through the centuries.

Some of the greatest feasts that the Church still celebrates honoring Mary are based on events that were never written in Scripture, at least not in the canon of the Bible.

The feast of the Nativity of Mary, for example, which is celebrated on September 8 every year, is based on the (noncanonical) gospel of James. We know that by the sixth century the feast was already being celebrated in Syria, spreading to the whole Christian Church as a major feast in the next two centuries.

There is no better example for the importance of tradition, however, than the feast of the Assumption of Mary.

Mary's Death or Assumption

There is no document by which we can formulate a definite opinion about Mary's death. There isn't even a certain tradition to guide us.

Church historian Caesar Baronius (d. 1607) in his historical accounts, known as his *Annals*, refers to a passage in the *Chronicon of Eusebius*, or Chronicle of Eusebius of Caesarea. Because of this source, Baronius comes up with the supposition that Mary died in 48 A.D.

Yet there is an ancient Christian tradition, probably the oldest among all the feasts of Mary, that declares that Mary did not die, but instead was assumed or taken up directly to heaven. By allowing this to happen, God assured that Mary's body, which gave birth to the Son of God, did not suffer decay through death.

Holy Mother
"Then he called the archangel Gabriel and sent him to the virgin Mary, at whose consent the mystery was wrought, in whom the Trinity clothed the Word with flesh. And though Three work this, it is wrought in the One; and the Word lived incarnate in the womb of Mary. And he who had only a Father now had a Mother too, but she was not like others who conceive by man. From her own flesh he received his flesh, so he is called Son of God and of man.
—John of the Cross in "The Incarnation" (d. 1591)

In fact, the Roman Catholic, Eastern, and Oriental Orthodox churches all believe that Mary's body and soul were together taken into heaven after the end of her earthly life. The Assumption of the Virgin Mary has been a favorite subject for artists for hundreds of years.

Celebrated as a memorial feast at first by the early Christians, by 602 A.D. the Emperor Maritius confirmed the feast as the "Falling Asleep of the Mother of God," as it is still known today in the Byzantine rite Church.

Whether she died and was assumed into heaven, or whether she was simply assumed, the bottom line and the common belief is that Mary's body was assumed into heaven at the end of her earthly life.

Ultimately, as you can see, this is another mystery of faith believed by Christians for almost two thousand years.

But one piece of evidence of her assumption that might at least partly satisfy our need for rational proof is the fact that no Christian community has ever claimed her relics—her body.

How do we explain that churches in various parts of the world claim to have whole or pieces of the relics of James, Peter, Paul, but not Mary? If it was plausible to have Mary's body, it stands to reason that surely someone would have claimed it!

In the Catholic church this truth of faith regarding the assumption of Mary was proclaimed a dogma by Pope Pius XII in 1950 and is today a major Marian feast in the church. In the Eastern churches the date is celebrated as the Dormition, or the falling asleep, of Mary. But both churches commemorate the event as a feast day on August 15.

In our modern world, many countries such as France, Italy, Greece, and Spanish-speaking countries in Latin America celebrate the feast of the Assumption of Mary as a public government holiday! And the celebration always includes religious parades and festivals to celebrate the day.

The Least You Need to Know

- Mary was present on the day of Pentecost when the first community of disciples received the Holy Spirit.

- Pentecost was the last recorded event in which she participated.

- For Peter, Paul, and early preachers, Mary was the evidence for the Incarnation, Jesus being both fully human and fully divine.

- The Christian Church celebrates the assumption of Mary into heaven in both body and spirit.

Part 4

Knowing Mary

There is a point or new phase that we reach in a relationship where only time can allow us to get to know the other person better. At some point after we get to know the facts, the details of someone's life—place of birth, ethnic culture, family data—the only way to continue to grow in intimacy in the relationship is by experiencing the other person. We must simply be together and witness the character of that new friend.

We've already outlined places and stories where we find Mary mentioned in Scripture, the particulars that we know about her and her life. And in this part we will spend time with some of the character traits and personwality descriptions that make up a clear picture of who Mary was. She described herself as the Lord's servant. She was called blessed among all women by the angel Gabriel and by her kinswoman Elizabeth. The early Christian community proclaimed her "Mother of God" and "Mother of the Church." And she was the first believer.

I Am the Lord's Servant

In This Chapter

- ◆ Let it be
- ◆ A handmaid or servant
- ◆ Believing in angels
- ◆ Reframing life

Among the many character traits that can describe Mary of Nazareth, one of the most heroic is her open heart and her willingness to let God direct her life. Mary lived out having an open heart with her whole being, like a musician expressing deep and heartfelt emotion through performing a song.

That's why often Mary is remembered and even described as the handmaiden of the Lord, the words that she spoke to the angel Gabriel at the Annunciation: I am the Lord's servant.

In this chapter we will explore some of the ways Mary lived this attitude throughout her life.

Mary Leads the Way

Three words, spoken three times in Scripture.

Let it be.

These words were spoken by God in the story of creation that is told in the book of Genesis. The creator of all things proclaimed let there be light, and a sky, and an ocean so that the dry land may appear. Every time he created something new in the world, he proclaimed, let it be.

These words were spoken by Jesus in the Garden of Gethsemane on the night before he died. Aware that they were looking for him to arrest him, Jesus prayed with all his being begging his Father to spare him from the suffering that was to come.

Holy Mother

"The dignity of every human being and the vocation corresponding to that dignity find their definitive measure in union with God. Mary, the woman of the Bible, is the most complete expression of this dignity and vocation. For no human being, male or female, created in the image and likeness of God, can in any way attain fulfillment apart from this image and likeness."

—John Paul II, 1988

Jesus prayed, "Abba (O Father), you have the power to do all things. Take this cup away from me. But let it be as you would have it, not as I." (Mark 14:36) Trusting in his father's goodness, even in the face of suffering, Jesus said "Let it be."

And theses words were spoken by Mary of Nazareth when the angel Gabriel first announced her pregnancy, telling Mary that she would conceive by the power of the Holy Spirit and that her child would be the son of the Most High. "I am the servant of the Lord," Mary responded. "Let it be done to me as you say." (Luke 1:38).

Let it be! Three simple words, full of intensity and the ability to transform the world.

Let It Be Done to Me

My pastor calls these three words—*let it be*—Mary of Nazareth's favorite prayer, and it probably was.

Even though we only hear Mary actually say them once in Scripture, we know she continued to pray them by how she lived her life, by the stories we've heard about her.

Image of Mary with angels, stained glass, from the Cathedral of Our Lady of Perpetual Help in Oklahoma City.

© Anamaría Scaperlanda-Ruiz

No doubt, Mary also taught her son these words, telling Jesus stories of God's mighty power and God's abundant mercy. By sharing this depth of her faith with Jesus, Mary passed on to her son not only the rituals of her Jewish faith, but also the rich spirit of it.

Their God, a mighty God, praised in Scripture and *liturgy* by their Jewish ancestors, brought light out of darkness and put stars in the sky.

He created the creatures of the sea and the animals that roam the earth. He controls the day and the night, and desires goodness and wellness for his people. He delivered their fathers and mothers of the faith from slavery and the desert, bringing them in safety to the Promised Land.

> ### Lord Knows
>
> The word **liturgy** is a Greek composite word that originally meant *a public duty*, from *leitos*, meaning "public," and *ergo* or "to do."
>
> In Hebrew Scriptures, liturgy was used for the public service of the temple. In Christian use it became all the public services of the Church—the rites, ceremonies, prayers, and sacraments, as opposed to private devotion. In the Eastern Churches, however, the term is restricted to the main service only, the sacrifice of the Holy Eucharist.

Mary believed in a good God, and that was the basic truth upon which everything stood in her life. This is the God she shared with her son Jesus, and the God that her life proclaims!

Ultimately, however, Mary not only said the words *let it be* in prayer, she was also willing to live out their consequence!

Mary's Ultimate Act of Faith

It is one thing to say "I believe in God," and another to live it.

Mary knew that each human being is accountable, that what we do, how we live, and the choices we make are never without consequence. So by choosing to say to God, "Let my life be your will, and not mine," meant she was willing to live through that end result—not even knowing what that meant!

When Mary responded to the angel with the words, *let it be done to me as you say*, she was able to do so because her life's foundation included two important factors.

Mary believed in God, in a good and merciful God. Her image of the creator of the universe was of a mighty and holy being, whose mercy to his people lives on from age to age. And, because this was her understanding of God, Mary was willing to put her entire life in his care—and her son's life as well!

Mary trusted her God so completely, so deeply, in fact, that she called herself the servant of the Lord. This understanding of "servant," then, is not actually about submissiveness. It is instead about trusting in God's goodness. But it does include Mary's willingness to place the direction of her life in God's hands—all of it. No matter what "surprise" came her way.

Becoming a mother while still a virgin. Giving birth to the Son of God. Wise men from the east coming to pay her son homage. Listening to her husband's dreams—even when it meant leaving her home and family and living as refugees.

In every new situation placed before her, Mary was able—and open—to see that reality, whatever it was, as part of God's will for her life and the lives of those whom she loved.

She didn't have to, you know. She chose to say "yes" over and over. But just because her yes was a *prayer* did not prevent her from being accountable for the consequences of that yes, in every situation—even standing at the foot of a cross watching her son die.

Mary was willing to turn her will and her life over to the care of God, and she did so deliberately and consistently, because in the midst of a crazy world, she trusted in the goodness of her creator.

> ### Sunday School
>
> **Prayer** is lifting the mind and heart to God in praise, in petition, in thanksgiving, or in intercession on behalf of others before God. Prayer can be individual, or it can be communal. It can be mental or it can be vocal. It can be liturgical or informal. In the words of Saint Augustine, "prayer is communication with God."

Alone with God

We know that Mary was a woman of prayer who made time to be alone with her God.

Her responses as recorded in Scripture tell us a lot about Mary's prayer life, both in what she said and how she acted.

A modern-day home altar or prayer corner with images of Mary and Jesus surrounded by prayer candles and flowers.

© *María Ruiz Scaperlanda*

In addition to her "let it be" response, and her beautiful canticle in reply to Elizabeth's greeting (which is discussed in Chapter 24)—we also hear how Mary treasured all the things that she experienced with her son, and reflected on them in her heart. (Luke 2:19 and Luke 2:51)

To reflect is to pray! Mary stored things—especially things that didn't make sense to her or that she did not understand—in her memory, taking them to her heart for prayer and reflection.

We also glimpse Mary's spirit of prayer in that only someone who is strengthened in prayer can respond to life's curveballs with the openness and willingness that Mary did.

To surrender her will to God, no matter how much she trusted and had confidence in her creator, was Mary's greatest act of prayer.

The Trouble with Angels

In an episode of the television sensation *Touched by an Angel* with Della Reese and Roma Downey, Monica the angel (Downey) turns to her charge (the person she's sent to take care of) and tells her in Downey's lovely Irish lilt, "In times like these, when a storm comes up quickly and you need a lamppost to cling to, you don't want to waste your time deciding which lamppost it's going to be. This is not time to put your faith in luck or fate … only God."

Every week, Monica and her fellow angels dropped into people's lives and essentially helped them remember the basics. There is a God. He exists whether we say he does or not. And God loves you and wants to walk with you, no matter where you are or who you are.

Perhaps the main reason why *Touched by an Angel* was such a popular and long-standing production (nine years) is because instinctively, we all know these truths.

But sometimes we need to be reminded, and the Bible is full of stories describing the many ways that God sends his people messages and messengers to jog our heart's memory.

In both dreams and real life, Mary was familiar with the reality of angels. I expect they were a fundamental aspect of her life, a reality that she was aware of far beyond the few instances we know about from Scripture.

God's Messengers

According to a recent poll, at least 69 percent of Americans say that they believe in angels. And more than 50 percent acknowledge that they have had a presence of a guardian angel in their life.

The three angels in the TV show *Touched by an Angel*, a man and two women, resembled in many ways the heavenly messengers in both Hebrew Scriptures and the New Testament. No, not because we know what these heavenly beings look like, but because these angels were messengers from God who came into people's lives when they needed it the most.

Sometimes they brought a message of good news, even though the news didn't appear good on the surface—like Mary's pregnancy.

Sometimes they warned and directed believers about dangers, or asked them to be open to God's hand in something that was about to happen. Mary's family flight into Egypt is a good example.

Lord Knows
Christians do not worship Mary, and do not take her as a god. Worship is the adoration and reverence given to God alone. Mary is venerated by the Christian church as a way of honoring her as the mother of Jesus Christ.

Angels exist to help God by becoming one more avenue through which he speaks to his beloved people. As always, the listener has the option to hear and believe, as Mary did—or not.

But their mission is always rooted in God.

And with That, the Angel Left

Aside from the awesome announcement that her son would be Son of God, perhaps the most crucial part of the Annunciation story is found in the final sentence in that story.

When Mary says, "I am the servant of the Lord. Let it be done to me as you say," there is no verbal response from the angel Gabriel.

But as Luke 1:38 notes, "With that the angel left her."

Can you hear it? With *that*, with her consent, *after* her "yes"—the angel left her!

Like so many stories in Scripture and in real life involving angels, the angel Gabriel delivered what under any circumstances would be provoking news! He also assured Mary of God's intimate and personal love for her, a woman who was full of grace.

But Gabriel's job was done, completed, as soon as—and only after—Mary gave her "okay."

Mary gave her consent in spite of the fact that she was asked something so big, so incomprehensible, that Mary didn't and couldn't completely grasp its meaning and ramifications.

This was true for the early believers, too. The proposition that a man who was born of a simple and ordinary Jewish woman from Nazareth could be the Son of God had to be beyond implausible.

But like Mary, each person who heard the outrageous story of Jesus of Nazareth—whether from heavenly beings or by human witness—had to make a choice.

Even in something so major as sending his son to be born in the world, God needed Mary's yes, her assent, to his action in her life.

Reframing the Lives of Christians

I think sometimes we take for granted the deliberate act of consent that Mary essentially made every time she responded to a new situation in her life.

We do Mary of Nazareth a disservice by making it sound like she had some sort of superhero powers that allowed her to say yes to God over and over.

What makes Mary most remarkable is, in fact, the reality that she was human, like us. A daughter. A mother. A wife. A friend. A Jew. A believer.

And like us, seeing God in every life situation was not like driving on cruise control through life. It was more like city traffic, with lots of stops, crazy drivers, unexpected delays and detours, and always, road construction.

Putting her daily life in God's hands was a deliberate choice on Mary's part, and most often, it was a response to a traffic situation she would have never predicted, or chosen.

My friend Judy is very good about pausing to realize, to become conscious, that the situations and the interruptions of her life in a busy office setting are a "God thing." Like Mary, she is aware that to believe that God is at work in this world, right now, means that every phone call and every traffic detour can either be a random interruption, or it can be God's grace trying to reach her!

> ### Holy Mother
>
> "The mood of springtime informs the church's interior; nature's blossoming, the warm air of May evenings, human gladness in a world that is renewing itself—all these things enter in. Veneration of Mary has its place in this very particular atmosphere, for she, the Virgin, shows us faith under its youthful aspect, as God's new beginning in a world that has grown old. In her we see the Christian life set forth as a youth—fullness of the heart, as beauty and a waiting readiness for what is to come."
>
> —Joseph Ratzinger, *Seek That Which Is Above* (Ignatius Press, 1986)

It's all about how we see life. It's what psychologists call "reframing" our perspective to allow for a different reality. Similarly, in business management this is called the "reframing matrix," a formal technique used to look at problems from a new and different perspective in order to expand the number of options you see for solving a problem, and therefore finding a solution.

As far as the situation goes, nothing, in fact, is different, except for our perception. And yet, everything changes.

The Copernican Revolution

In the ancient Ptolemaic model, accepted for over 1,000 years by the vast majority of the world, the earth was the centre of the universe and all celestial bodies rotated around it.

Under this system, it was believed that all heavenly bodies are attached to crystal spheres, which rotate around the Earth, with the moon having the innermost sphere.

Then comes Nicolaus Copernicus (d. 1453 A.D.), a Polish mathematician and economist whose main occupation was as church canon, governor, and administrator. Copernicus, for whom astronomy was a hobby, turned the entire theory upside down—asserting that the planets revolved around the sun for light and heat, not the earth!

Copernicus's theory that the sun is the center of the solar system was a scientific revolution, and one of the most important discoveries ever. Besides being the starting point of modern astronomy, his perspective opened up science to consider that there are other possibilities than the ones taken for granted—or the ones judged by appearance.

This unprecedented opening to a different perspective in scientific thought is the sort of radical outlook that Mary lived.

Transforming Our Perspective

Mary lived the equivalent of a Copernican revolution in how she approached life and how she lived out her personal situations.

She did not think that the world revolved around her, as we would say today. In Copernican language, she did not believe that the earth, herself, was the center of the universe!

Her focus was on God as the sun, the central point. And her decisions were based on this perspective.

In Marian understanding, not only does every detail in life revolve around God, but also He is the source of the detail and of all life.

Imagine how different all the stories would be if Mary had chosen differently, if she had not consciously acknowledged with words and actions that God was in control!

This attitude about Mary's life was based on her core belief that God's choices for her were ultimately better than anything she could ever do for herself. It was a free and open acknowledgement that God was and is the center of the universe.

Mary's Month

As early Christian believers developed liturgy and ritual, finding ways to honor Mary as the mother of God was a fundamental and natural form of popular devotion. One of the most long-standing traditions of popular devotion has been to dedicate the month of May to Mary.

In many cultures, as the seasons and the weather changed, the month of May was a time for celebrating the bloom of new life, and it was often dedicated to a female goddess.

In Roman culture May was dedicated to Flora, the goddess of bloom or blossoms. The Romans celebrated in May *ludi florales*, or floral games, asking Flora to bless all that blooms. Similarly, the Greeks dedicated May to Artemis, the goddess of fertility and fruitfulness.

Although a devotion to Mary over the course of thirty days is more ancient than we can verify in origin, the practice of honoring Mary in May, in particular, dates back to medieval times.

In Spain, for instance, Alphonsus X, the King of Castille (1221–1284 A.D.) known as "el sabio," the wise one, celebrated "Cantigas de Santa Maria," or canticles to Mary. Over time, special devotions to Mary were organized for every day of the month.

A May Crowning

One of the particular ways that towns and church communities celebrate their devotion to Mary is by crowning a statue of Mary with flowers.

In some cultures, such as with Hispanics, this practice is also carried on at home, where families set up a small May altar in honor of Mary.

In the United States the tradition of Mary crowning was once very popular, especially before the 1960s when many changes took place in the Catholic Church worldwide.

Lord Knows
Councils are assemblies of the leaders of the church (in modern times the bishops) from around the world in order to consider matters of concern to the universal church. The first council is described in the fifteenth chapter of the book of Acts, as apostles and presbyters gathered in Jerusalem to discuss what requirements were to be placed on Gentiles who became Christians.

But the practice of honoring a statue of Mary with a wreath of blossoms dedicated to Mary is still celebrated in many churches and schools to this day.

The traditional ceremony for a May crowning around the world centers on school children leading the service with a processional, sometimes ethnic dresses, and a wreath of fresh flowers or a formal crown (depending on the culture) that one child gets to place on the statue of Mary.

In some church communities, celebrations such as May crownings and other Marian rites, also become moments for Mother-daughter celebrations around Mary, the model of what it means to be a Christian woman.

The Catholic Church has an official liturgical rite called the *Order of Crowning*, that may take place at any time of the year. It is usually followed, however, for solemnities and feasts of Mary or in the month of May.

On Venerating Statues

It was back at the church Council of Nicea in 787 A.D. that the Christian church declared it was proper and fitting to venerate images of Christ, of Mary, and of the saints. This is, then, an ancient practice of the Christian churches in both the East and the West.

As the official rite for the *Order of Crowning an Image of the Blessed Virgin Mary* explains, "Coronation is one form of reverence frequently shown to images of the Blessed Virgin Mary …. It is especially from the end of the sixteenth century that in the West the practice became widespread for the faithful, both religious and laity, to crown images of the Blessed Virgin."

Ways to Celebrate

There are many simple ways to honor Mary in May (or any other month!), but here are a few specific suggestions:

◆ Plant a Mary garden—Usually a garden dedicated to Mary will include some form of statue of Mary, placed in a place of honor.

Besides a statue of Mary and other familiar type of garden additions (fountain, birdbath, birdfeeder), what defines a Mary garden is the type of flowers that are planted in it.

Some examples of Marian flowers are: marigolds, also named as Mary's bud; lily of the valley, still called *maiglockchen* or may bells in Germany; foxgloves, called Our Lady's thimbles in medieval times; and roses, which have been associated with Mary for centuries. The lily has not only been associated from ancient times with Jesus and Mary, it is also called Madonna lily in many parts of Europe.

Roses of three colors are especially linked with Mary: white, as symbol of her joy and purity; red for her suffering; and yellow, or golden, for her glory.

◆ May baskets—I am not sure of the ethnic or date origin of this tradition, but it involves making simple baskets to be given as anonymous gifts.

The baskets, filled with flowers, homemade notes and prayers, and candy, are meant to be left anonymously on doorsteps of friends or neighbors, usually on the first day of May.

Mary in the garden at Little Portion Hermitage in Arkansas.

© *María Ruiz Scaperlanda*

◆ Family crowning—Just as its name implies, a family crowning would be a simple ceremony where the family in some way honors Mary and prays together, preferably placing an image or statue of Mary in a place of honor. Even at home, school-age children can make a crown and lead a procession with flowers!

◆ Pray the Hail Mary—or any other traditional Marian prayer every day, individually or as a family.

The Hail Mary is probably the best-known and oldest Marian prayer. The first part of the prayer comes straight from the Gospel of Luke, and the second part of the verse was added years later to conclude the prayer.

Therefore, Christians pray, "Hail Mary, full of grace, the Lord is with you" (the words with which the angel Gabriel greeted Mary, Luke 1:28), "Blessed are you among women and blessed is the fruit of your womb" (the greeting given to Mary by her cousin Elizabeth, Luke 1:42), "Holy Mary, mother of God, pray for us sinners now and at the hour of our death" (added by Christians in the fifteenth century).

While there are many and varied traditions in every culture, there are, ultimately, no universally defined or correct ways of honoring Mary. What we choose to do and how we choose to do it should be personal, reflecting our own understanding and relationship with the one who is mother to us all.

The Least You Need to Know

- Mary's "let it be" transformed the world.

- Her servant attitude was rooted in trusting God with her whole being.

- Mary placed God at the center of her life, and her choices reflected that attitude.

- Traditionally, the Christian church has honored Mary by dedicating the month of May to her.

Chapter 13

Blessed Are You

In This Chapter

- ◆ Who is Zechariah?
- ◆ Announcing the birth of John
- ◆ Blessing Mary
- ◆ A voice crying in the wilderness

The Gospel of Luke begins not with Gabriel's angelic announcement to Mary about the birth of Jesus but with an angel of the Lord announcing the birth of John to his father, Zechariah.

Who is this John? And why did he get announced first?

We'll talk about that in this chapter. Everything matters here. Even the order in which the stories are presented by the Gospel writer is meant to tell us something about John the Baptist's role in Scripture, and how he fits into the story of Mary and Jesus of Nazareth.

Family Ties

The infancy narrative in Luke's Gospel opens by introducing two rather unknown characters, a husband and wife named Zechariah and Elizabeth, who "were just in the eyes of God, blamelessly following all the commandments and ordinances of the Lord." (Luke 1:6)

Holy Mother

"One by one the lights in the chapel would be extinguished until there were left only the vigil light at the altar and the shaded lamp that illuminated the statue of the Virgin Mary. When everything else was dark the nuns began to sing. For Gabrielle, this was the moment that made every next day possible .... It seemed to her then that every convent, monastery and remotest mission on the planet was somehow brought into her own chapel and the pure voices she heard close to her were but the top level of sound in the cry for mercy that was welling up at that moment to the Mother of God from every place where vowed ones lived behind walls. Their eyes of trust like those of children in the dark, thousands upon thousands of them, seemed to be looking out through her own, fixed on the single lighted figure to which the voices sang O dulcis Virgo Maria."

—Kathryn Hulme, *The Nun's Story* (Little, Brown & Co, 1956)

Zechariah, a priest of the priestly class of Abijah, and his wife, Elizabeth, were childless because Elizabeth was sterile, and they were both too old to have children.

Like other famous childless couples from the Hebrew Scripture who conceived children because of divine intervention—Abraham and Sarah (Genesis 16) and Elkanah and Hannah (1 Samuel 1–2)—their barrenness in this story is used by God to show that, indeed, God can do the impossible.

As you will see, the Zechariah story parallels in many ways the announcement of that other unlikely birth announced to Mary of Nazareth by the same angel, Gabriel. But the story of John and his parents is much more than a mere literary device by Luke. It is meant to bring light to the special and unique role that Zechariah's son, John, was to play in the story of Jesus.

Who Is Zechariah?

One day as Zechariah was performing his priestly duties in the Temple, he entered the *sanctuary* of the Lord to offer incense while the full assembly of people prayed outside.

An angel of the Lord appeared to Zechariah there, in private, standing at the right hand of the altar of incense.

Zechariah was "deeply disturbed" and overcome with fear. But the angel said to him, "Don't be afraid, Zechariah, your prayer has been answered. Your wife Elizabeth will conceive a son whom you shall name John, and he will be great in the eyes of the Lord. He will be filled with the Holy Spirit from his mother's womb, and one day, he will bring many of the sons of Israel back to the Lord their God. Your child will open the hearts of many and prepare the people for the coming of their Lord." (Luke 1:12–16)

> **Sunday School**
>
> A **sanctuary** is the term used for the building itself when referring to a sacred place, such as a church, temple, or mosque. It is also used to identify a consecrated area where sacred objects are kept, as in the holiest part of a sacred space. In a Christian church, it would be the area where the altar is located.

The angel's reminder that God had heard Zechariah's prayers is a beautiful echo of Zechariah's name, which means "Yahweh has remembered."

Like Mary, Zechariah was stunned by the news brought by the angel, and he began to honestly say what he was thinking.

Zechariah's response and what he finds most disturbing, however, are comical. He is not bothered by the angelic appearance or even by the apparently prophetic role that Gabriel predicts for his new son.

Zechariah is stuck at the idea that he and Elizabeth were going to have a baby.

"My wife and I are too old," he told the angel. "How am I to know this? How can I believe?"

The angel Gabriel's reply to him might sound harsh, at first, even short-tempered. "I am the angel Gabriel who stands before God, and I was sent to bring you these good news," Gabriel says to Zechariah, "but you have not trusted my words."

"Until the day that this child is born," the angel declares, "You will be unable to speak."

Whether Gabriel's response to Zechariah is really meant as a punishment or not, the fact is that it becomes a very effective literary device. It builds suspense, beginning on that day and continuing up until the big announcement of John's birth.

At different points in the Gospel the text says that Zechariah was speechless, mute, unable to speak. But he must have also lost his hearing because in Luke 1:62 we are told that his family tried communicating with him by using signs, which they wouldn't have had to do unless he could not hear what they were saying.

Imagine the scene. Zechariah goes into the sanctuary as he normally does and he comes out unable to speak to the people. He can't even bless them, which means he can't complete the liturgy that he began.

Lord Knows

On the one hand, incense is a substance that produces a unique and fragrant odor when burned. But symbolically, incense has been a symbol of prayer for centuries. The book of Exodus in the Hebrew Scripture has specific guidelines on how and when to burn fragrant incense. It was offered daily on the golden altar in the holy place, and on the great Day of Atonement was burnt by the high priest in the holy of holies. (Exodus 30)

Clearly, this got the people's attention. Something extraordinary and supernatural had taken place. What had occurred? What had Zechariah done?

For nine long months Zechariah was speechless. Then suddenly, after the birth of his son, he regained his ability to communicate. Every indication suggests that Zechariah was well respected, someone to whom others would listen. How much more must they have listened after so long a silence. The Lord had Zechariah's attention, and he had the attention of those around him.

Zechariah's Work in the Temple

Participating in the burning of the incense, which took place at the conclusion of the sacrifices in the Temple, was regarded as an especially important and prestigious task for a Temple priest.

Part of what made this particular task so special is that most of the tasks that the priests did daily took place in the Temple courtyard, not in the sanctuary itself. Only the kindling of the lamps and the burning of incense took place within the sanctuary.

The incense was burnt upon a golden altar in the center of the sanctuary. Although the priest was accompanied by fellow priests to the top of the steps leading into the sanctuary, the officiating priest—in this case Zechariah—entered the sanctuary alone.

The other priests would have waited for him to come out at the courtyard, with the crowd assembled there, mostly made up of people who had brought sacrifices to the Temple. According to the description in the Talmud, "When all had gone he offered the incense, prostrated himself [in adoration] and went out [of the sanctuary]" (Mishnah, Tamid 6:3).

Although the incense was offered in the morning and the afternoon, the second offering was considered of greater importance than the morning offering.

Luke does not specify whether Zechariah's vision took place during the morning or the afternoon ceremony, but because the afternoon incense was more important, it makes sense that the vision would have taken place then.

Why Elizabeth?

While all this was going on with Zechariah, Elizabeth's side of the story is only one paragraph long.

When Elizabeth conceived, she went into seclusion, keeping to herself for five months. Infertility was considered a humiliation, and even a punishment.

Elizabeth, whose name means "My God is fullness," declared about her pregnancy, "the Lord is clearly acting on my behalf. By giving me this child, he has taken away the humiliation of being barren and removed the criticism and censure against me." (See Luke 1:24–25)

The Visit

After Gabriel's announcement, Mary set out for the hill country to visit her kinswoman, Elizabeth. We're not told the name of the town, only that she went to a town in Judah, in the southern regions.

As soon as Mary entered Elizabeth and Zechariah's house and Elizabeth heard her voice, the baby in Elizabeth's womb leapt with joy!—for she was filled with the Holy Spirit.

Stained glass image of Elizabeth greeting Mary, with Joseph and Zechariah in the background. From the Cathedral of Our Lady of Perpetual Help in Oklahoma City.

© María Ruiz Scaperlanda

Elizabeth's Greeting

It must have been an incredibly moving moment, full of emotion, as Elizabeth cried out, "Blessed are you, Mary, among all women, and blessed is the baby in your womb." (Luke 1:42)

Recognizing without explanations the reality before her, Elizabeth added, "How is it that I am chosen to receive the mother of the Messiah, that she would come to me? My baby leapt within with joy the moment he heard your voice! Oh, Mary ... blessed are you because you trusted what the Lord said to you, and it is now being fulfilled." (Luke 1:43–45)

Through the grace of the Holy Spirit, Elizabeth interpreted the leaping of John within her womb, and in just a few sentences, she praises Mary's trust and fidelity to the work of Lord in her life by using the word *blessed* three times.

Blessed Be

The word *blessed* has several meanings, each with a little different emphasis, in Scripture. It is sometimes used as a synonym for praise, as in, "I will bless the Lord at all times; his praise shall be ever in my mouth." (Psalm 34:1)

Lord Knows

What do we know about the adult John the Baptist? John was a Jewish prophet who in the Gospels baptized and prepared the way for Jesus. He was also a hermit who devoted his life to prayer and lived in the desert. John was put into prison and beheaded by Herod Antipas at the request of Salome, his niece, who asked for John's head in return for her dancing before Herod. Jesus called John "the lamp, set aflame and burning bright." (John 5:35)

Blessed is also used as a term of good fortune, to express a wish or a desire that all things good be with the person or thing. "The blessing of the Lord be upon you! We bless you in the name of the Lord!" (Psalm 129:8)

A blessing is the means of consecrating a person or a thing to some sacred purpose, too, as when Jesus "took bread, blessed it, broke it, and gave it to his disciples." (Matthew 26:26)

A blessing is as well a rite or a ceremony, in which prayers are performed in order to sanctify a person, event, or thing by dedicating it to God. This practice has always been a part of religious tradition. In fact, in the very first story in Genesis God blessed each new aspect of his creation at the end of each day.

Giving blessings is still a part of modern rituals, especially in public services where a minister not only praises God in blessing, but also blesses the community at the end of each Sunday service.

But conferring a blessing is not restricted to clergy. As it did with Mary and Elizabeth, a blessing can also take place in the home, away from a public liturgy. Parents, for example, can bless their children each day, or the family can bless and pray over a specific person in the family with a special need or situation.

In that short passage of Scripture, Elizabeth unfolded several types of blessings on Mary, and on the child within her. She gave praise for the wonder taking place in Mary. She wished her well. And she consecrated the child growing in Mary!

We will talk in Chapter 24 about Mary's response, popularly known as "the Magnificat," named so because of the first words Mary says in response to Elizabeth's greeting, "my soul magnifies the Lord!" But for now, let's go back to the story of John's birth.

Mary remained with Elizabeth about three months, and then she returned home.

Full of Grace

As we've said before, grace is that quality or condition that makes us holy. Or better yet, it's what reminds us that we are holy and that we are connected to the transcendent, to all things divine.

Elizabeth and the child within Elizabeth's womb recognized this in Mary because she was, indeed, full of grace—but not only because Mary carried the Son of God in her womb.

Like us, Mary had to be deliberate and purposeful in deciding to be open to God and to divine grace. And she did so through her posture of openness, her attitude of "yes," even to what she did not understand—which had to happen quite frequently!

What Is This Amazing Grace?

I often think that what makes grace most amazing is the fact that in addition to grace being that connection and recognition of the divine already within us, grace is also a sort of spiritual fuel that propels us forward.

It comes in the form of the right words said at the right time. Or running into a friend when we've been thinking about her. Or hearing encouragement when we need it the most. Or receiving an unexpected bonus on the same week that our car breaks down.

Grace usually leaves us with at least a bit of awe.

Grace is that force constantly at work that reminds us that God is present. God is here. God is in charge. Much in the same way that God was present for Mary at the Annunciation, or when she heard Elizabeth's greeting, or when the shepherds came to worship her newborn child.

Grace is also that unexplainable peace that embraces us when we turn to God in our need. Mary was conscious of that powerful divine presence.

And we are reminded of this every time we hear how she treasured, reflected upon, and pondered the events of her life in her heart.

The Lord Is with Thee

A modern word that is often used to explain the unexplainable spiritual connection to divine grace in our lives is serendipity!

But serendipity is, by definition, more about luck. And luck is not deliberate. It is a chance happening—often a good one, mind you, but still a coincidence, something that just "happened" to turn out a certain way.

On the other hand, there is providence and grace.

Mary was aware that those amazing "coincidences" that happen in our life, those unexpected and fortunate discoveries, are reminders of God's providence and presence in the world. She was conscious, as the angel Gabriel said of her, that the Lord was with her—and this made her blessed and full of grace!

John, Son of Zechariah and Elizabeth

Elizabeth gave birth to a son, which would have been a surprise to her since the only person who knew it was a boy was her husband—but Zechariah had not been able to speak!

Her neighbors and relatives rejoiced with Elizabeth and thanked God for the miracle of a child birthed by an old woman who was thought to be sterile. And they rejoiced with her at the mercy of God poured upon this family.

Following Jewish practice, friends and family gathered on the eighth day for the child's *circumcision* and for his naming, assuming that the baby boy would be named after his father, Zechariah.

But when the time in the rite came to name the child, Elizabeth intervened, announcing that the child was to be called John.

The people must have looked at her like she was crazy—and presumptuous!

It was not up to the mother to name the child or to lead the rite of circumcision, but imagine doing so in the home of a Temple priest!

Remember that at this point Zechariah remained mute and deaf, so he wouldn't have known what was being discussed.

> **Sunday School**
>
> The religious rite of **circumcision** (the removal of the foreskin of males) was traditionally done on boys eight days after birth in both the Jewish and Muslim traditions. Circumcision was considered a sign of the Jewish people's consecration to God, a special badge that set them apart from others.

"They" (the relatives and friends who have now become a motley crew!) turn on Elizabeth pointing out the obvious, "Where did you come up with the name John? None of your relatives has this name."

And when it became obvious that they were not going to get the answer they thought they should get, they turned to Zechariah, and: "using signs, they asked the father what he wished him to be called." (Luke 1:62)

He Is to Be Called John

As soon as Zechariah understood the question that he was being asked, he motioned for someone to give him a writing tablet. Although he was unable to hear what Elizabeth had said, Zechariah wrote with firmness the words, "His name is John." (Luke 1:63)

This announcement, notes Luke, "astonished them all."

To make it even more exciting, at that exact moment Zechariah recovered his senses and became able to speak again—and the first thing he did was to "speak in praise of God." (Luke 1:64)

Astonishment. Wonder. Amazement. Stunned with surprise. Can we begin to imagine what the people gathered there that day thought of the entire turn of events?

I assume that along with feeling flabbergasted and perhaps embarrassed by their role in the events, the crowd must have also been pretty alarmed.

The next sentence in the story tells us that "fear descended on all in the neighborhood; throughout the hill country of Judea these happenings began to be recounted to the last detail. All who heard stored these things up in their hearts, saying, 'What will this child be?' and 'Was not the hand of the Lord upon him?'" (Luke 1:65–66)

Did you catch the phrase we've already heard twice now with regard to Mary? They stored these things up in their hearts, as Mary did at the birth of Jesus, and again at finding her lost child in the Temple. A master storyteller, Luke uses the same exact saying here, word for word, this time referring to "all who heard" the story about the child John and his parents Zechariah and Elizabeth.

I propose that here the words "all who heard" can also be understood as all who are open to hearing what these events were really all about! Over and over they remind us that nothing, no situation, is impossible for God, and that this is a God who takes care of and is mindful of every detail in a person's life—and how one person's details connect with others who come in contact with him or her, like Mary and Elizabeth!

Zechariah's Canticle

The next thing to come out of Zechariah's mouth has been traditionally called the *Benedictus* (from the Latin for *blessed*, the first word that he speaks), or simply Zechariah's canticle. Monks around the world to this day sing this poetic hymn daily at morning prayers.

Filled with the Holy Spirit, the same description Luke used for Elizabeth, Zechariah began to praise God in a poetic discourse that parallels (in beauty and importance) Mary's Magnificat, her response to Elizabeth's greeting.

"Blessed be the Lord the God of Israel because he has visited and ransomed his people," Zechariah began. "He has dealt mercifully with our fathers and remembered the holy covenant he made … we should serve him devoutly and through all our days be holy in his sight." (Luke 1:68, 72, 75)

Then Zechariah revealed a prophecy about his own newborn child, John, who would grow into the next major prophet, becoming the voice to announce the coming of Jesus: "And you, O child, shall be called prophet of the Most High; For you shall go before the Lord to prepare straight paths for him, Giving his people a knowledge of salvation in freedom from their sins." (Luke 1:76–77)

As author Michael O'Neill McGrath reminds us in *Blessed Art Thou: Mother, Lady, Mystic, Queen* (World Library Publications, 2004), prophets speak in the day what they have heard in the darkness, in that place deep within where the Holy Spirit's voice is heard. And most prophets, even one-time voices like Zechariah, often hesitated and questioned at first before their voices became strong and confident.

That's what happened to Zechariah in this story.

The Opposite of Cursed

The birth announcement of John and the stories told about his parents, Zechariah and Elizabeth, are much more than a mere parallel to the Jesus, Mary, and Joseph story.

Even the way the events are placed in the Gospel narrative—going back and forth between John and Jesus—the Gospel writer skillfully and inseparably connects the two stories.

As the story of John's birth announcement and birth unfold, Jesus' birth announcement and birth narrative develops. We can't separate one from the other.

Setting aside all the theological and literary explanations for this weaving together of the two stories, there is a very important reality that they present about Mary.

We've already heard how Elizabeth's greeting clarified and proclaimed Mary's unique role and her graced spirit. She is the mother of our Lord, Elizabeth declares!

But Elizabeth's son, too, will play an important role in the Jesus story. Luke tells us that "the child grew up and matured in sprit. He lived in the desert until the day when he made his public appearance in Israel." (Luke 1:80)

John the Baptist

John became a powerful and gifted prophet, so much so that some wondered whether John might be the Messiah. (Luke 3:15)

Luke does not tell us the meaning of John's name: "Yahweh has shown favor." Yet from the beginning, we become conscious that this child was chosen, favored by the Lord.

The fact that we know John is related to Jesus in some way (their mothers are "kin," probably cousins!) is not what's important.

Like the larger-than-life prophets of the Hebrew Scripture, John is God's prophet. But John's message was bigger—more urgent! He sets in motion the period of fulfillment, whose main figure, of course, is Jesus the Christ.

For years preceding Jesus' public ministry, John preached and baptized all who were willing to repent—which explains why he's known as John the Baptizer or John the Baptist. His message was urgent and insistent, "Repent. The waiting is over. The Lord is coming. He is near!"

Just as Elizabeth was the first to publicly proclaim the reality of Mary's nature as the mother of God, her son John announced the coming of Jesus, the Messiah.

John told his followers: "I am baptizing you in water, but there is one to come who is mightier than I. I am not fit to loosen his sandal strap. He will baptize you in the Holy Spirit and in fire." (Luke 3:16)

> **Holy Mother**
>
> **The Hail Mary or Ave Maria**
>
> Hail Mary, full of grace
> The Lord is with Thee
> Blessed are you among women
> And blessed is the fruit of your womb, Jesus.
> Holy Mary, mother of God,
> Pray for us sinners
> Now and at the hour of our death
> Amen.

What's the Blessing?

Zechariah's canticle was not just a song of thanksgiving at the birth of a child. He and his wife were undoubtedly blessed by the arrival of their son, John.

But it was much more than that. From the first words that Zechariah said when he was given his voice back, he praised the Lord, the God of Israel, for his love and faithfulness to his people.

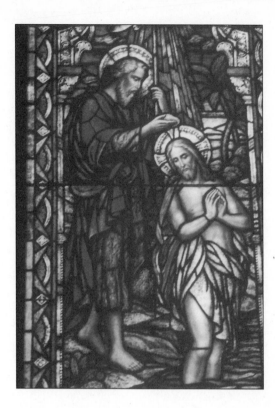

Stained glass image of John baptizing Jesus from the Cathedral of Our Lady of Perpetual Help in Oklahoma City.

© María Ruiz Scaperlanda

Zechariah's canticle remembered the prophets and their father Abraham, and the mercy of God from age to age—culminating with the arrival of the Dayspring, the Messiah, who comes to shine light in the darkness, and "to guide our feet into the way of peace." (Luke 1:79)

This is the blessing that Zechariah proclaims. This is the blessing that Elizabeth recognized. And this is the blessing that Mary makes known with her life.

The Least You Need to Know

- The angel Gabriel announced to Zechariah that his wife Elizabeth was pregnant.

- Because Zechariah did not trust Gabriel's words, he was mute until the circumcision of his son, John.

- Elizabeth declared Mary "blessed among all women."

- John the Baptist was a prophet sent by God to announce the coming of the Messiah.

Chapter 14

Holy Theotokos! Mary the Mother of God

In This Chapter

- ◆ Affirming the Incarnation
- ◆ Church councils and synods
- ◆ Heresies and errors
- ◆ Mary as Mother of God

It is hard to conceive what life was like for those early Christians. On the one hand, their experience of Jesus meant they had come to know something so amazing, so powerful, that they wanted to share it with anyone who would listen. They had encountered the Messiah, the Son of God, who had come into the world through a woman so as to be one with humanity in all things. These Christians were willing to die when persecuted in order to profess this truth about God's love.

At the same time, these early Christian communities had to deal with defining and finding language to express this and other truths of their faith. Every time this early community of believers gave vocabulary to their faith, they formulated a theology of what it means to be a Christian.

In a very real way, they defined the Christian faith by living through the questions as they unfolded.

This chapter discusses the importance of identifying Mary as the "Mother of God."

Not Mere Name Calling

The letters by Paul in the New Testament, written to those first Christian churches, are a beautiful example of the passion and the excitement that thrust Christianity forward.

They are also a powerful illustration of how the Christian faith developed a living theology, a formulated set of beliefs that defined Christianity as a religion separate from Judaism.

In this Christian theology, the expression and understanding of love embodied in a God in human form was central to the message of being a follower of Jesus. The Incarnation, the fact that God loved the world so much that he chose to become fully human, was the foundation of this truth. From here, all Christian theology began to unfold.

And Mary was a fundamental and central figure in this reality.

Not Just Mother, but Mother of God

Obviously, honoring Mary as the mother of their Savior would have been important to the disciples and the early Christian church.

But Mary was not only the human mother of a great prophet—although she was clearly that!

When she consented to be impregnated by the Holy Spirit, Mary of Nazareth also agreed to be the human mother of the Son of God.

Elizabeth said it first when she greeted Mary at the visitation: "Blest are you among women! Blest is the fruit of your womb! Who am I that the mother of my Lord should come to me?" (Luke 1:42–43)

Honoring Mary as the mother of their Lord, the Mother of God, was not merely about giving Mary a special place or a special title. For the early Christian community, as is true for the Christian faith today, to call Mary the mother of God testifies and proclaims the belief that Jesus was indeed divine.

Fully Human, Fully Divine

The word *incarnation* never actually appears in the Bible. But the incarnation is the theology, the mystery of faith, that Paul described in his letter to the Philippians, one of the epistles in the New Testament.

Paul says it this way: "Though he was in the form of God, [Jesus] did not deem equality with God something to be grasped at. Rather, he emptied himself and took the form of a slave, being born in the likeness of men. He was known to be of human estate, and it was thus that he humbled himself, obediently accepting death, death on a cross!" (Philippians 2:6–8)

The certainty that God the Most High, the creator of the world, humbled himself to take on human form is mind-boggling for any one. But it would have been a preposterous proposition to the Jews and Gentiles to whom Paul and Peter and those early preachers spoke.

Lord Knows

There are two Eastern churches: the Eastern church, separated, which broke away from its Roman Catholic roots in 1054; and the Eastern church, Catholic, which follows the Eastern rites or liturgies but is still in union with the Catholic church today.

The largest group of the separated Eastern churches is the Orthodox church, which holds many matters of faith, liturgy, and tradition in common with the other Eastern church, but accepts only the first seven ecumenical councils of the church.

The Incarnation states that Jesus Christ, the Son of God, is fully divine and at the same time fully human. And Mary, who conceived the Son of God, was placed at the heart of this truth.

Another way to view this is as a circle of faith. The belief in the Incarnation led the Christian church to honor Mary as the Mother of God. And declaring Mary as the Mother of God testified right back to the belief that Jesus was both fully human and fully divine!

John Chrysostom

John Chrysostom (d. 407), a noted Christian bishop and eloquent preacher in Syria and Constantinople, is specially remembered for his homilies, hymns, and prayers.

John lived during a time when much was being defined about the Christian faith, and he was a central part of this foundation.

The Liturgy of St. John Chrysostom, still used by Orthodox and Byzantine Catholics almost 1,600 years after it was written, includes a litany known as "The Little Ektenia" (prayer of petition), which goes like this:

> O only begotten Son and Word of God,
> who art immortal,
> yet didst deign for our salvation
> to be incarnate
> of the Theotokos and ever-virgin Mary;
> and without change wast made man;
> and wast crucified also,
> O Christ our God,
> and by thy death didst Death subdue;
> who art one of the Holy Trinity,
> glorified together with the Father and the Holy Spirit:
> Save us!

The Orthodox church honors him as a saint and counts him among the Three Holy Hierarchs, together with Basil the Great and Gregory the Theologian.

The Catholic church considers John Chrysostom a saint and a "Doctor of the Church," an honorary title that identifies theologians whose teachings and saintly life have significantly and effectively contributed to the Christian faith.

On This Day in History

But in those first few centuries of Christianity not everyone agreed about the definitions and practices that make up the Christian faith.

These errors which led some away from the faith are known as *heresies*, a term we will discuss shortly.

What happened, however, is that when these specific communities challenged the body of believers with mistaken ideas, it forced Christianity to make deliberate and specific statements about what it believed.

In essence, these divisions helped give clarity to the language of the Christian faith.

For example, Saint Irenaeus (c. 130–202), bishop of the region of modern-day Lyons, France, wrote a number of books refuting the teachings of various groups whose principles did not conform to Christian beliefs. His most famous book is titled *Against Heresies* (c. 180), in which he stated that the teaching and tradition of the "Roman See" was the standard for belief.

By this Irenaeus meant that, in cases of theological disagreement, the Christian church should look to Rome and to its leader, the Pope, because he is the successor to Peter, the head of the apostles, who was martyred in Rome in the mid-60s. The word "See" comes from the Latin *sedes*, which means "chair." Each diocese (a district or region) is called a see and is under the jurisdiction of a bishop.

> **Sunday School**
>
> A **heresy** is a religious doctrine that develops contrary to the doctrines of Christianity. From the Greek *hairesis*, the word can mean either a choice of beliefs or a group of dissident believers. The word *heresy* is also used to describe an opinion or doctrine in philosophy, politics, science, art, and so on which deviates with those generally accepted as authoritative.

What's a Church Council?

As early as the second century, Christian bishops convened in area gatherings they called synods or councils. At these meetings, which have continued to take place throughout the history of the Christian church, the bishops discussed issues of faith and took action on defining a common doctrine or belief.

From the beginning, these ecumenical councils used as a model the Council of Jerusalem (described in the book of Acts, chapter 15), which took place in 51 A.D. At that gathering, under the leadership of Peter, Christians decided that converts to the faith were not required to follow the rules and ordinances outlined by the Hebrew Scriptures, specifically the Jewish laws on dietary regulations and regarding circumcision.

The Christian councils have also been the settings where the assembled church produced a creed—a common rule of faith to be accepted by all the church communities.

The Apostle's Creed

Around the year 100, something called the Apostle's Creed was developed as an outline or blueprint of all Christian beliefs. This formula of faith was especially needed as the Christian faith continued to spread throughout the Roman Empire.

The Apostle's Creed was not so named because it originated with the twelve original apostles, but rather, because it reflected the teachings of the apostles. It is made up of 12 separate statements of faith.

The Apostle's Creed was meant to be professed by all converts before being baptized, so it was essentially a baptismal affirmation.

Although it had several variations over the centuries, the Apostle's Creed basically stated:

> I believe in God, the Father almighty,
> Creator of heaven and earth.
> And in Jesus Christ, his only Son, our Lord;
> who was conceived by the Holy Spirit,
> born of the Virgin Mary,
> suffered under Pontius Pilate, was crucified,
> died, and was buried. He descended into hell;
> the third day he arose again from the dead;
> he ascended into heaven, sits at the right hand of God, the Father Almighty;
> from thence he shall come to judge the living and the dead.
> I believe in the Holy Spirit, the holy catholic Church,
> the communion of saints, the forgiveness of sins,
> the resurrection of the body, and life everlasting.
> Amen.

The word *catholic* in this creed (and the one in the following section) does not mean the Roman Catholic church, but the universal Christian church as a whole.

The Nicene Creed

Ecumenical councils were also formal gatherings where the church discussed and addressed how to take action against what it considered errors of the faith or heresies.

When a priest named Arius in the fourth century, for example, began to question and eventually deny publicly Jesus' divinity (what is known as the Arian heresy), the Christian church convened at the Council of Nicaea in 325 A.D. and adopted a creed much more sophisticated than the Apostle's Creed—known as the Nicene Creed.

The Nicene Creed, still said every week at Sunday liturgies, declares:

> We believe in one God, the Father, the Almighty, maker of heaven and earth, of all that is seen and unseen.
>
> We believe in one Lord, Jesus Christ, the only Son of God, eternally begotten of the Father, God from God, Light from Light, true God from true God, begotten, not made, one in being with the Father. Through him all things were made. For us and for our salvation he came down from heaven: by the power of the Holy Spirit he was born of the Virgin Mary, and became man. For our sake he was crucified under Pontius Pilate; he suffered, died, and was buried. On the third day he rose again in fulfillment of the Scriptures; he ascended into heaven and is seated at the right hand of the Father. He will come again in glory to judge the living and the dead, and his kingdom will have no end.
>
> We believe in the Holy Spirit, the Lord, the giver of life, who proceeds from the Father and the Son. With the Father and the Son he is worshipped and glorified. He has spoken through the prophets.
>
> We believe in one catholic and apostolic Church. We acknowledge one baptism for the forgiveness of sins. We look for the resurrection of the dead, and the life of the world to come.
>
> Amen.

Since the fifth century, the Nicene Creed has been the only creed in liturgical use in the Eastern churches. And the Western church adopted it by the end of the eighth century.

Holy Mother

Mary, Mother of God, we salute you. Precious vessel, worthy of the whole world's reverence, you are an ever-shining light, the crown of virginity, the symbol of orthodoxy, an indestructible temple, the place that held him whom no place can contain, mother and virgin. Because of you the holy gospels could say: Blessed is she who comes in the name of the Lord.

—St. Cyril of Alexandria (c. 376–444)

What's It Got to Do with Mary?

Besides the fact that it outlines the beliefs of the Christian faith, the big deal about the Council of Nicaea and its proclamation of the Nicene Creed is that it clearly defined the divinity of Jesus and the reality of the Incarnation.

In fact, the language in both creeds makes clear that Christianity was based on Jesus Christ as the only son of God, conceived by the Holy Spirit—and born of the Virgin Mary!

Because Jesus was truly God and Mary was Jesus' mother, Mary was honored and venerated since those early centuries with the title of mother of God.

The image that follows, from the eleventh-century Benedictine monastery in Santo Domingo de Silos, Spain, portrays Mary as the mother of God.

Mary's most popular pose is as a mother holding a baby Jesus, as she is here in this sculpture from Santo Domingo de Silos in the province of Burgos, Spain.

© María Ruiz Scaperlanda

Council of Ephesus in 431

One year after the death of St. Augustine, and one year before St. Patrick arrived in Ireland, the Third Ecumenical Council in the history of the Christian church gathered in Ephesus.

This particular gathering became a major moment in the Christian church's understanding of Mary—and it made fundamental proclamation about her son, Jesus the Christ.

Nestorius and Nestorianism

In the year 430 A.D., St. Cyril, patriarch of Alexandria, accused Nestorius, the bishop of Constantinople, of heresy.

This was not a situation where an ordinary person just happened to disagree with a small aspect of the Christian faith.

Nestorius was a bishop, the leader of the church in Constantinople—and he formulated public declarations that significantly differed from the professed Christian set of beliefs.

What's a Heresy?

A heresy is a religious opinion or doctrine that stands contrary to the doctrines of Christianity.

The word heresy comes from the Greek *hairesis*, which can mean either "a choice of beliefs" or "a group of dissident believers."

In the early centuries of Christianity, there were several serious heresies that disrupted and splintered the unity of the church.

One of the earliest, the Gnostic heresy (c. 125), for instance, stated that Jesus only appeared to be, but was not, a true man.

At the other extreme, the Arian heresy (c. 325) denied the divinity of Christ!

So what did Nestorius do?

Nestorianism

One tradition says that Nestorius's infamous act took place on Christmas day of 428 A.D. Others are not so sure of the date. But whenever it happened, Nestorius, who was at the time the newly installed bishop of Constantinople, condemned in his preaching the title of Theotokos for Mary, declaring that she was the mother of Jesus, but not the mother of God.

Nestorius claimed that Mary was the mother of Christ's human side, his human nature, but that she could not be the mother of God. He also eventually said that only Jesus' human side (Jesus the man, not Jesus the God) suffered and died on the cross.

Lord Knows

Augustine of Hippo, a saint and a Doctor of the Church, was born in Tagaste, a provincial Roman city in North Africa, in 354 A.D. Augustine's mother, Saint Monica, was a devoted Christian and his father was a pagan. After many years searching for the meaning of life, Augustine converted and was baptized in 387. He eventually became a bishop and one of the most influential theologians in the Christian church. He wrote many books including his famous *Confessions* and *City of God*.

Nestorius declared that Mary would from then on be named "Mother of Christ" in his "see" or diocese (the church in Constantinople).

But the people of Constantinople rejected their bishop's denial of a treasured belief. Both lay leaders and priests immediately took a stance and challenged Nestorius's statements about the nature of Jesus.

By making Jesus into two different persons and separating the man Jesus (human) from the divinity of Jesus (God) but still sharing one body—Nestorius denied the reality of the Incarnation.

As we discussed in Chapter 5, the Incarnation, which literally means *enfleshment*, is central to the Christian faith. It is the belief that Jesus, the second person of the Trinity, "became flesh" when he was divinely conceived in the womb of Mary. In the Incarnation, the divine nature of the Son was united with the human nature in one, undivided, divine person: Jesus.

As Cyril of Alexandria declared, "I am astonished that the question should ever have been raised as to whether the Holy Virgin should be called Mother of God, for it really amounts to asking, is her Son God or is he not?"

Denying Motherhood Denied Divinity

Ultimately, even a heresy as threatening as Nestorianism became an opportunity for the clarification and development of Christian doctrine.

In this case, the church gathered at Ephesus realized that denying Mary the title of Mother of God denied specifically Jesus' true nature—his complete humanity and his complete divinity.

The Council of Ephesus officially assigned Mary the title of *Theotokos*, a name that means "Bearer of God," or "mother of the Son of God made man."

Calling Mary the "Mother of God" was not invented at the Council of Ephesus. Not only had many early church theologians (including the theologian Origen) used the title of Theotokos, but the title had also already become a part of church hymns and liturgical prayers.

But the Council of Ephesus was nevertheless a significant milestone!

The council of Ephesus was the moment in history when the Christian church, under the pressure of a serious heresy, professed and defended the shared truth that Mary gave birth to the Son of God.

When the Council of Ephesus refuted Nestorius, tradition has it that Christian believers in Constantinople took to the streets, enthusiastically chanting, "Theotokos! Theotokos!"

A Visual Proclamation

One of the ways that Christians throughout history have portrayed this affection and respect for Mary has been by incorporating her image into public places, usually in the form of statues, paintings, and street shrines. Check out the following photo from Italy.

The lovely city of Assisi has many beautiful examples of public devotion to Mary, such as this street shrine.

© *María Ruiz Scaperlanda*

Holy Mother
The Virgin Mary, being obedient to his word, received from an angel the glad tidings that she would bear God. —Irenaeus in *Against Heresies* (180 A.D.)

Perhaps no other city portrays this ancient devotion like Rome.

After Ephesus in 431, Pope Sixtus XIII rebuilt a basilica (a major cathedral church) dedicated to the honor of the Holy Mother of God. St. Mary Major, as the basilica church is known, remains the largest church in the world honoring God through Mary, and the oldest church in the West dedicated to Mary.

Standing atop one of Rome's seven hills, the Esquiline, Saint Mary Major and its fifth-century mosaics have survived many restorations. The dedication of the church of Saint Mary Major is a liturgical feast celebrated yearly on August 5 in the Roman Catholic calendar.

The opening prayer of the feast of the dedication of Saint Mary Major affirms, "Lord, pardon the sins of your people. May the prayers of Mary, the mother of your Son, help to save us, for by ourselves we cannot please you. Grant this through our Lord Jesus Christ, your Son, who lives and reigns with you and the Holy Spirit, one God, for ever and ever."

Always Pointing to Jesus

The veneration of Mary as the Mother of God has always been especially popular in the Eastern church, where art and liturgy proclaimed in joyful song the mystery of the Incarnation through Mary.

In Theotokos, as well as in all her other proclaimed titles, the important thing about Mary is that, in her actions and her words, she always leads us to Jesus.

The Least You Need to Know

- Theotokos, or Mother of God, is the oldest title officially given to Mary.

- Although she was a part of church history before then, Mary was officially declared Mother of God in 431 A.D. at the Council of Ephesus.

- The many heresies in the early centuries of Christianity confused and divided Christian communities.

- Declaring Mary as Mother of God was necessary in order to defend the Christian church's belief in the Incarnation.

Chapter 15

Mary, the First Christian

In This Chapter

- Why do we call Mary the first Christian?
- Who says she's first?
- Defining *disciple*
- Making her our model

Christ was not part of Jesus' proper name, but a description of his divine mission. The word *Christ* comes from the Greek translation of the Hebrew *Messiah*, which means "anointed," as in the Anointed of God.

It might seem like an unusual title for a Jewish mother from Nazareth, but Mary is often described as the first Christian, the first to embody the spirit of Christ.

In this chapter, we will focus on the title of disciple and why we call Mary the first disciple of Jesus, the first Christian.

Always First in Line

The name *Christian* was first used about the year 43 A.D., to refer to the followers of Christ at Antioch, the capital of Syria. The term was originally actually used by the pagans as a condescending term, an insult!

But it soon began to be used to refer to anyone who professed belief in the teachings and divinity of Christ.

Sunday School

Those who accepted Jesus' message to follow him are called his **disciples.** The word *disciple* comes from the Latin *discipulus,* or "pupil," from *discere,* "to learn."

Obviously, Mary would not have been labeled a Christian, at least not in the same way we use the term today.

But Mary was clearly a follower of Christ. Like the twelve apostles and the other *disciples* of Jesus, Mary believed that her son Jesus was, indeed, the Christ, the anointed one of God.

The Annunciation Was the Beginning

As shocked as Mary had to be when she heard the announcement by the angel Gabriel that she was to conceive and give birth to the Son of the Most High, it was Mary's simple yet profound "yes" that enabled God's plan of salvation to take place.

We call Mary the first Christian because this honest and generous response to God's announcement profoundly changed the course of history.

Both literally and figuratively, Mary was the first human to acknowledge the shocking and amazing reality that God so loved the world that he chose to become human, like us, in all things but sin.

Quite plainly, Mary's "yes" altered forever our experience and understanding of God.

After Jesus was born, God can no longer be some entity "out there" or "up somewhere." He is a God who chose to become one of us, out of love for his creatures.

This is not just a theological statement. It is a life-changing truth! And Mary of Nazareth was the first to embody this truth, the first to welcome and accept it!

That's why we call her the first Christian.

Saying "Yes" Made Her a Disciple

The fact is that without Mary's final consent, there is no birth story.

No, I'm not suggesting that everything regarding God's plan of salvation for us would have stopped if Mary had not said "yes."

Nothing is impossible for God!

But God needed Mary's consent if this plan was to take place. And Mary did say "yes."

The word *disciple* means *learner,* and although it is used in reference to other prophets (disciples of Moses or disciples of John the Baptist), in the New Testament it is almost exclusively used for the disciples of Jesus.

In the four Gospels, the word disciple is sometimes used in reference to the twelve apostles, and often it is used as a synonym for *believer of Jesus.*

In the Acts of the Apostles, *disciple* became exclusively used to designate the Christian converts: the believers, both men and women.

Some disciples were called personally by Jesus. Others simply chose to follow the Messiah, believing that Jesus was the Son of God.

Mary's invitation to believe came in the form of Gabriel's perplexing announcement that she would conceive the Son of God by the power of the Holy Spirit.

And Mary chose to believe in the unbelievable.

Like Mary of Nazareth, a disciple is one who follows the teaching of Jesus, not only in New Testament times, but in any century.

Name Calling

When my children were young, it was not unusual to find them "debating" about who would be first—to the car, to get dessert, even to give mom a hug, a unique and curious competition I never discouraged!

In reality, however, why does it matter whether we call Mary "first" or not?

Well, Mary was not only a member of the early community of believers, she was the number-one person to hear, accept, and respond to the announcement that God the Most High chose to send his own son to be born of a human mother.

What a scandalous proposition!

A Disciple Is ...

Yet this "scandal" is exactly what we hear Peter proclaim on Pentecost, a day the apostles experienced together with the mother of their Lord.

Those first Christians, disciples of Jesus the Christ, had the good fortune of having Mary of Nazareth still present in their midst. (Acts 1:12–14)

I can only imagine what a blessing it must have been to have Mary gathered with them as they prayed, as they shared the ways that God was speaking to them in their lives—and as they struggled with how to give witness to the mystery and the glory of God that they witnessed with their eyes and felt with their hearts.

Like those who listened to Jesus' parables or witnessed one of his miracles, it was not enough to recognize that Jesus was the Messiah.

> **Lord Knows**
>
> In the first chapter of Luke, the angel Gabriel greets Mary with the words: "Rejoice, O highly favored daughter! The Lord is with you. Blessed are you among women." (Luke 1:28) Because she was blessed among all women, and the mother of Jesus, Mary is sometimes referred to as the Blessed Mother.

After this reality was accepted, some sort of response was required!

To call Mary the first disciple is simply to acknowledge that she was the first person to be presented with this radical proposition of a God made man, and the first one to struggle with a personal response to this reality.

We know that in Mary's case, it meant that she agreed to give birth to Jesus, in spite of being unmarried, in spite of being a virgin, in spite of not knowing what exactly this would do to her life!

In reality, this is not all that different from the proposition of faith I, too, face. Either I believe that nothing is impossible for God—or I don't. Either I believe in a God who so loved the world that he would be willing to become completely human like me in all things but sin—or I don't. Either I believe, or I don't.

I don't mean to oversimplify the choice, because there is nothing easy or simple about it. Yet making that choice is the heart of the Mary story.

Obedience as Model

After Jesus' resurrection and ascension into heaven, it was up to his followers to share the good news of God's love and salvation with the rest of humanity.

And every person who heard the truth of Jesus and accepted it was faced with a response, an act that would inevitably define and transform his or her life.

To become a disciple of Jesus required a change in one's basic understanding of faith, based on obedience to what one heard.

To obey, as we have already discussed, is to listen. It is not only an act; it is a posture or attitude to life.

On the day of Pentecost recorded in the Acts of the Apostles, when Peter finished his exhortation to the crowd regarding Jesus, those who listened were "deeply shaken." They asked Peter and the other apostles what they should do.

"You must reform and be baptized, each one of you, in the name of Jesus Christ," Peter responded, "that your sins may be forgiven; then you will receive the gift of the Holy Spirit. It was to you and your children that the promise was made, and to all those still far off whom the Lord our God calls." (Acts 2:38–39)

The first to listen, to obey, and to embrace the way of discipleship was Mary, the mother of the Messiah. And so we naturally turn to her to be our model in how to live the life of a disciple.

Christians across cultures and across time have used images like the one that follows from Zaragoza, Spain, as a way of remembering Mary and the truths of faith that she models for all believers.

This image of Nuestra Señora del Pilar *from the Cathedral in Zaragoza, Spain, speaks in a particular way to this community and this region.*

© *Phillip Reilly*

Follow the Leader

The oldest written reference to Mary in Scripture actually dates back to the mid-50s A.D. Saint Paul writes in his letter to the Christian church in Galatia: "When the designated time had come, God sent forth his Son born of a woman, born under the law, to deliver from the law those who were subjected to it, so that we might receive our status as adopted sons." (Galatians 4:4–5)

Because Mary said "yes" to this shocking proposition of faith, she became an example of how to live this mystery and apparent contradiction in every believer's life.

When confronted and presented by the story of Jesus of Nazareth, a man born of a woman yet fully God and fully man, the early believers must have gone through a very similar progression to the one Mary experienced after the angel Gabriel's announcement.

Surprise. Feeling troubled. Wondering how this could be true. And ultimately, wondering what this "news" would mean in their lives.

In the end, it is important to recognize that Mary is the first Christian because she was the first to believe the improbable idea that Jesus was the Son of the Most High—and it is a truth that Mary professed throughout her life.

Holy Mother

Mary's "How can this be?" is a simpler response than Zechariah's, and also more profound ... Mary proceeds—as we must do in life—making her commitment without knowing much about what it will entail or where it will lead. I treasure the story because it forces me to ask: When the mystery of God's love breaks through into my consciousness, do I run from it? Do I ask of it what it cannot answer?

—Kathleen Norris, *Meditations on Mary* (Penguin Putnam, 1999)

The One, the Only

Because from his birth to his death Mary of Nazareth was present at every major event we know of in Jesus' life, it only makes sense that we ponder her, her actions, and her life, in a special way.

In a very real and practical way, Mary modeled Christianity like no one else can!

Mary was a faithful, prayerful Jewish woman who made God the center of her life—and whose life was transformed because of Jesus.

Isn't this what being a Christian believer means?

Amen! Yes, I Believe

Mary's consent, however, was more than an acceptance. It wasn't about letting something happen to her, but about a conscious and deliberate act, a choice.

It was a statement of faith: "yes, I believe!" And in this way, Mary set the precedent for the rest of us.

And from the very beginning, the early Church recognized Mary's unique role in the story of Jesus—and her ability to lead us to him.

Like going to a friend we know will understand and even help us name what we're feeling, the stories of Mary from the gospels provide us with insight and discernment about what it means to live as a follower of Jesus.

Mary experienced first all the difficulties, the sense of awe, the power, and the complexity of having Jesus in her life. Because she lived it first, her example can show us the way as we, too, choose to make Jesus central to our everyday living.

When faced with moments of uncertainty or struggle, I ask myself what a woman I admire would do in that situation. It could be my best friend or my mother or my grandmother.

Whether I can literally ask them or not is not the point.

When I open myself to the question—what would she do as a woman and a mother if she were in my place?—I allow myself to think outside the box, to imagine possibilities beyond the particular situation.

It also helps me because I trust these women's judgments and I know that bringing them into my life today can guide me, whether they are across state lines or watching me from heaven.

In previous chapters, we've already looked at important moments in Mary's life as they are described in Scripture.

But the bottom line is this: much in the same way that I hear myself in someone else's story, we find in the Scripture stories with Mary themes and emotions that are familiar to us all. They are our everyday life.

And they can bring us to a new understanding, a new awareness about the world, and about ourselves, if we begin by asking the questions.

The Art of Surrender

Mary of Nazareth has been portrayed in countless ways and given many emphases over the past two thousand years.

She has been called a feminist, a modern woman, a traditional woman, a working woman, a working mother, an at-home mother, a revolutionary, and even a radical activist.

One of the ways Mary is described that I find most troublesome involves the word *surrender*.

I must admit that if we say Mary models for us how to live surrender, it's not too far-fetched to picture a feeble, submissive, weak young woman.

But is that really what it means to say that Mary surrendered to the will of God in her life?

Not Giving Up

The word *surrender* means so much more than giving up or even submission. And neither of those qualities are the driving force of Mary's "yes."

To surrender means to stop trying to be in charge, to stop fighting reality. It means to recognize that there already is a God, and that I'm not it!

> **Lord Knows**
>
> The Serenity Prayer (which is also an integral part of the Alcoholics Anonymous program and other 12-Step-based recovery groups) is as follows:
>
> God grant me the serenity
> To accept the things I cannot change,
> Courage to change the things I can,
> And wisdom to know the difference.

It means to willfully acknowledge and concede that God is in charge, not me.

This act of surrender took place at the scene of the Incarnation. Mary was confronted with a reality that she did not choose. She heard a message from God, and did not dispute it. She asked questions of the angelic messenger, but did not argue. She was troubled, but did not lose heart.

Mary trusted that the God who created the universe was also intricately involved in creating and shaping her reality. God was in control. That's what Mary's surrendered "yes" acknowledged.

In doing so, Mary did not kneel down in weakness and frailty giving up her power.

Instead, Mary bowed down in humble surrender recognizing and praising the greatest of all powers, the hand of the Creator. It's a subtle but significant distinction!

The First Step

Every day of the year, across the nation and the world, literally, members of Alcoholics Anonymous and other similar 12-Step support groups gather to acknowledge this same reality, and that identical reliance on a higher power taking care of the world.

As the first step of Alcoholics Anonymous reveals, "We admitted we were powerless over alcohol—that our lives had become unmanageable."

As the program emphasizes, only after this monumental first move can a person journeying toward recovery move to the next step, which affirms: "We came to believe that a Power greater than ourselves could restore us to sanity."

This surrender, by the way, is not a reality that is good only for people suffering from addiction, or even for those affected by someone else's addiction—but for everyone.

There is so much irony in saying that one is letting go of what one ultimately cannot control!

But whether one acknowledges it or not, the reality remains that one is never in control. That reality won't change!

When I did consent and surrender to God, as Mary did, my attitude and my perception about God's ability to act in my life and in my world were completely transformed.

Mary—very much like recovering addicts!—understood that placing her entire will and life in God's hands allowed her to grow in health and wellness and spirit.

Making a Choice

Mary's "yes," therefore, was not an act of defeat, but a choice based on personal confidence and strength.

With each new situation, Mary surrendered herself and her new reality to the care of God—and in doing so, she showed us the way of discipleship.

No matter what decision I face, whether a job offer or plans for dinner, I can ask for guidance and for the clarity to see God's hand already present there. Undoubtedly, this is what Mary did every time she "pondered" and held the events of her life in her heart.

In order to live this spiritual path, like Mary, I ultimately choose to surrender to both what I know and what I do not see. My confidence is rooted in my ability to make a good choice because I trust the reality that God is in control.

This takes practice. Or as I tell my children, practice makes better!

Holy Mother

There are large truths about the human condition at work in recovery, an experience had by so many people that it should be added to our sum of knowledge, even when it sounds the stuff of mystery. AA is a spiritual practice, a way of life. But in our culture, I think, well-worn phrases like "powerlessness" and "higher power"—used out of context—can get in the way of understanding that.

—Krista Tippett, host of *Speaking of Faith* on National Public Radio (Newsletter, August 25, 2005, on "Spirituality and Recovery")

In Chapters 20 and 21 we will discuss how Mary can help us see prayer and meditation as two ways that can help us grow in understanding and in our ability to surrender our will and our lives to God's care.

As anyone in a program of recovery can testify, this is an ongoing process, not a one-time act. So is choosing to have a thankful heart, an attitude of thanksgiving.

Like a toddler who bends down to see and admire the flower growing in the crack of the sidewalk, the more I practice living with thanksgiving, the more I am able to experience joy and to see God already present in the details of my life.

Every time I seek a companion in my lifelong journey of faith, I find Mary.

The Least You Need to Know

◆ Mary is called the first Christian because she was first to believe in the Son of God.

◆ Mary's "yes" transformed the world.

◆ Like Mary, each person who hears the story of Jesus has to make a choice.

◆ Surrendering is an act of faith.

Chapter 16

Mother of the Church

In This Chapter

- Mary and the disciple at the cross
- A mother for all
- Queen of Heaven
- Rediscovering Mary

Mary's relationship with the body of Christian believers has been one of extremes. There was a time when so much emphasis was placed on Mary as mother of God and Queen of Heaven, that devotion to Our Lady became disorderly. Mary is not co-equal with God. The real Mary, in fact, would not have approved of the reality that at least for some, she was no longer a way to Jesus, but she had become the destination itself.

But the Christian church has also experienced the other extreme, where Mary has been basically taken out of the story of salvation. She is avoided. Ignored. As if there could have been a baby Jesus at the nativity story without his mother!

In recent years, a concerted effort has been taking place in the Christian faith community to become conscious once again of Mary—of her role, of her gifts, and of her well-deserved place standing next to her son. Instead of dividing Christianity, Mary brings us together and points us to Jesus.

Indeed, Mary's rightful place and most important one is where she stands at the foot of Jesus' cross.

This chapter reminds us that Mary has always been the Mother of the Christian church.

Beneath the Cross Stood Mary

In Chapter 10 we looked at the Scripture reference placing Mary at Jesus' crucifixion from the Gospel of John, and its importance within the Passion Narrative.

We heard that "Near the cross of Jesus there stood his mother, his mother's sister, Mary the wife of Clopas, and Mary Magdalene." (John 19:25) The Gospel of John is also the only text that has Jesus talking to his mother as he's dying on the cross.

What we will discuss is how this passage has been interpreted for centuries by the Christian church as a message from Jesus not just for the people at that moment, but for all Christian disciples.

Behold Your Mother

Seeing his mother standing there by the cross, along with the disciple whom he loved, Jesus said to Mary, "'Woman, there is your son.' In turn he said to the disciple, 'There is your mother.' From that hour onward, the disciple took her into his care." (John 19:26–27)

Even though these few lines are described basically void of emotion, the moment that John captures in these verses is truly loaded with all sorts of ideas and images—and scholars have been interpreting the symbolism in this text since it was first written!

At one level, there is the literal, actual act initiated by Jesus of entrusting Mary and the beloved disciple to each other, of making sure that two people whom he loved dearly would turn to each other in their need and in facing an unknown future after the cross and his death.

In a very real way, Jesus was acknowledging a relationship that already existed between Mary and all of his disciples, not only his beloved one. Mary, who so often traveled with Jesus and no doubt fed and hosted the whole brood of them at her home many times, was already "Mother" to them, individually and as a group.

But in that particular exchange, Jesus went much further, giving his mother and her expansive and loving heart not only to that disciple, or even to the immediate group of disciples, but to the whole world.

Christian tradition has long interpreted those four words to Mary, "there is your son," as symbolic of his desire that Mary's motherhood be a gift to all Christians.

Just as she was mother to the first disciples, and to that eager group of early Christian believers, Mary remains today mother of the whole Christian church.

Just as Mary said "yes" in her desire that the Word of God be born in her, literally, she can show us how to say "yes" figuratively, allowing that same Word of God to be born in our hearts today.

We can turn to her as a model to help us learn what it means to live day by day as a follower of Jesus, and as a Church we turn to Mary as the mother of all believers.

Mary and the beloved disciple at the foot of the cross, a scene at an Irish cemetery.

© *María Ruiz Scaperlanda*

In a letter to all the bishops of the world, Pope Paul VI said it this way: the Blessed Virgin Mary "now continues to fulfill from heaven her maternal function as the cooperator in the birth and development of divine life in the individual souls of redeemed men. This is a most consoling truth which, by the free consent of God the All-Wise, is an integrating part of the mystery of human salvation; therefore, it must be held as faith by all Christians" (1967).

Queen of Heaven

At the Annunciation, the angel Gabriel told Mary that her son would receive the throne of David his father, and "he will rule over the house of Jacob forever, and his reign will be without end." (Luke 1:32–33)

Christian converts in those early centuries would have been especially aware of the words of the prophet Isaiah about the child who would have vast and eternal dominion "from David's throne, and over his kingdom." (Isaiah 9:6) And it would have been natural to honor the mother of their king.

As in all the aspects of her life, Mary remains always connected with Jesus. To regard her as Queen of Heaven would have been a logical conclusion in light of how it directed attention to Jesus as King of kings and Lord of lords.

Whether in time of triumph or more especially in time of crisis, the Christian church found it natural to address prayers of petition and hymns of praise to Mary as the Queen of Heaven.

This devotion was not so much a new title bestowed on Mary as it was an instinctive response to the mother of their Lord, and it is evident in the ancient documents of the church, but especially in the ancient liturgical prayers, hymns, and practices.

What Early Writers Said

In the fourth century, Ephrem of Syria (d. 373) was the first to describe Mary as "Lady" and "Queen," a practice that has remained in the soul of the church.

St. Ephrem prayed, "… Majestic and Heavenly Maid, Lady, Queen, protect and keep me under your wing lest Satan the sower of destruction glory over me, lest my wicked foe be victorious against me."

Gregory Nazianzen (d. 390), bishop of Constantinople and a contemporary of Ephrem, called Mary the "Mother of the King of the universe," and the "Virgin Mother who brought forth the King of the whole world."

Three hundred years later, Prudentius of Tarazona, a hermit in modern-day Spain, declared that the Virgin Mary marvels "that she has brought forth God as man, and even as Supreme King."

Another Spaniard and contemporary of Prudentius, Ildephonsus of Toledo (d. 667), gathered together almost all of Mary's possible titles of honor in this one salutation: "O my Lady, my Sovereign, You who rule over me, Mother of my Lord … Lady among handmaids, Queen among sisters."

For an ancient writer of the Eastern church, Mary became, "favored Queen," "the perpetual Queen beside the King, her son," whose "snow-white brow is crowned with a golden diadem."

During the eleventh and thirteenth centuries there were many hymns and prayers created in honor of the Virgin Mary, and a special devotion developed for her under the title of "Queen of Heaven."

For hundreds of years, artists have produced artistic interpretations of the "Coronation of Mary," a moment not quoted in Scripture and based on tradition, when Jesus himself crowns his mother as Queen of Heaven.

Jesus crowning Mary as Queen of Heaven has been a popular theme for artists, such as this stained glass image from Our Lady of Perpetual Help Cathedral in Oklahoma City.

© Anamaría Scaperlanda-Ruiz

Welcome to My Life

For those first believers and the early Christian converts, honoring Mary in their memory, in song, and in prayers was a way of passing on the story of the Son of God, and of proclaiming the mystery of Jesus' humanity and divinity brought together in the Incarnation.

Honoring her also was a way of remembering that an ordinary woman named Mary of Nazareth was chosen by God to have a special place in the history of salvation.

Look at it this way. Never before or since has God become flesh in a woman to dwell among humanity! And if we accept that Jesus Christ is the Son of God, then it stands to reason that Mary must be honored as unique and "blessed" among all the women, across time and humanity.

Mary's motherhood, her singly unique role in the story of Jesus, is the fact and the meaning that all Christian traditions share. And to those early believers, it simply made sense to include her in their faith life.

Mother for All Christian Faith Traditions

For the first thousand years, Christianity thrived and flourished as one universal church, despite tensions with temporal rulers, the fall of the Western Roman Empire, and internal dissension caused by the great heresies of the time.

Over time, a division began to develop between the Eastern and the Western parts of the Church. This is now known as the East-West Schism or the Great Schism, which culminated in 1054 with the leaders of both sides excommunicating each other.

Everyone knows of the next major split to take place in the Western church, which we call the Reformation.

It is interesting to point out that Mary was not an issue in any of these major divisions in Christianity.

In the Eastern church, for example, Mary remains a central figure of the faith—and her role as mother, queen, and intercessor is prominently honored.

This was also true to a lesser extent in the Protestant tradition, although contemporary Protestantism has shied away from Mary in fear that she might detract from Jesus Christ as the main focus of salvation.

The first sixteenth-century Protestant reformers, however, did not oppose or challenge the Church's devotion to Mary, but instead took Marian doctrines for granted.

Martin Luther, for instance, was very fond of Mary.

He spoke of Mary's grace and humility, and her willingness to allow God's plan to be carried out through her. "Not only was Mary the mother of Him who is born [in Bethlehem], but of Him who, before the world, was eternally born of the Father from a Mother in time and at the same time man and God."

Luther defended Mary's virginity as part of the mystery of Jesus coming into the world. "It is an article of faith that Mary is Mother of the Lord and still a virgin," he wrote. "Christ, we believe, came forth from a womb left perfectly intact."

Ironically, the original Protestant Reformers were actually in agreement over many of the ideas that are now considered divisive Marian theology. The teachings of these reformers continued to affirm, for example, the virginal conception, Mary's divine maternity, as well as her perpetual virginity.

Although these Reformers sought change from any Medieval excesses in piety or devotional practices, they remained in agreement on Mary's unique and honored role, as well as on Marian theology.

Big Title for an Ordinary Reality

Seeing Mary, as the Mother of the whole Christian church was a part of the understanding, the living practice of the body of believers—long before the Reformation or the Great Schism divided the church.

These doctrines and beliefs on Mary, and the titles which they propose, such as Mother of God, Virgin Mary, and Mother of the Church—are based on and directly point to Jesus. This is exactly how Mary would have wanted it!

Ultimately, honorary titles like the ones that Mary has been given are nothing more than a human attempt to give words to an idea that we're often not sure how to express. But the essence of the idea remains the same.

Mary was the mother of Jesus, the Son of God. Mary said "yes" to Jesus being conceived in her by the power of the Holy Spirit. And Mary was given to and claimed by the whole Church as mother of all believers.

Pray for Us

When I was a young child, it was very moving for me to hear my grandmother's voice late at night praying. She always ended her evening ritual the same way, offering in prayer a litany of names that she commended to Mary, asking for her motherly intercession. I will never forget the butterfly flying in my stomach whenever I heard my grandmother's voice saying my name.

Having someone pray for us is a humbling and highly intimate act.

Our Intercessor

The apostle Paul was adamant in his instructions that Christians pray for each other: "I urge that petitions, prayers, intercessions, and thanksgiving be offered for all men … Prayer of this kind is good, and God our savior is pleased with it." (1 Timothy 2:1, 3)

In his letter to the church community in Ephesus, he said: "At every opportunity pray in the spirit, using prayers and petitions of every sort. Pray constantly and attentively for all in the holy company. Pray for me that God may put his word on my lips, that I may courageously make known the mystery of the gospel—that mystery for which I am an ambassador in chains. Pray that I may have courage to proclaim it as I ought." (Ephesians 6:18–20)

And in his letter to the Romans he again requests prayers for himself: "I beg you … for the sake of our Lord Jesus Christ and the love of the Spirit, join me in the struggle by your prayers to God on my behalf." (Romans 15:30)

Praying on behalf of one another, as Paul describes in these few examples, was intrinsic to the understanding of Christianity from the very beginning.

As the apostles and many of the early disciples were martyred for their faith, asking for the prayers of intercession from heaven from these holy men and women in heaven became a regular part of their liturgical and personal formal prayers.

And adding requests for Mary's intercession was a no brainer to Christians. Who better to speak to God on behalf of us or our needs than the mother of Jesus?

She touched his heart at Cana, and she continues to touch his heart on behalf of others in need.

Not Mediator

It's all about using the right words.

Although Jesus is the mediator, the way of our faith, Christians have always prayed for one another, interceding before God for the one for whom they are praying. This is similar to an older sibling interceding on behalf of the youngest child when she's in trouble with Mom or Dad!

The word *mediation*, from the Latin *mediatus*, not only means to intervene or to act as an intermediary, but it also suggests the act of promoting reconciliation or compromise.

Jesus is the one and only mediator in the Christian faith. Some Protestants object to asking Mary or the saints in heaven for their help. I can go directly to Jesus, they say, I don't need Mary or the saints.

Asking for Mary's intercession is comparable, in a very real way, to asking our friends or family to pray for us, to mediate on our behalf through their prayers. The "place" where the prayers end up is always the same, regardless of who is joining us or interceding for us.

But we are always thankful when we hear that someone has been praying for us because we are reminded that we're not alone in the journey.

In other words, asking for prayers from Mary and other holy men and women has always been within the instructions that we read in Scripture, to "pray in the Spirit" through "intercessions" and "prayers and petitions of every sort."

And in the Eastern Church

From early in its history, the Eastern church has had a deep and personal love for the Virgin Mary. And it has embraced in a special way the image of Mary as intermediary of God's grace on behalf of "unworthy sinners" who make up the community of believers.

Many popular Marian feasts celebrated in the Western church originated in the Eastern church, and many prayers are simply translated paraphrases of their Eastern originals. The Byzantine *liturgy*, in particular, is rich with Marian hymns, odes, and prayers.

The Byzantines have hundreds of *kontaks*, or short prayers based on Scripture, and thousands of canons honoring Our Lady. Some of the famous Eastern church composers of Marian hymns include Gregory of Cappadocia (d. 345), John Chrysostom (d. 407), and Ephrem (d. 373), who is often described as Mary's first poet and hymnodist.

> ### Sunday School
>
> A **liturgy**, notes the dictionary, is a prescribed form or set of forms for public religious worship. With reference to Christianity, however, the word *liturgy* is also used to mean a specific type of religious worship—the celebration of the Sacrament of the Eucharist, also referred to as the Lord's Supper or the Holy Eucharist.

The Akathist Hymn (seventh century) remains one of the most beautiful songs of praise of all times in honor of the Theotokos, the Mother of God.

It is a lovely example of Eastern devotion to Mary, with parts of it sung in Byzantine churches on the first four Saturdays of Lent, and the entire long hymn (which fills nearly 30 pages of an ordinary pamphlet!) sung on the fifth Saturday, known as Akathistos Saturday.

Another beautiful hymn traditionally sung at the dismissal of *compline* (evening prayer) on Mondays and Wednesdays during Lent in the Byzantine rite proclaims: "All those who with faith flee unto thee, with thy mighty hand dost thou shelter, O pure one, as thou art good; no one else have we who sin as a perpetual intercessor for us with God in dangers and sorrows, we who have been burdened down with our abundant sins, Mother of God in the highest, Wherefore we all fall down before thee; rescue us, thy servants, from adversities" (Dismissal Theotokion, Tone 2).

Some Eastern Christians celebrate the feast of the "Protecting Veil of Our Lady," a feast that celebrates Mary's intercession on October 1.

Sunday School

Compline, from the Latin word meaning *to complete,* is the final of the seven times of day at which canon law prescribes that certain prayers are to be said by monastic communities. Compline may be recited or sung just before retiring for the day, which explains where the name comes from.

The feast, which dates back to the year 910, is based on a story that took place during a terrible epidemic in Constantinople. A man named Andrew had a vision of the Mother of God as he prayed at church, where Mary was with John the Baptist and John Chrysostom.

In his vision, while Mary was suspended over the sanctuary she removed the veil from her head and spread it out, as if to protect the entire city. According to the story, at that moment, the plague that had been ravaging Constantinople ended.

According to historians, a widespread notion in the Eastern church has always been that Mary and her maternal influence could, in effect, turn away Christ's just anger and obtain mercy for sinners.

A good example of this idea is the popularity of the Theophilus legend. In this story, translated into Latin in the eighth century, a man named Theophilus bargains away his soul to the devil in order to get a lucrative job. But when he is near death, Theophilus implores the Virgin Mary to get back the contract, which Mary does after contending with the devil. In this story, Theophilus dies forgiven and avoids eternal hell.

Rediscovering Mary

The controversies and arguments that took place following the Reformation have generated, at best, a deep silence regarding Mary.

Somehow, Mary became lost in all the shuffle and redesigning as traditions split within traditions and the Christian faith became not one but many groups.

In terms of remembering Mary, it became especially difficult to find her memory anywhere within modern fundamentalism and other Bible-only-based religions—which had no room for Mary or for history steeped in tradition.

What modern Protestantism has feared is "Mariolatry," the elevation of Mary to a status approaching Christ's.

But all of that is changing.

Books by Protestant pastors and theologians addressing Mary and her importance to the Christian faith are numerous. *Theology Today*, a predominantly Protestant Journal from Princeton Theological Seminary, defended the fact that they devoted an entire issue to Mary with an editorial entitled, "The Church's First Theologian."

And Pope John Paul II, a great admirer and promoter of Mary until his death in 2005, publicly and frequently emphasized that Mary is a source of Christian unity— and that Marian feasts celebrated by the church serve as pointers on our common Christian journey.

Remembering Mary's assumption into heaven, for example, "is an invitation to look up, to gaze at Mary who is glorified in body, so that we can regain the true meaning of life and be encouraged to walk on its path with trust," said the pope. Mary has already gained what we as Christians all hope and yearn for, to be raised up one day and joined body and spirit with Christ. This is the union that Mary lets us glimpse and hope for.

Perhaps the most encouraging and exciting changes, however, are coming from mainstream Protestant traditions, as both preachers and scholars are openly and publicly engaging Mary as a central part of the Christian faith—right where she belongs.

Today's Protestant Tradition

Beverly Roberts Gaventa, a professor of New Testament Literature at Princeton Theological Seminary, is one of the driving forces in bringing Mary back into Protestant theological and biblical discussions.

Gaventa, who was one of the main interviewees in a recent *Time* magazine article on Protestants and Mary (March 2005), has written extensively on the mother of Jesus from a Protestant perspective.

What is perhaps most healthy about Gaventa's approach is that she addresses what she calls "Protestant anxiety" regarding a possible overemphasizing of Mary's role by addressing all the questions head-on.

Still, Gaventa would disagree with the Catholic and Orthodox emphasis that the exchange between Jesus, his mother, and his beloved disciple symbolize Jesus giving Mary and her unique motherhood to the whole church.

Instead, she concludes that the scene at the cross is both symbolic and emotional, but emphasizes that its primary function is "to complete the crucifixion's separation of Jesus from all that belongs to his earthly life."

The point of that story for her is that it symbolizes the culmination of Jesus' return to his Father. For Gaventa, the exchange involving Mary and the beloved disciple completes the physical stripping that had been taking place throughout the passion.

Ultimately, biblical interpretation is always open to discussion.

But what strikes me as most important about Gaventa's work, however, is the fact that it is taking place at all!

Like popular author Kathleen Norris, Gaventa brings her Protestant upbringing and understanding to the table—and she makes it known that Mary is an intricate part of understanding our faith, theologically, liturgically, and devotionally.

Time magazine makes it sound even more dramatic, declaring that the "long-standing wall around Mary appears to be eroding."

This is not because Protestants are converting or even reclaiming all the ancient devotions of Christianity, but because "a growing number of Christian thinkers who are neither Catholic nor Eastern Orthodox have concluded that their various traditions have short-changed [Mary] in the very arena in which Protestantism most prides itself: the careful and full reading of Scripture."

Lord Knows

Litanies in the Eastern church are always a part of the official liturgy, and they have at least three different forms: *Synaptae* (Collect), *Ektenie* ("intense" prayer of intercession and pardon based in part on Psalm 50) and *Aitaesis* (intercessory prayer for peace, pardon and protection).

In the liturgy of the Western church the word *litany* is derived from *litania*, meaning "prayer of invocation" or "intercession." It also meant, up to the twelfth century, that it involved a procession.

Even the publishing world is changing. Although one evangelical publishing house predictably shied away from publishing a Marian guide for teens by author Shannon Kubiak for fear of elevating Mary, a second one picked up. Even the title of Kubiak's book—*God Called a Girl: How Mary Changed Her World and You Can Too*—is remarkable and indicative of how things are changing.

As long as Christians are open to rediscovering their roots in Christianity's first 1,500 years, Mary will remain a central and vibrant character in the Christian story.

And in the meantime, from *Christianity Today* to the *Christian Century*, everyone will keep talking about Mary!

Mary in Orthodox Christianity

In the Orthodox church, Mary's role as the Mother of God is very important. The Orthodox church honors Mary as the first Christian, as she wholeheartedly accepted God's mission for her.

The church honors in a special way Mary as God-bearer, Theotokos, who gave birth to Jesus, the only begotten Son of God.

In the words from the Orthodox liturgy, "It is truly meet to bless thee, O Theotokos, who art ever blessed and all-blameless, and the mother of our God. More honorable than the Cherubim, and more glorious beyond compare than the Seraphim, thou who without stain barest God the Word, and art truly Theotokos: we magnify thee."

According to the Greek Orthodox Archdiocese of America, in the Orthodox church, the Theotokos is "highly honored as expressed in praises recorded in the Scriptures with qualities mirrored in the Magnificat."

Despite the high honor and the highest admiration, which the Orthodox church bestows upon the Virgin Mary Theotokos, however, it does not teach either her Immaculate Conception, or her bodily Assumption into heaven, celebrating instead the Dormition of Mary.

The Feast of the Dormition of the Theotokos and Ever-Virgin Mary is celebrated on August 15 each year. The Feast commemorates the repose (dormition) or "falling-asleep" of the mother of Jesus and the translation or assumption of her body into heaven.

According to the story, all the apostles except for Thomas returned to Jerusalem to see Mary at the time of her death. As they gathered at her bedside at the moment of her death, Jesus himself descended and carried her soul into heaven.

Mary's body was then taken in procession and laid in a tomb near the Garden of Gethsemane. When the apostle Thomas arrived three days after her repose and asked to see her body, they found the tomb to be empty. The bodily assumption of the God-bearer was confirmed by the message of an angel, and by her appearance to the apostles.

The Eastern Orthodox church venerates the Theotokos as "holder of Him Who is illimitable … and infinite Creator."

It was noticeable at Pope John Paul II's funeral on April 8, 2005, that the Ecumenical Patriarch Bartholomew I and other heads of self-governed Eastern churches were present.

This marked the first time for many centuries that an Ecumenical Patriarch attended the funeral of a pope. Many considered it a significant sign that the dialogue toward reconciliation that John Paul II so much wanted, might already have started.

The Least You Need to Know

- ◆ At the cross, Jesus gave Mary as mother to the whole body of believers.
- ◆ From the first centuries, Mary has been called Mother of the Church and Queen of Heaven.
- ◆ The liturgy of the Eastern church is especially rich in Marian devotion.
- ◆ Mary as Theotokos, God-bearer, is highly honored and venerated in the Eastern Orthodox church.

Part 5

Naming Mary

One of the things that makes Mary exceptional, and quite puzzling to most people, is the fact that she is known by so many names! Our Lady of this and Mother of that—what in the world is that all about?

Like any woman, Mary wears a million hats, each describing an aspect of who she is. But in Mary's case these names also usually include ideas that need a little bit of explanation and understanding. In this part we will discuss things like what it means to be the "patron" of something or someone or some country! What is up with all those unusual apparitions and people claiming to see Mary around the globe? And why do particular countries or ethnic groups lay a claim on Mary and give her a personal name?

Chapter 17

Will the Real Mary Please Stand Up?

In This Chapter

- ◆ One woman
- ◆ Titles and names
- ◆ Patron of her children
- ◆ Appearing now

The Virgin Mary is both one woman and many.

To understand this reality, we have to learn to see how Mary fits within the church universal, acknowledging the myriad cultures, races, and nationalities that have embraced Christianity in the past two thousand years.

In addition to discussing the many names given to Mary (and why), we will also explore in this chapter the concepts of patronage and apparitions with regard to Mary.

Many Names, Still One Mary

The fact that Mary is honored with so many specific names and titles can be confusing. After all, there are hundreds!

Some names refer to her qualities or attributes. Others are specific to a city or a country. A few examples are Our Lady of Solitude, Our Lady of Victory, Virgin Mary of Guadalupe (Mexico), and Mother of Mercy.

She might be known by many names, but she is still the same Mary of Nazareth.

The Titles Don't Change the Person

I teased our niece recently, telling her that after her first baby is born, she will lose her name and forever become "Kayden's mom." And of course, I am only half-kidding.

Depending on whom I am talking with, I can be, and often am, called many names (Mrs. Scaperlanda, Mama Scap, Maria, Mom). Sometimes I am described by my ethnicity or my place of birth (a Cuban-American, a Hispanic, a Cuban).

And it doesn't happen often, but sometimes I will be introduced by names that refer to my "titles" or my profession (a published author, a Master's in English).

None of these names change who I am. They are simply a way of connecting with me in some sort of personal form, or perhaps even a form of intimacy.

Holy Mother

O Mary, beautiful Flower of Mount Carmel, fruitful Vine, Splendor of heaven, Virgin Mother of the Son of God, assist us in our present necessities (mention your intentions).

O Star of the Sea, come to our aid and show yourself a Mother to us. O Holy Mary, Mother of God, Queen of Heaven and Earth, we humbly ask you from the bottom of our hearts to help us, for nothing can withstand your powerful intercession. O show us that you are our Mother."

—Chaplet of Our Lady of Mount Carmel

This, too, is true of Mary.

As Christianity spread and ideas became formulated into theological concepts, early disciples attempted to describe and define what it means to be a Christian.

Just as important as the theology was the experience of Christianity. It is in this category that we find Mary.

Mary of Nazareth was not a concept to be defined and filed away in a book; she was a person that Christian women turned to for guidance and support in their mothering. It was to Mary that they went, knowing she understood suffering and the anguish of experiencing violence.

The evolving understanding of Mary in Christianity is really not about knowledge as much as it is about relationship. And it was that personal experience that eventually gave birth to the theology!

Differences in Christianity

From its birth, the spiritual path that we call Christianity involved not one, but many cultures and ethnicities.

In fact, the book of Acts and the letters that make up the rest of the New Testament are filled with directives, explanations, and advice by the apostles for communities that were struggling with diversity.

Many of those personal differences involved cultural, ethnic, and national background. For example, one of the first questions that the new Christians had to address was whether gentiles (non-Jews) would be required to become Jewish before they could become Christian!

Some of the questions faced by these early disciples were directly related to the different ethnic and cultural backgrounds of the communities in which they traveled and preached. And it all happened very fast.

In spite of harsh and violent persecution, Christianity spread rapidly within and outside the Roman Empire.

As the map that follows shows, by the year 180 A.D., there were Christian communities evident across northern Africa; in modern-day Spain, Belgium, and France; in parts of modern-day Germany; in Eastern Europe; and in Asia Minor.

Think about it. This was a mere 150 years after Jesus' death—and within the lifetime of some who authored the gospels!

Now bring Mary into the picture.

This map, drawn by Adolf Harnack, shows the spread of Christianity at 180 A.D.

(Public domain. Digitized from Adolf Harnack, The Mission and Expansion of Christianity in the First Three Centuries, translated and edited by James Moffatt, second edition, vol. 2 [New York: G. P. Putnam's Sons, 1908]. ccat.sas.upenn.edu/rs/maps/1)

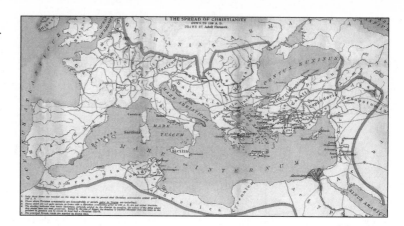

Why So Many Names?

Even within the United States today, the differences are obvious from one part of the country to another. The distinctions are cultural, religious, and ethnic. The weather is different. The landscape and the music vary. Even the way people dress. There are different lingoes, accents, and even languages between New York City and northern New Mexico, for example. Well, you get the idea.

As Christianity spread across different regions, landscapes, and cultures, it was accepted by people of different colors speaking different languages. And the way Christianity was experienced by each particular group became personal.

This was true for each Christian community's relationship to and experience of Mary.

Much the same way that you might keep a dear friend's picture on your bookshelf, Christians throughout the centuries created icons, paintings, and sculptures of Mary, some of which are still preserved in catacomb walls, cemeteries, homes, and houses of worship.

These images of Mary frequently resembled the culture and the people where they resided, in style, skin color, design, and of course the setting in which they were placed.

The Black Madonnas

In general, the term *Black Madonna* refers to a type of Marian statute or painting with dark or black features.

Although the images are believed to be of medieval origin (twelfth to fifteenth century), their exact creation is often not traceable. In most cases, the popularity of the images is mostly due to their alleged miraculous abilities.

The image of Our Lady of Czestochowa, Poland, is among a small group of the better-known "Black Madonnas."

Image of the Black Madonna of Czestochowa, Poland, sometimes called Our Lady of Jasna Gora, the name of the monastery were the original is found). This representation is from St. Anne's Church in Krakow, Poland

© Brian J. McMorrow

According to legend, the image of Czestochowa was created by St. Luke, the author of the Gospel. Helena, the Queen-mother of Emperor Constantine, found the icon in Jerusalem and brought it to Constantinople in the fourth century, where it remained for five centuries.

After that, the icon was allegedly transferred among the royal houses until it made its way to Poland, and became the possession of St. Ladislaus in the fifteenth century.

Over the years, the image was damaged by invading Hussites, Tartars, and even a robber, who drew his sword and inflicted two deep gashes on the cheek of the Blessed Virgin. And according to the legend, the slashes and damages to the image always reappear despite repeated attempts to repair them.

In addition to Czestochowa, some of the most famous "Black Madonnas" include Our Lady of Guadalupe in Mexico City (which we will discuss in Chapter 18), Our Lady of Tindari in Sicily, and Our Lady of Montserrat in Spain.

Not all images of Mary are as distinctively defined or categorized as the Black Madonnas.

But the main point is this: although every image of Mary has clearly represented the era, culture, race, or ethnic background of its artist, it has also spoken volumes about the Christian community where it was (and is) venerated.

These representations over the centuries continue to convey a beautiful message about the trans-racial, universal reality of Christianity, including its Mother Mary.

A Big, Big Lap

In 1964, a woman named Helen Cordero of the Cochiti Pueblo in New Mexico created a seated grandfather figure as a special gift for her grandfather. The clay figure, a man with his mouth open with several children climbing on his lap, was meant to honor the contribution that he made to the whole family through his storytelling.

For the Pueblo Indians, whose family history and songs have been passed orally from generation to generation, the storyteller clay figure became the perfect symbol.

Cordero did not invent clay figures, a pottery form that dates back from long before Columbus reached this side of the world.

But her inspiration in creating storyteller figures initiated a renaissance of clay images that has led to the creation of many forms and styles of storytellers: grandmothers, mothers, bears, owls, dogs, turtles, even Koshare clowns.

And today, storyteller figures are made by potters from every Pueblo, as well as Navajo and other Indian nations. Each storyteller differs in color, style, and substance, based on the particular Pueblo that its artist comes from. For example, a storyteller from the Isleta Pueblo would be of pastel colors. Potters from Santa Clara Pueblo often make small animal storytellers from blackened, polished clay. And one from the Taos Pueblo might be made of micaceous clay, like the one pictured here.

A storyteller clay figure from the Taos Pueblo.

© *Michael Scaperlanda*

The storyteller image is a beautiful metaphor for Mary of Nazareth. Not only does she have a lap big enough for all her "children," but it's a lap that is open to any color, any ethnicity, any religion, any nationality.

Mary is for everyone.

Sometimes she will be depicted with dark skin, other times she will be oriental, often she is European white. She is always shaped and colored to represent the nationality or ethnic background of the particular community that claims her. Sometimes she will be dressed like a queen, other times as simple as a peasant. Sometimes she will be presented within a specific moment in Jesus' life, or sometimes standing alone with arms raised in prayer. With a halo or with a basket of fruit. With child or with angels.

This mirror image of Mary, like the assorted and unique storyteller figures from the different Pueblos, represent the faith and the vision of the artist and his community.

And they remind us that what's important is what she represents, what made her who she is—even if we don't know exactly what she looked like. Or perhaps that is why we don't know anything about Mary's physical appearance, so that she could continue to belong to everyone, crossing all barriers that divide us as Christians and as humans.

Who Needs a Patron?

A *patron* is a holy man or woman who is venerated as a special intercessor (before God). The patronage they are given is usually designated (by occupation, profession, or special needs) as the result of popular devotion and a long-standing tradition.

There are patron saints for everything—a city, a country or continent, professions, hobbies, physical or spiritual conditions, even events.

The church has made official designations for relatively few patrons. Most of these people, in fact, are known and remembered—and assigned their particular attribute—out of devotion, and sometimes in spite of historical details.

Whether by career or background, the patronage connected to a holy man or woman is in some way related to their story.

The patron of academics, for example, is Thomas Aquinas, a thirteenth-century theologian with a multitude of volumes to his name. And the patron of blindness or eye disease is Lucy (d. 304), whose name means (bringer of) light and whose eyesight was restored before her death after having her eyes taken out as part of being tortured for being a Christian.

Francis of Assisi (d. 1226) is patron of all kinds of things—peace, animals in general, the environment, ecology, zoos! Francis was, indeed, a lover of animals and nature, and you often find him as a standing garden figure or bird feeder in yards.

Sunday School

A **patron** is, literally, someone who supports, protects, or champions someone or something, a sponsor or benefactor. In church language, a patron saint is a holy man or woman who is venerated as a special intercessor before God.

Claiming Her Is a Personal Thing

Mary, under many different names, is by far the most popular patron.

For instance, Our Lady of Mercy is claimed as patron by the people of Barcelona, Spain—and by people named different variations of Mercedes or Mercy.

Our Lady of Good Counsel is venerated as the patron of Albania, and of enlightenment.

The image of Nuestra Señora de la Soledad, Our Lady of Solitude, was unexplainably dropped in the seventeenth century in the town of Oaxaca, Mexico, and it remains patron of the region.

And the figure of Our Lady of Knock, patron of Ireland, miraculously appeared at Saint John the Baptist church in County Mayo, Knock, Ireland, as an image seen by a group of witnesses as ablaze in light.

Almost always, the specific name given to that personification of Mary has a particular image of Our Lady attached to it.

For example, Nuestra Señora de la Caridad, Our Lady of Charity, is the patron of my homeland, the island of Cuba. A statue of Our Lady is said to have appeared miraculously in the early 1600s floating in the ocean. It was found by two Spanish brothers and a black slave boy near the town of El Cobre (named after the copper mines) in Cuba.

The image was attached to a board, completely dry, and bore the inscription "I am the Virgin of Charity," the name that it has retained. But the representation of Nuestra Señora de la Caridad del Cobre usually also includes the three young men in a boat who found the small statue.

This mosaic of the image of Nuestra Señora de la Caridad del Cobre, *Our Lady of Charity of el Cobre, decorates a street wall in the city of Pinar del Río, Cuba.*

© María Ruiz Scaperlanda

Now Appearing

In 1991, *Life* magazine became one of the first in the mainstream media to acknowledge the countless unexplainable, miraculous phenomena that occur regularly worldwide.

In addition to angel sightings and other miraculous events, the cover story, "Do You Believe in Miracles?" devoted a large section of the article to apparitions of the Virgin Mary, a topic that is seldom reported—at least in the form of being taken seriously.

Weird and downright bizarre reports of Marian apparitions are many.

In November of 2004, for instance, a piece of popcorn shaped like the Virgin Mary was auctioned on eBay. And a Canadian woman said she saw the Blessed Mother and baby Jesus on a Lay's Smokey Bacon chip.

In April of 2005, the New Zealand Herald reported that dozens of people began to gather near a Chicago highway underpass to see what they believed was an image of the Virgin Mary on the wall. She was immediately dubbed "Our Lady of the Underpass." Enough people stopped that the local police put up temporary barricades to prevent people from driving and parking in the area.

There is nothing normal about those kinds of "apparitions."

What About Recognized Marian Apparitions?

Because of all the close encounters of the bizarre kind, when it comes to discussing apparitions and other supernatural phenomena, most of us react with at least some level of embarrassment and deep skepticism.

But there are places such as Lourdes, France; Fátima, Portugal; and Mexico City, where accounts of Mary's apparitions have survived the intense scrutiny of the local church.

An apparition is exactly what it sounds like, an appearance of a heavenly being—Christ, Mary, a saint, or an angel—to a human or a group of people. Heavenly apparitions have been recorded throughout history, and the Bible is full of those kinds of stories. As we've previously discussed, angel appearances are many in the gospels—as well as in the Acts of the Apostles.

According to the Marian Library's website, the first testimony of a Marian apparition was recorded by Gregory of Nyssa (d. 395), who reported that Mary appeared in the third century to Gregory Thaumaturgus (d. 270).

Nearly 80,000 visions of Mary have been claimed since then, yet less that 2,200 have received official recognition by the Catholic church.

Apparitions have been reported in every continent on the planet, by seers from all walks of life, and every age. The places of apparitions range from cities and churches to homes, caves, and fields.

The Apparitions of Kibeho, Rwanda

Here's a good example of a recent apparition. Between 1981 and 1983, there was a very active period of apparitions in the region of Kibeho with people claiming to have seen visions of the Virgin Mary and Jesus.

Although there were many more after them, the original three visionaries were young women (ages 16, 17, and 21) who said the virgin appeared to them with the name "Nyina wa Jambo" ("Mother of the Word" or "Mother of God"). The 21-year-old, Marie-Clare, was killed 12 years later during the 1994 ethnic violence in Rwanda.

Mary often spoke of the importance of prayer and of saying the Rosary, and she emphasized to the visionaries the importance of loving one another. In one of her messages, Mary was reported saying, "Nothing is more beautiful than a heart which offers its suffering to God. Pray, pray, pray. Follow the Gospel of my Son. Do not forget that God is more powerful than all the evil in the world. Share. Do not kill. Do not persecute. Respect the rights of man because if you act contrary to those rights, you will not succeed and it will come back against you."

Reported apparitions go through a long and thorough process of investigation that begins at the local level with a committee of experts that meticulously investigates the events and carefully interviews the seers.

Even after the long investigation process, the most official statement that the church makes about any apparition is simply to classify it as "worthy of belief" or "not worthy of belief."

In the case of Kibeho, it took twenty years for the local church to give its formal conclusion that "there are more reasons to believe in the apparitions than to deny them."

> **Lord Knows**
>
> The Catholic church never declares officially that an apparition is real or authentic. After a long and thorough investigation, the most that the church will pronounce about any reported apparition is simply a classification. It will be either "worthy of belief" or "not worthy of belief."

Part of the criteria that the church takes into consideration when evaluating any report of an apparition involves how the apparition has strengthened the life of faith and prayer of the community, and whether the message of the visionaries is in conformity with Scripture and with the living tradition of the church.

All of these were judged favorable in Kibeho, where the church officially declared that there is a supernatural character to the apparitions, with the local bishop granting approval of faith expression (prayer and devotion) associated with the apparitions. The Marian sanctuary built in Kibeho was named the Shrine of Our Lady of Sorrows.

Is That a Catholic Thing?

Belief in apparitions, regardless of your religion, is not a matter of faith or morals. This means that even officially, the church permits it, but it doesn't require it!

Apparitions are considered private revelations given to an individual person as reminders of some particular truth already revealed by Jesus. The message of any apparition, in fact, is always meant to bring attention back to faith in Christ.

Most genuine apparitions, the kind that have been validated by the local church, bring a special message to the world through the words spoken by Mary to the seers. Mary's messages have been to a large extent continuously the same, urging believers to return to prayer, to do penance, and to seek a genuine personal conversion.

Throughout the history of Christianity, believers have always had a strong need to experience Mary in the midst of daily life. At no other time is this truer than in times of affliction and need.

It's no surprise, then, that these visitations by Mary are frequently connected with people who are experiencing some kind of crisis in their local community, or in the world at large.

This was clearly the case in Rwanda, a country whose people have been ravaged and sacrificed by ongoing ethnic wars.

Whether in dramatic or simple ways, the truth is that God reaches out to each of us every day, yet how we interpret or recognize these messages is always a matter of personal awareness.

The Least You Need to Know

- ◆ Mary is called by many names, but is only one person.
- ◆ Throughout history, images of Mary have resembled the specifics of the local culture and its people.
- ◆ Mary is, by far, the most popular patron.
- ◆ Apparitions are appearances by Mary or other heavenly beings that always bring reminders of prayer, conversion, and a renewal of faith.

Chapter 18

A Woman of Many Hats

In This Chapter

- ◆ Watching over us
- ◆ Our Lady of …
- ◆ Famous apparitions
- ◆ One with the lowly

In addition to artistic images, the body of Christian believers has expressed its experience of Mary over the centuries through the specific titles and names that have been given to her. In this chapter we will look at certain examples and what those names profess about Mary.

We will also look at three well-known places where Mary is said to have appeared, and how the experience of those apparitions continues to shape the faith and the devotion of the Christian church, sometimes hundreds of years after the fact.

Like Any Other Mother

My friend Judy suggested to me that perhaps the reason why there have been so many experiences of Mary the mother of Jesus with so many different people in so many different countries is simply because Mary wants to make sure that all her children know that she claims them!

I think there's a lot of truth to that. That sounds just like something that a loving, thoughtful mother would do, aware of her children's individual and personal needs.

Just as each child in a family has a different and unique personality, different needs and desires, the Christian communities of faith from the beginning sought to express who they were as Christians within their own distinctive, one-of-a-kind view of the world.

And as mother of the whole Christian church and mother of all Christians, like the tender grandmother of a large brood, Mary is many things to many people.

Descent over Bethany

I opened the beautiful glossy picture book to the first full-page illustration and impulsively raised my eyebrows. Imagine an orange-colored oblong Mary, perched in the sky with four angels, two above and two below her, floating among puffy white clouds.

Below her, picture a busy modern beach, complete with pink and white beach umbrellas, a couple of lifeguards, beach chairs, teenagers tanning in the sun, and cap-wearing men reading at the edge of the water.

It's like nothing I had ever seen! And immediately I found myself drawn into the scene, smiling at the details in the story. A pair of flip-flops is forgotten in a corner. A young child lost in his own world of pail, shovel, and sand. Little birds stand by a half-washed-out sand castle, and a little person with arms outstretched in the water waves for a lifeguard. The almost-drowning person is the illustrator of the book, it turns out! And it was that experience that inspired the rendition of Mary that he titled *Descent over Bethany*, as in Bethany Beach in Delaware.

Here's how artist Michael O'Neill McGrath described what he experienced: "I imagined Mary hovering above our heads. Some of us on the beach that morning were merely soaking up the sun, sipping lemonade and wondering where to have dinner that evening, while others among us were nearly drowning. Life is like that, isn't it? Birth, death, and the ordinary stuff in between happen at the same time, packing every moment of our day with mystery."

We are continually and simultaneously given glimpses, he added, both of serpents and of all things godly, including "the woman so holy we assume she is in heaven watching over us like a lifeguard."

This is the Mary that the Christian church has experienced for the past two thousand years, a holy woman, a mother so loving and devoted that she will be wherever we are, even at the beach!

Mary has been a continuous, active presence in a journey that began with her son and continued through his disciples. For over two thousands years, she has been mother and friend, disciple and model, to every Christian who sets on the journey.

And sometimes that experience has been captured for the rest of the world to see through art, words, and liturgical prayers.

Mary on Stamps

Before looking at some of Mary's popular names and famous apparitions, I want to point out an interesting and unusual expression of Mary in our modern culture—Mary on stamps.

The first stamps were used in Great Britain in 1840 as a way of simplifying the process of sending mail. Before that time, the system was that the recipient of the mail paid a charge according to the distance involved.

The first detachable and adhesive stamp was issued on May 1, 1840, and it featured the image of Queen Victoria, without naming the country. To this day, British stamps are known by the figure of the reigning monarch! Within a handful of years, stamps spread rapidly to other countries. By 1847, stamps were adopted in the United States.

By 1865, an article in the "Stamp Collectors" magazine proposed that the word *philately* be used to describe the newfound pastime of studying and collecting postage stamps.

The first stamp commemorating Christmas was a Canadian stamp issued on December 7, 1898. It featured a map of the British Empire and the words "Xmas 1898."

> **Sunday School**
>
> **Philately** is the collection and study of postage stamps, postmarks, and related materials. Within philately is a subcategory called religious philately, which is dedicated to collecting stamps with a religious theme. And within religious philately, Marian philately is the specific study and collection of stamps related to Mary.

*This is the first stamp com-
memorating Christmas. It
was issued in Canada for
Christmas 1898.*

*(Public domain. www.udayton.
edu/mary/resources/
marystamps.html)*

Throughout the twentieth century there were many Christian themes on stamps. The first stamp portraying Mary was issued in Bavaria and is dated February 14, 1920.

*The first stamp illustrating
Mary was issued in Bavaria
in 1920.*

*(Public domain. www.udayton.
edu/mary/resources/
marystamps.html)*

The stamp featured a famous Marian column that stands on Munich's Marienplatz (Mary's Square), commemorating Maximilian I's victory over the Turks in 1620, and honoring Mary as patron of Bavaria.

Later that same year, Liechtenstein issued a Mary stamp. And in 1936, Estonia printed the first stamp with a Nativity image.

The United States printed its first Mary stamp for Christmas 1966. It featured a painting by Hans Memling (d. 1494) titled *La Madone et l'Enfant* (see the Madonna and Child in the image that follows). Every year since then the United States has issued an image of Mary related to the Nativity, usually featuring a Madonna, Mary with a baby Jesus.

This painting by Hans Memling from the National Gallery of Art in Washington, D.C., was the first image of Mary used in a United States stamp.

(Public domain. www.udayton. edu/mary/resources/stamps/ stamps_usa.html)

Qualities and Attributes

Some of the most beautiful names given to Mary have to do with attributes or personal qualities that Christians have experienced about their heavenly mother.

One of the ways that people were able to express these names and reflect on Mary's specific attributes was through litanies—a prayer in the form of responsive petitions. To pray a litany, the leader or cantor recites a list of names to which the congregation responds with a request for prayers; for example, "Blessed Virgin Mary, pray for us. Mother of Christ, pray for us."

The Litany of the Blessed Mother, also called the Litany of Loreto, is probably the most famous in this prayer form. Through a long list of colorful titles and names, a litany becomes a powerful prayer tool for reflecting on Mary and becoming aware of her presence in the ordinary of our lives.

I will give examples of Marian prayers in Chapter 21, including the Litany of Loreto. In the next sections I will discuss three of the names that are commonly found in litanies and other prayers.

Mother of Mercy

Mercy is such a powerful word. It attempts to define someone's personal disposition to kindness, thanksgiving, and a forgiving heart. Above all, it speaks of compassion. Not in the form of impersonal charity, but the kind that is based on empathy, or feeling with, someone else.

The first person believed to have used the title "Mother of Mercy" in reference to Mary was St. Odo (d. 942), the Abbot of the Benedictine monastery in Cluny, France, who was himself known for his loving charity.

Mercy is what you experience as deep accepting love when you are sincerely forgiven after you have hurt someone you love, or the sense of gratefulness you feel by someone's unexpected generosity.

To honor Mary as the Mother of Mercy is to remember and acknowledge the kindness and generosity of a loving mother who never ceases to pray for us from heaven.

Our Lady of Perpetual Help

The image of Our Lady of Perpetual Help is very easy to recognize because of its distinctive style. As you can see in the following figure, it is in a Byzantine design, with a gold background, and probably dates back to the thirteenth century.

Mosaic of Our Lady of Perpetual Help from the Cathedral of Our Lady of Perpetual Help in Oklahoma City.

© *Anamaría Scaperlanda-Ruiz*

The image of Our Lady of Perpetual Help clearly represents the Mother of God holding Jesus, with two archangels in the background. Over the figures in the picture are Greek letters that form the abbreviated words Mother of God, Jesus Christ, Archangel Michael, and Archangel Gabriel, respectively.

In addition to it being a beautiful representation of Mary, devotion to Our Lady of Perpetual Help emphasizes Mary's desire and readiness to be of help, to assist in a special way when her children are most in need. Her presence is perpetual—forever!

She is the best friend you call first when there is an emergency. She is the person you can always count on to be present at your time of need.

It is no wonder this image and the love it embodies has been a source of Christian devotion and prayer for hundreds of years.

> **Lord Knows**
>
> Benedictines are those who follow the spiritual Rule of Saint Benedict, a contemplative way of life dedicated to prayer, work and hospitality, written in the sixth century by their founder Saint Benedict (d. 547). Benedict is considered the founder of Western monasticism.

Queen of Peace

The evocative title of "Our Lady Queen of Peace" or simply "Queen of Peace" is one of Mary's most popular names. Just do a search on Google for *Queen of Peace* and watch over five million hits show up!

Schools. Churches. Nursing homes. Hospitals. Cemeteries. The frequency of these words' occurrence says a lot about our desire for inner peace; we find ourselves attracted to places with that name and that attribute from our birth all the way to our burial!

We seek peace, that sense that tells us that all is well with the world, and that we are exactly where we are supposed to be. But it's much more than that. We hope for a sense that goodness prevails within us and around us, and it is peace that assures us of its presence.

We feel this peace when we watch a newborn resting in her mother's arms, sit under a tree and look up at its branches, or are held so contentedly by someone who loves us that time stands still.

Mary not only asks us to pray for peace, she joins us in our quest to find it. Our Lady Queen of Peace reminds us that her son said "seek and you shall find … ask and it will be given to you … knock and the door will be opened." It is God's promise.

Sacred Pilgrimage

A *pilgrim* is not a traveler or a tourist on a journey, but rather, someone who journeys (usually a long distance) to some sacred place as a religious observance or devotion.

Sunday School

A **pilgrim** is a person on a journey—a traveler, a wanderer, a sojourner. A pilgrim journeys to some sacred place, as an act of religious devotion. A person who undertakes a journey on a spiritual quest is making a pilgrimage.

A pilgrim seeks to connect an unexplainable but very real inner yearning with an external journey.

People have been making pilgrimages to sacred sites since very early in Christianity. In Eusebius's (d. 341) history of the church, he recounts that Bishop Alexander made a pilgrimage from Cappadocia to Jerusalem in 217 A.D.

We will talk more about the purpose of pilgrimages in relation to Mary in Chapter 20. Here are three places that have become very popular pilgrimage destinations because of appearances by Mary—in each case, to some very unlikely people!

Each of these places has a unique image of Mary associated with it, as well as a special name that Mary provided to the seers during the apparitions.

But usually Mary is described by having her name be related to the location where the apparition took place, such as "Our Lady of …" and adding the name of the place.

No matter how many names she accepts, however, Mary is only one person. We are always referring to the same woman, Mary the mother of Jesus, the Lady from Nazareth.

Our Lady of Lourdes

Perhaps the most famous of all Marian apparitions were the ones to 14-year-old Bernadette Soubirous in 1858. Bernadette lived in Lourdes, France, at the foot of the Pyrenees, in a town of approximately 4,000 people.

On February 11, Bernadette, her sister Toinette, and their friend Jeanne were looking for firewood for the family when Bernadette heard a rustling sound of wind behind her. When she turned around, Bernadette saw a beautiful young woman wearing white with an azure sash and yellow shoes. The woman was standing in front of a grotto (small rock cave) smiling at Bernadette.

The lady motioned for Bernadette to come close, and signaled for her to pray by signaling with a *rosary* that hung on her arm. (We will talk more about rosaries in Chapter 21). After Bernadette said the Rosary, the lady disappeared into the grotto.

Three days later, Bernadette returned to the grotto of Massabielle with several young girls after Sunday Mass, and the lady appeared to Bernadette as the girls said the Rosary, but she still said nothing.

On February 18, Bernadette returned, this time with two adults. As they recited the Rosary together, the lady appeared to Bernadette and asked her, "Would you do me the kindness of coming here for fifteen days?"

Mary appeared 18 times to Bernadette at the grotto of Massabielle between February 11 and July 16, 1858. She repeatedly invited Bernadette to pray, recommending penance and prayer for all people as the only way to obtain pardon for the sins of humankind. A spring miraculously came forth from a site where the Lady told Bernadette to dig on the thirteenth apparition.

The lady who appeared to Bernadette was someone that Bernadette described as beautiful, and she spoke to Bernadette in her native Bigourdian dialect. Bernadette was a young girl, with no formal education, who heard the lady identify herself as "I am the Immaculate Conception," words that she could not understand, but were very meaningful to the local priest!

Sunday School
The word **Rosary** refers both to the prayer method in which the Lord's Prayer and the Hail Mary are repeated in a designated pattern—and to the actual string of beads that is used for counting during the prayer. We will discuss how the Rosary works in Chapter 21.

Approximately five million people from 150 countries visit Lourdes and its 15,300 inhabitants every year, making Lourdes the second most important city in France in the hotel trade.

The Lourdes spring and the beautiful church built next to the grotto is one of the most popular pilgrimage sites in the world. Many who come to Lourdes are seeking some sort of healing (physical, mental, spiritual) from the water.

Since March 1, 1858, the church has recognized 65 miracles from the waters that still flow at Lourdes, and there have been over 5,000 other "unexplained healings."

The following image is a replica of the Lourdes grotto, one of the most visited spots at the University of Notre Dame in South Bend, Indiana.

Students pray at the Lourdes Grotto at the University of Notre Dame, a replica of the original site in France.

© *Anamaría Scaperlanda-Ruiz*

Our Lady of Fátima

In May of 1917, the third year of the First World War, Portugal had joined France, Great Britain, and the United States to fight the military forces of Germany. The pope at the time, Pope Benedict XV, wrote a letter urging all the children of the world to ask Mary, Mother of Mercy, for peace for the world. On the thirteenth day of that same month, three young children from a small town in Portugal received a visit from Mary.

Lucia dos Santos (10) and her cousins Francisco (9) and Jacinta Marto (7) were tending sheep in the valley of Cova da Iria, near Fátima, when they saw a sudden flash of lighting, followed by a great ball of light that came toward them and transformed into a beautiful woman wearing a white dress.

The lady was smiling at them, holding a rosary in her right hand, and she told the children not to be afraid. When Lucia asked the lady where she came from she responded, "I come from heaven."

The lady asked the children to return to that spot on the thirteenth day of every month until October, and she asked them to pray the Rosary every day.

A month later when the children returned they were accompanied by about sixty people. When the lady appeared to the children, the witnesses could not see the apparition, only a tree's branches bent as if weighted down. All the people heard a loud sound at the end of the vision, like that of a rocket taking off.

Mary's message to the children was mainly a request for prayer, especially the Rosary. The lady identified herself as Our Lady of the Rosary, and she asked for devotion under the title of her Immaculate Heart. She also asked that the people of Russia be consecrated to her under this title.

Mary requested that a chapel be built at that site, which now sits next to a huge basilica in the town of Fátima.

This is the first small chapel built at the site of the Marian apparitions in Fátima, Portugal, which still sits next to the main large church where the bodies of the seers reside.

© María Ruiz Scaperlanda

Two specific things have made the Fátima apparitions extra famous.

The first is the miracle of the sun, which took place on the day of the final apparition in October before a crowd of approximately 70,000 people. The sun lost its color, became a silver disk in a multicolored sky, and began to dance in the sky as the crowd screamed in terror, wept, and prayed. According to witnesses, the sun zigzagged through the sky for ten minutes, stopping three times before returning to its place in the sky.

During that time, the children received four consecutive visions: Jesus giving his blessing to the world; Our Lady of Sorrows; the sacred family; and Our Lady of Mount Carmel with a scapular in her hand.

The second thing that made Fátima famous was that the children received three secrets, which the lady entrusted to Lucia dos Santos (d. 13 February 2005) as the main and longest-living seer. The first two secrets were revealed in 1927 in a memoir.

The first prediction was that a second, more terrible world war would take place. The second warned that if Russia did not convert, it would spread its errors throughout the world and many nations would be annihilated.

The third secret Lucia wrote down but did not disclose, asking that it not be revealed before 1960. The handwritten text was kept at the Vatican from 1957 to 2000, when it was finally published alongside an interpretation of the secret by Pope John Paul II. The secret described Lucia's final vision of a "bishop dressed in white, we had the impression it was the Holy Father," going up a steep mountain toward "a big cross of rough-hewn trunks" with other bishops, priests, and religious people. Before reaching it, "the Holy Father passed through a big city half in ruins and prayed over the souls of the corpses he met on his way," Lucia wrote.

"Having reached the top of the mountain, on his knees at the foot of the big cross he was killed by a group of soldiers who fired bullets and arrows at him." The others walking with the pope were also killed, and angels standing beneath the cross gathered the blood of the martyrs, put it in "a crystal aspersorium" as if it were holy water, "and with it sprinkled the souls that were making their way to God."

Pope John Paul II in his published interpretation of the third secret of Fátima said that he believed the vision referred specifically to the 1981 attempt on his life, and he credited Our Lady of Fátima with saving his life when he was shot in St. Peter's Square in Rome.

Our Lady of Guadalupe, Mexico City

Juan Diego Cuauhtlatoatzin is the only person in history to have been gifted by Mary with her portrait. And his image of *la morenita*, the dark-skinned Lady, is America's very own—474-year-old—picture of the Mother of God.

On Saturday, December 9, 1531, Juan Diego, an Aztec Christian convert, was walking on his way to Tlatelólco to attend Mass. But when he reached Tepeyac hill, a former sanctuary to the Aztec goddess Tonantzin, Juan Diego heard beautiful music, like that of songbirds, and then a woman's voice calling him by name, "Juanito, Juan Dieguito!"

Juan Diego followed the voice to the summit of the hill where he saw a radiantly beautiful woman who called him to come closer.

The Lady spoke to Juan Diego in his native Náhuatl language, saying, "I am your Compassionate Mother, yours, for you yourself, for everybody here in the land, for each and all together, for all others too, for all folk of every kind … here I shall listen to their groanings, to their saddenings; here shall I make well and heal up their each and every kind of disappointment, of exhausting pangs, of bitter pain."

The Lady asked him to go to the palace of the Bishop of Mexico and tell him that she had commissioned Juan Diego with the message that a church should be built on that hill.

Juan Diego immediately obeyed, but the bishop did not believe Juan Diego's story.

Juan Diego returned to the hill to tell her that she should send someone else, someone of a higher class and with more stature than him—someone who would be believed.

The Lady listened, smiled, and persistently asked him to go back and tell the bishop that it was the Mother of God who sent him.

The next day Juan Diego obediently returned to the bishop's palace to speak with the bishop, who asked him many questions. Finally, the Bishop told Juan Diego that in order for him to believe that Mary the Mother of God had sent Juan Diego to him, he needed a sign.

Juan Diego told the Lady of the Bishop's response, and she in turn promised that when Juan Diego returned, she would present him with a sign to offer the Bishop.

Mary asked Juan Diego to climb up to the top of the hill, where he had first seen her, saying that there he would find the sign. Juan Diego did as she said, and discovered a miraculous garden of roses in December.

He gathered the roses and took them to the Lady, who arranged them in his *tilma* (a traditional blanket woven from the fibers of maguey). The lady told him to take the flowers to the Bishop as the sign that he had requested.

When Juan Diego reached the Bishop's Palace in Mexico City, he entered and prostrated himself before the bishop as he had done previously, telling him the whole story, with every beautiful word that the Lady said to him, including the details of gathering the flowers that very morning.

As Juan Diego opened his tilma to unwrap the flowers that were to be the sign for the bishop, an image—a portrait of the Lady—suddenly appeared as if painted on his tilma. The bishop and all who were in the room immediately dropped to their knees in awe and reverence at the Lady's beautiful image, which looked just as Juan Diego had described the Virgin Mother.

Yet One of a Kind

I can tell you the stories of many apparitions. I can tell you the details of what happened. I can let you know what the Lady said to each seer, and how the seers were received. I can even quote to you the estimated number of visitors and pilgrims who travel to these places and others where Marian apparitions are said to have taken place.

Yet it is impossible to measure the impact that these apparitions have had and continue to have on the Christian faith and the Christian community.

Pilgrimage sites are not particular to Christians. Many world religions have a developed devotion related to pilgrimages. And not all Christian pilgrimage sites are related to Mary or to Marian apparitions, but a lot of them are.

Millions of pilgrims each year feel a need to be where Mary had been, to stand where she stood, to be connected with her in a personal way. Sometimes they go seeking healing. Sometimes it's remorse or a desire for forgiveness. Often they go with a special prayer request in their hearts.

The story of Juan Diego and Our Lady of Guadalupe is a beautiful example of what makes Mary special to her people. Perhaps the most remarkable aspect of that first apparition in the "New World" is that Mary's Aztec Indian identity validated and empowered not only Juan Diego, but also the sense of personhood and culture of all the indigenous population.

Mary has many names because she is present to all her children. Like the *Descent over Bethany* beach, Mary comes to her people in their daily need. She speaks to their heart, and she does so in their own native language. She brings them a message of salvation, and always a sense of hope.

And the people respond by naming Mary, by giving her the attributes and qualities that they have experienced through her.

The Least You Need to Know

- Mary is given titles that signify her personality traits.
- Sometimes her name refers to a place where there has been a modern apparition of Mary.
- A pilgrim is someone who makes a physical journey to a sacred place.
- Millions of people make pilgrimages every year to holy sites associated with Jesus, Mary, and the saints.

Chapter 19

The Heart of the Matter

In This Chapter

- ◆ Defining Mary's image
- ◆ The early church on Mary
- ◆ What some of the saints have to say
- ◆ On venerating images

There was a time about a thousand years ago in the Christian church when the issue of sacred images or statues became a big source of controversy. It was such a big deal that there were actually wars between those who wanted to destroy and remove sacred images from the expression of the faith and those who did not.

The Christian faith traditions, which have retained the practice of visual art in their churches and homes, including sacred images, are sometimes accused of "worshipping idols" and "venerating images" of Mary and the saints.

Why do some churches have so many pictures and sculptures of Mary? And why are they all so different? In this chapter, we'll portray a few examples of how Christians have attempted to grasp and represent their experience and understanding of Mary throughout the centuries.

Extreme Makeover

New York City's famous Metropolitan Museum of Art (or "the Met," as it is casually known), recently purchased a remarkable piece of art that created a lot of talk in the art world. It was the Met's most expensive acquisition to date, costing more than double what the museum had spent on any previous acquisition.

The little picture (only eleven inches high and eight inches wide) is painted in tempera and gold on a wooden panel. It is an early Renaissance image titled *Madonna and Child* by Duccio di Buoninsegna.

One of the things that art experts say is remarkable about this picture is that its artist, from Siena, Italy, was in some way breaking the rules that marked centuries of "Byzantine rigidity and impersonal, hieratic forms" to allow a personal and intimate moment between Mary and Jesus.

> ### Holy Mother
>
> Let us, my daughters, imitate in some way the great humility of the Blessed Virgin, whose habit we wear. However much we humble ourselves, we fall short of being daughters of such a Mother and brides of such a Spouse.
>
> —Teresa of Jesus (d. 1582)

On the one hand, the picture is quite traditional as far as Byzantine art goes. It has a dominant gold background, and the two figures are not exactly lifelike.

But this is not a traditional two-dimensional iconic representation. There's an element of reality in how the two images interact that changes everything.

In the picture, Mary is holding the child in her left arm, looking at him with a melancholic glance full of tenderness. And Jesus reaches out a tiny hand to her face, as if to gently push aside the veil that covers her head.

Cleaning Up Her Image

There have been many moments in Christian history when historic and global events change everything about how people function and see the world.

A world war. The Copernican revolution. Walking on the moon. A major natural disaster like a tsunami or the New Orleans flood following hurricane Katrina.

Like major personal events that shift and reframe how we see the world and how we respond to it, these global moments do that, in a very real way, for human thinking as a whole.

Knowing that, it makes perfect sense that how humanity sees and responds to God is also altered during such paradigm shifts. Whether the event is personal or global, we find ourselves wondering where God fits within it.

Because historically speaking Mary's relationship with Christianity has been so relational, there have been many different "reframings" in how Mary is perceived over the centuries.

Duccio di Buoninsegna's *Madonna and Child* (dated c. 1300) represents one of those moments—and is a beautiful symbol of a subtle but very real shift that was taking place in Christianity's perception of Mary.

By breaking away from the formal and rigid posture and its impersonal quality, the artist is showing a glimpse of emotion, and inviting emotion from the viewer.

A Reflection of Virtue

Duccio, as he is known in museum circles, was a near contemporary of Dante, who is famous for (among many things) writing in the vernacular, in Italian, rather than Latin!

This made the writing at least somewhat more accessible to the people.

Much in the same way, Duccio's art is meant for the general population, not just for those who could understand the illustration. And so the Mary in this painting is familiar, personal, even intimate.

It's almost a redefinition of the meaning of *virtue*.

The quality of virtue can refer to many qualities (patience, generosity, or compassion), but it is itself a basic goodness, a moral excellence, a righteousness.

Mary has always been recognized as a virtuous woman, a true model of discipleship and womanhood. But by allowing her humanity, her mothering, to appear, her virtue is no longer something unattainable or something to shoot for and never reach.

> **Sunday School**
>
> **Virtue** is the quality of doing what is right and avoiding what is wrong. Virtue is moral excellence, goodness, and righteousness. It is also a particularly effective quality, such as the virtue of patience.

If Mary was like me, then I, too, can grow in virtue and in goodness. She is no longer a detached model—much in the same way that we refer to unreachable beauty of the women on magazine covers!—but instead, she is an example that we can copy and imitate.

In the Beginning

In many ways, Mary came across as more reachable at the beginning of Christianity.

Perhaps it's a like a pendulum effect, where we go through one extreme and we have to realize we're at the other extreme before we are aware that we're out of balance.

Mary's humanity was an important and critical element for those early Christians. Understanding how God the Most High would be birthed of a human woman was the heart of the matter, the central point of the incarnation.

Yet as Christianity sought to define these ideas, sometimes shifts and different emphases occurred.

Images of Mary have always been important in Christianity, and they reflect how those believers related to the Mother of God. Sometimes she is depicted as queen, sometimes as mother, sometimes as one of the disciples, sometimes as a little bit of all those—or something entirely different.

Obviously, however, we can only ultimately live, understand, and respond to the world within the reality that we know. If no one had walked on the moon, then we would have a hard time conceiving that it could happen!

So how Christians related to Mary at any given point in history, like anything else in life, is intricately woven within the personal reality of the Christian church in that particular time and place.

This street shrine in Chile, South America, is a good example of how the local Christian community brings Mary into their town by creating a public display of affection for her (see the image that follows).

What Early Historians Say About Mary

Ephrem of Syria is known as Mary's first poet, and he had a great devotion to her.

His writings show a great desire to embrace a very real and familiar understanding of this woman, who became the bearer of the creator of the universe!

Ephrem was born in the Mesopotamian city of Nisibis, an outpost of the Roman Empire, toward the end of the third century. The Christian community that Ephrem lived in was shaped by the reign of Constantine and by the doctrines of the Council of Nicea.

A street shrine or grotto dedicated to Mary in the coastal town of Papudo, Chile, South America.

© *María Ruiz Scaperlanda*

Ephrem's writings reveal the fact that he actively sought to defend orthodox Nicene Christianity against numerous Gnostic sects—and his writings and voice made him a great influence in the Christian church. He is considered the patron of spiritual directors and spiritual leaders. And he is the only Syrian recognized as a Doctor of the Church in the Roman Catholic tradition.

Ephrem lived through the peaceful years of Constantine, when Christianity was the official religion of the region. But he also lived through the years of persecution that followed, and he ultimately had to move to Edessa, where he died in 373.

> ### Lord Knows
>
> Giaus Flavius Valerius Aurelius Constantine, commonly known as Constantine the Great or Constantine I, is an important figure in the history of Christianity. In 325, Constantine fully legalized Christianity for the first time in the Roman Empire. He is sometimes referred to as "the first Christian emperor."

Because he sought to speak out against Gnosticism, it makes sense that one of Ephrem's most frequent themes is the Nativity—the act where God came into the world as fully human and fully divine in the person of Jesus. (See Gnostic heresy in Chapter 14.)

Here are a few verses from one of Ephrem's Nativity Hymns. Listen to his desire to understand both the human reality and the divine intervention of the Incarnation!

> By power from Him Mary's womb became able
> to bear the One who bears all.
> From the great treasury of all creation
> Mary gave to Him everything that she gave.
> She gave Him milk from what He made exist.
> She gave Him food from what He had created.
> He gave milk to Mary as God.
> In turn He was given suck by her as human.
> Her arms carried Him, for He lightened His weight,
> And her bosom embraced Him, for He made Himself small.
> Who would be able to measure his grandeur?
> He diminished his measurements corresponding to the garment.
> She wove it and clothed in it Him Who had taken off His glory.
> She measured and wove for Him Who had made Himself small."

[Hymn 4, 182–188]

What Some of the Saints Say About Mary

As you can imagine, throughout the history of Christianity, Mary was a common subject of theologians!

But some of the most beautiful and spiritual expressions of Mary's virtues were written by men and women who have been declared official saints by the Christian church.

Here are a few examples:

> Our Lord ... was not averse to males, for he took the form of a male, nor to females, for of a female he was born. Besides, there is a great mystery here: that just as death comes to us through a woman, life is born to us through a woman.

—St. Augustine (d. 430)

Human beings will never comprehend sufficiently the anguish and immensity of Mary's sorrows. Very few Christians partake of those sufferings and even fewer offer any consolation to her.

—St. Bridget of Sweden (d. 1373)

Do not marvel at the novelty of the thing, if a Virgin gives birth to God

—St. Jerome (d. 419)

In anxiety, in trouble, in danger, think of Mary, invoke her sweet name. Let it be always on your lips and always in your hearts. With Her as guide we cannot be lost; with Her as our intercessor we shall never despair. Give Her your hand, she will support and protect you.

—St. Bernard (d. 1180)

Do not be afraid of loving the Blessed Virgin too much. You can never love her enough. And Jesus will be very happy, because the Blessed Virgin is His Mother.

—Thérèse of Lisieux (d. 1897)

And He who had only a Father
Now had a Mother too,
But she was not like others
Who conceive by man.
From her own flesh
He received His flesh,
So he is called
Son of God and of man

—St. John of the Cross (d. 1591)

> **Holy Mother**
>
> It is her "genius" to have described herself as handmaid and not as mother or bride or helpmate or daughter. In doing so, she embraces each and every form of service that is worthy of God. He can form from her everything that pleases him.
>
> —Adrienne Von Speyr (d. 1967)

Hail, holy Lady,
Most holy Queen,
Mary, Mother of God,
Ever Virgin;
Chosen by the most holy Father in heaven …
Hail, his palace.
Hail, his Tabernacle.
Hail, his Robe.
Hail, his Handmaid.
Hail, his Mother.
And hail, all holy virtues.

—St. Francis of Assisi (d. 1226)

Maternity itself is glorified through her. Every woman who wants to fulfill her destiny must look to Mary as ideal … That woman who, everywhere she goes, brings along with her the Savior and enkindles love for Him will fulfill her feminine vocation in its purest form. Basically … woman's intrinsic value lies in making room within herself for God's being and works.

—St. Edith Stein (d. 1942)

Do not labour, I pray to you, to describe with charm of fancy and eloquence of style each trait of Mary's character. Of whatever privilege you speak, or of whatever dignity, it is enough to have said once, 'Mary, of whom is born Jesus'.

—St. Thomas of Villanova (d. 1555)

So pleasing to God was Mary's humility that He was constrained by His goodness to entrust to her the Word, His only Son. And it was that dearest Mary who gave Him to us.

—St. Catherine of Siena (d. 1380)

Ask Mary for the grace to love our Lord as she loves Him and to remain faithful to Him in life and in death.

—St. Bernadette (d. 1879)

Images in Christianity

One of the ways that as humans we preserve our memories of people we love and care about has always been to create some sort of image (a photograph in our modern world!) of that person that will remind us of them on a day-to-day basis.

The same is true for Jesus, as well as for the holy men and women in the church.

Believers wanted to retain a sense of their memory that reflected their understanding, their experience of God, of Jesus, of the martyrs of the faith, and of course, of Mary.

And so they created images.

The Christian church has always emphasized that it is God who gives the images, and not the people who invent them. They are meant to be visible signs of the divine, and always lead us to that encounter with God.

In the Christian Tradition

An image can refer to a living thing, as in Genesis, where it is stated that God created humanity, male and female, in his own image. (See Genesis 1:26–27)

Theologically speaking, in fact, God—who could not be imagined or named in Hebrew Scripture—gave us an image of himself when he gave us Jesus, his son!

Yet most of the time, and for our purpose here, the term "image" is used to mean an inanimate thing like a painting, a carved figure, or a sculpture.

An image is not an idol. In its essence, an idol is an invented or imagined person or entity, a caricature.

An image, a sacred image, is meant to remind us of God and of godly people. It is not an end in itself.

Sacred images have been a part of the culture and worship of the Christian church from the beginning. The art in the catacombs speaks to this reality.

A Family Album

In Christian art, images are meant to help people understand the importance of God or something related to God. And making images of the angels, Mary, and the saints, who are not God, are important in helping us understand God, what God has done for us, and the meaning of God in our lives.

A sacred image, no matter what kind, is always a window into the divine, one that can be akin to how Jesus' humanity is a window to the divine!

Walking into a church and seeing the images and art portrayed in it is like walking into a giant life-size family album. The windows tell stories about God's people and about God's actions in the world. Sometimes they are stories from the Bible. Other times (see the following image), the window tells the story about a holy person who is remembered in the Christian church.

> **Lord Knows**
>
> An idol and an image are completely different things. An idol is an image that becomes an object of worship, and therefore a false god. To worship an idol is to adore the object itself. A sacred image is a reproduction of a person, a symbol, meant to remind us of God and of God's role in our lives.

The sculptures, windows, and paintings can be both prayer and educational aids in the sense that they explain an aspect of the faith or tell a story about a moment or person in Christianity.

This stained glass window shows Juan Diego and the image of Our Lady of Guadalupe in his tilma, from the chapel at the Casa Juan Diego Catholic Worker House in Houston, Texas.

© *María Ruiz Scaperlanda*

Yet perhaps most important, they tell the story of the Christian family. Every time you walk into the building, you are reminded that you, too, belong to this family of faith.

Over there is Francis who lived in Assisi a long time ago and who loved God with all his heart. And over here is Joseph, who was Jesus' earthly father and protector.

And here, that is Mother Mary, Jesus' mom, and our heavenly mother, who keeps an eye on us from heaven and is always available when we need her to come to our aid.

Through these images we understand that we are home and are all one Christian family.

The Least You Need to Know

- How Christians have understood and related to Mary's virtues has been both formal and intimate, depending on the moment in history.

- Ephrem of Syria was Mary's first poet.

- Christians don't venerate images, but instead venerate the person whose image is represented.

- Sacred images are a life-size family album of the Christian faith.

Part 6 Praying with Mary

Most of us have seen prayer beads of some kind, sometimes even in the form of a rosary hanging from a rearview mirror. Prayer beads like the rosary are an ancient prayer tool used by the world's major religions across the centuries as a medium for spiritual awareness.

But in addition to the Rosary, there are other prayers and prayer tools that are associated with Mary, such as making a pilgrimage to a certain site or shrine, iconography, ethnic festivals and feasts, and exploring Mary in the various forms of art. This final section looks at how Christians have experienced the heart of Mary, and how they have discovered her in prayer.

Chapter 20

Walking with Mary

In This Chapter

♦ Intercessory prayer

♦ Mediatrix

♦ Marian and other pilgrimage sites

♦ The communion of saints

We've already touched on the subject of Mary as intercessor of our prayers, and why it was so natural for the Christian community to build on that prayer tradition by including Mary and the martyrs for the faith. Following Paul's admonition to pray for one another, they instinctively included in the practice the woman they grew to know as simply "Mother."

In this chapter, we will look at the oldest Marian prayer, and how Marian intercessory prayer has been an accepted aspect of the Christian faith for centuries.

We will also look at pilgrimages and statues, as examples of prayer tools that are often connected with Mary, although not restricted to Marian devotion.

Not Like God, but Mother of God

It might sound immensely silly, but it's amazing how many Christians are afraid of Mary. Not in the sense that she has super powers or that she could or would do anything to us, but certainly in the sense of being frightened. As if including her as part of our daily faith would in some way detract from God.

This must certainly seem sad to Mary herself, whose entire life was focused and dedicated to God her savior, to whom she sang praises (see Luke 1:46–55) in word and deed.

> **Holy Mother**
>
> Tender Virgin, most serene,
> Thee we hail as Heaven's Queen;
> Unto thee, on bended knee,
> Trusting, call for charity.
> Be our hope and refuge sweet,
> Humbly bending at thy feet;
> By thy prayers our bosoms
>   cleanse,
> Bring us tears of penitence.
>
> —Medieval hymn

Inviting Mary into our faith life by asking for her prayers of intercession is obviously not required of our Christianity!

Mary is not like God. She never claimed to be. She honored and revered her God and Savior as master of the universe and of her life.

No one has ever claimed that Mary is like God, not even the Catholic and Orthodox churches, who have welcomed Mary into their homes without interruption for the past two thousand years.

But anyone who is interested and who seeks her will find "Mother" waiting for them with open arms.

Not Divine

I might be hammering this point to death, but with the history attributed to Mary you can never be too sure.

Calling Mary Mother of God, Mother of the Church, Queen of Heaven, or any other title that she has received as a gift from her children in no way suggests that Mary is divine in nature. Mary is not a goddess. She lives in heaven, but she is not a god.

Look at where we find her in Scripture: taking care of her child, listening to Jesus preach, at the foot of the cross, gathered with the early disciples in prayer. She is always supporting, looking after, cooperating with God's plan through Jesus.

Look at the experience of Mary since the end of the apostolic age. The prayers in her honor praise her unique character and role, yes. But they also emphasize her mothering of all Christians, her aid and encouragement as we walk this earthly journey.

Look at how she has reached out to the church universal. In all the honored stories of apparitions, her messages remind people to turn *to* God, to pray, to repent and come back to the one who loves us, and to build a place of worship to come together and remember these truths as a faith community.

In all the ways that we have experienced and we continue to experience Mother Mary, she leads us to God and she reminds us that he is the path, the journey, and our ultimate destination!

Mediatrix

There is a term that you might hear with regard to Mary and intercessory prayer that I want to bring to your attention.

Calling Mary a *mediatrix* might sound exotic and even daunting. But mediatrix simply means, according to the dictionary, a woman who is a mediator!

Sunday School
Mediatrix, a woman who acts as a mediator, a woman who intercedes.

Throughout Christianity, Mary has placed herself between her son and humanity, advocating or mediating for her children's wants, needs, and sufferings.

Mary puts herself in the middle, and in that way acts as a mediatrix. And she does this not as an outsider, but as Mother. She knows that in her mothering she not only can point out the needs of humanity to her son, but in essence she has the right to do so!

A good example from Scripture that reflects this role well took place at the wedding at Cana. It was Mary's observation—her awareness, regarding the needs of the wedding party at that moment (they had no more wine!)—that led her to go to Jesus and "suggest" that he do something about it.

Jesus didn't seem ready to act on it, but it was Mary's "insistent suggestion" to which he ultimately responded—and that gave way to his first public sign, his first miracle. (See John 2:1–11)

This is why we say that Mary's intercessory prayers are what identify her as mediatrix.

Just as Christians pray for each other without fear that they are diminishing Jesus' unique role as Mediator, Christians should not fear Mary's intercession.

A Mother's Role: Intercessory Prayer

One of the hardest things I have faced as a mother as my children have grown up is to hear of a hardship or a difficult time that one of them is going through, and to be away from them.

I can't describe how hard that is for me, really. I can hear the pain in their voices, the distress in their words. I know that this is tearing them apart, and invading every area of their life. And yet, I can "do" nothing about it.

When they were little, I could simply pick them up and hold them. And while this act of "unison," this reminder that we were together, did not take away the pain, it certainly brought peace to both of our hearts—and often a smile to our teary faces.

Holding someone you love in prayer is the hardest of all weights to carry—I think even more difficult than going through suffering yourself.

This might sound commonsensical, but intercessory prayer is not the same as prayers for yourself. You are not asking for guidance or for enlightenment, spiritual gifts, or any sort of personal thing.

But intercession is also not just praying for someone else's needs. It's holding them in prayer in trust and confidence that God will take care of them and that whatever happens, it will be well.

Intercessory prayer reminds us that we're not in charge. That more often than not, there is nothing we can "do" for someone in need. We can, however, bring them to God and join the communion of saints in praying for them.

Intercessory prayers are a long-standing tradition in the Christian and Hebrew traditions.

Both Moses and Abraham interceded at various times on behalf of the Jewish people to God, asking him to show his mercy.

There are many instances of this as Moses led the Israelites out of captivity and into the desert. As they left the Red Sea, for instance, the people grumbled because they were thirsty, and Moses "appealed to the Lord" for them, and the Lord provided them instantly with fresh water. (Exodus 15:25)

The letters of Paul are full of his constant prayers for the struggling new church communities, as well as his requests for their intercessory prayers. As the New Testament shows us, from its earliest, the young church prayed for people, for safe travel, for spiritual growth, for healing, for understanding.

In Paul's words, "At every opportunity pray in the Spirit, using prayers and petitions of every sort ... Pray for me that God may put his word on my lips, that I may courageously make known the mystery of the gospel." (Ephesians 6:18–19) And in his letter to the Hebrews, "Pray for us: we are confident that we have a good conscience, wishing, as we do, to act rightly in every respect. I especially ask your prayers that I may be restored to you very soon." (Hebrews 13:18)

Communion of Saints

The phrase "communion of saints" is traditionally used to describe the invisible family bond shared by all the believers in Christ.

This of course includes those holy men and women who are in the Bible, those early Christians who died for the faith, and all the ones who have been officially given the title or name of saint because of what we know about them and about their lives.

But the communion of saints is much more than that. In addition to all the dead who are blessed in heaven, it also refers to all the believers who are pilgrims on earth right now.

The communion of saints describes the concept that believers on earth and those who are already in heaven are together one church, one body of believers, very much like the one that the apostle Paul describes in his first letter to the church in Corinth: "The body is one and has many members, but all the members, many though they are, are one body; and so it is with Christ ... You, then, are the body of Christ. Every one of you is a member of it." (1 Corinthians 12:12, 27)

Many of the ancient prayers of the saints refer to the communion of saints, often requesting prayers of intercession from all angels and saints. Sometimes the prayers make a point of naming Mary, as in, "with Mary and all the angels and saints ...."

But often Mary's intercession is assumed to be there by saying "in the communion of saints," as are all living and dead Christian believers.

Pray for Us

The oldest known Marian prayer (dating back somewhere between 200–350 A.D.) is known in Latin as *Sub tuum praesidium,* or *We Fly to Thy Patronage.*

The words are:

> We turn to you for protection,
> Holy Mother of God.
> Listen to our prayers
> and help us in our needs.
> Save us from every danger,
> glorious and blessed Virgin.

Clearly, for the early Christians and for believers since then, Mary was much more than "another saint" in heaven to ask for prayers.

She was, and is, Mother, the one to ask for protection. The one who will always listen. The one who stops what she's doing to help us. The one who keeps an eye on us and watches out for us from heaven.

Quotidian Mysteries

There's a wonderful little pamphlet, perhaps big enough to be called a booklet, called *The Quotidian Mysteries: Laundry, Liturgy and "Women's Work"* (Paulist Press, 1998) by Kathleen Norris, the award-winning author of *The Cloister Walk* (Riverhead Trade, 1997) and *Amazing Grace* (Riverhead Trade, 1999).

> **Lord Knows**
>
> Most of us know that a church is a building of worship. But a shrine, in reference to churches, is a place at which devotion is paid to a certain or specific venerated person, such as a saint. A shrine can be a church. But it can also be the tomb of a person.

Quotidian Mysteries is actually the text of a lecture that Norris gave in 1998 at St. Mary's College in Notre Dame, Indiana.

Norris begins by reminding us that the word *quotidian* means "occurring every day; belonging to every day; commonplace, ordinary."

And she turns to the ordinary, the everyday, as the way to holiness. "It is in ordinary life that our stories unfold ... stories of annunciation, incarnation, resurrection, and the spirit, the giver of life, who has spoken through the prophets and enlivens our faith," Norris emphasizes. "Christianity is inescapably down-to-earth and incarnational ... [it] asks us to place our trust not in ideas, and certainly not in theologies, but in a God who was vulnerable enough to become human and die."

And because we are human, she adds, we must find our way to God in the realm of the daily and the mundane, in the quotidian of our everyday existence.

What Norris describes in this great essay echoes Mary's life and her understanding of what it meant to be human. Although she gave birth to the Son of God, Mary remained a human, a woman, a wife, like us.

Our Christianity asks us to make all that we are, all that we are trained to do, our very quotidian existence available to God.

This is what Mary did. This was her "yes"! Not once at the Incarnation, but in all the human, quotidian events of her life. Mary chose to be, and remained, available to God.

And this is why we can humbly ask her to pray for us. Because in addition to being one of the holy people already in heaven, Mary understood and lived out her humanity to its fullest.

An Incarnational Church

At birthdays, we sing the same song and we blow out candles on a cake—every year. At weddings, we dress up in once-in-a-lifetime outfits and exchange symbolic rings. At New Year's eve, we bring in every New Year with whistles and cheers and a kiss from our loved ones. As humans, we like rituals!

And because we are a people of ritual, in addition to experiencing Mary through prayer and intercession, Christians over the centuries have sought to connect with Mary through tangible, concrete things.

Some of the ways that have become a part of church tradition are building special shrines and sanctuaries; making pilgrimages to holy places; and creating visual art, such as statues and paintings.

Shrines and Sanctuaries

The church has always regarded shrines, churches, and sanctuaries as important in the Christian life. From ancient records, we know that Christians preserved and visited, for example, the places where Jesus walked in Galilee—and in a special way, where he died.

This was also true for places for the first apostles; the places where they died and where Christians were martyred became some of the first "churches," as well as places where they gathered to pray and worship.

These holy sites often become places for Christians to travel to in pilgrimage.

More than fancy buildings or impressive structures—although they are often that, too—holy sites are "Oases of the spirit," in the words of John Paul II, places that invite us to meditate on the Word of God and of the ways that God is active in our lives.

Ideally, shrines are places where Christians revive their faith and where they go to become more genuinely aware of their Christian calling, the responsibilities that arise from that faith.

As I pointed out before, the concept of pilgrimage is prominent in all of the world's major religions: Christianity, Judaism, Hinduism, Islam, and Buddhism. In the Christian church, the tradition of making pilgrimages is an ancient custom with deep spiritual meaning.

Christians have been going to Jerusalem for hundreds of years to visit the tombs of the apostles and other martyrs, as well as sites related to Jesus.

Pilgrimages are not trips or sightseeing vacations, however. To go on a pilgrimage assumes an attitude of openness and renewal, and always the hope of conversion in the pilgrim's life.

El Camino de Santiago

The most recent "major" pilgrimage that I have made took place a couple of years ago when my friend Pat from Austin, Texas, and I decided to walk as much of the *Camino de Santiago* as we could.

> **Lord Knows**
>
> The "Middle Ages" is a very broad term used to describe the period in history between classical antiquity and the Italian Renaissance. It is often dated anywhere between 476 A.D. all the way to 1453!

El Camino de Santiago, or the way of St. James, is actually not a single path, but a thousand-year-old cluster of routes across Europe that converge in northern Spain, ending at the city of *Santiago de Compostela*, where the remains of the apostle James are said to be kept.

During the Middle Ages, *El Camino de Santiago* became one of three major Christian pilgrimage routes—and it remains the most popular long-distance trail in Europe, winding its way through France and the Pyrenees into Spain through the city of Pamplona. This is where Pat and I began our walk.

When all was said and done, Pat and I walked approximately 300 of the 500 miles that make up the Spanish part of the Camino, by walking every day for about three weeks—with some days off for resting, of course!

I'm not sure I can describe what exactly drew me to this particular pilgrimage. Perhaps it was my Cuban-Spanish roots, or maybe it was my first language, Spanish. Perhaps it was the walking itself, a practice that for me parallels in intensity and profundity to writing!

I can tell you that, from the start, it was obvious that I was where I was supposed to be—and that I was meant to walk that pilgrimage with Pat.

Mary was everywhere on the *Camino*. In addition to the beautiful pieces of art we found inside cathedrals, we saw her in side altars, in street shrines, and in town squares. Sometimes her image overlooked a town or sat silently on top of a hill. And we found her name all over the place. Street signs. City names. People. Bakeries. Songs.

Santa María la Real, from the twelfth-century Romanesque shrine of Santa María de Eunate, along the Camino de Santiago in Spain.

© *María Ruiz Scaperlanda*

Mary had clearly been keeping pilgrims walking to *Compostela* company for over a thousand years! And at the end of each walking day, I found comfort in looking and finding Mary at whatever town in which we spent the night. Sometimes she was that beautiful statue in the local church. Other times she was a song we heard, or a story told by one of our fellow pilgrims.

And more than once, she was the person who welcomed us to the *albergues*, or pilgrim hostels, where we stayed.

Naming Sites After Mary

When it comes to making pilgrimages, the journey itself is what transforms us—going to the destination, the moment when reaching the destination, and the journey home.

But the actual, physical shrine or building or site is an object important for the faith because it reminds us of God's constant presence by telling us its "story" of God's powerful activity at that moment in history.

Our visits as Christians to these holy sites become experiences that help us to discern our goal in life, which is our lifelong pilgrimage toward heaven.

Marian shrines, in particular, are centers of growth in that they remind us of Mary's example and of her eternal motherly intercession.

In the Catholic world, about 80 percent of all shrines and sanctuaries are dedicated to Mary—and millions of people visit them every year. The numbers are outstanding. Approximately ten million people visit Guadalupe in Mexico every year; five million go to Lourdes; and five million to the monastery in Czestochowa in Poland.

All of the sites of Marian apparitions have become admired pilgrimage sites. But they are above all communities based on hospitality and noted for prayer and a call for renewal in the Christian faith.

Making a Pilgrimage

People make pilgrimages for all sorts of reasons. Crisis. Sickness. Penance. Intercession. Curiosity. Faith. Doubt. Thanksgiving.

On that ancient pilgrimage road across northern Spain to *Santiago de Compostela*, there is a document hanging on the wall of one of the *albergues* that notes who is welcome as a pilgrim. The text, which dates from the twelfth century, says its doors are "open to all, well and ill, not only to Catholics, but to pagans, Jews, and heretics, the idler and the vagabond and, to put it shortly, the good and the wicked."

Whatever motive invites you to make a pilgrimage is not as important as what happens when you go—and how it transforms your life.

Pilgrimage sites are often places where believers go to seek spiritual courage to face a difficult moment in their lives, to pray for someone they love, or to give thanks for a special blessing.

Marian shrines, because they are related to Mother Mary, are unique in their invitation to seek from the Mother of God both an example of how to live—and her prayerful intercession for the pilgrim.

Nuestra Señora de la Macarena (Our Lady of Macarena) in Sevilla, Spain.

© *Phillip Reilly*

At their best, pilgrimage sites give us a taste of what it means to be a living and breathing member of the communion of saints. They are places that welcome the tired, suffering, needy traveler and offer hospitable mercy and compassion. They remind pilgrims that we are not alone in the journey, or in our prayers. And they are an example of what our own homes and lives can be in both hospitality and openness to God's hand in the quotidian of our life.

Ultimately, everything about pilgrimage is meant to be both symbolic and spiritually transforming—the preparation, the prayers at the shrine, the liturgical celebrations, as well as the return home!

Venerating Images and Places

I would like to make a final note about venerating images and places.

No person, government agency, or religious figure had to make an official announcement that the site where the Murrah Building stood in Oklahoma City was a local or national pilgrimage site. The same is true of the site where the World Trade Center's Twin Towers once stood in New York City.

> **Holy Mother**
>
> Thou our Maiden, thou who dwellest in Heaven
> We pray for thee, Mary delightful, that God may bless thee!
> Do thou, O Virgin, at day when we rise from our sleeping
> Speak soothingly for us to God, and when in distress we
> Cry for thee out of the night wherein we are prone,
> Struck down, do thou part us the darkness that we see thee.
> Be near us. And God's will be done!
>
> —D. H. Lawrence (d. 1930)

From the moment that these events impacted our lives, people came to see with their own eyes what no television or newspaper report could honestly ever convey.

From around the state, around the country, and around the world, people came to Oklahoma City, for years after the bombing, and long before it became a refined and beautiful national memorial, part of the National Park System.

Some skeptics would argue that people go to see these sights because they are just curious. But I think it's bigger than that. No one told these visitors to be silent. They intrinsically embodied a silence more powerful and effective than at any church I have been in.

Something inside us yearns to connect in a physical way with those things that have deeply and profoundly affected our lives. The sense of reverence, of veneration, for that physical place is simply self-evident.

Much in the same way, a statue or an image serves as a visual representation of something so big, so important, that we want to be reminded through all our senses; we want something we can touch, see, and feel with our hearts, minds, and hands.

Across the street from the Oklahoma City Memorial, there is a powerful white statue standing on a corner. The name of the monument is "And Jesus Wept," the shortest sentence found in the Bible. It features a standing Jesus with his hand covering his face in deep, profound sadness for the human tragedy that took place on that holy ground.

Most people who come to the memorial find themselves naturally attracted to this place, where they come to touch, to feel, to stand silently in prayer with the one who understands suffering. They come to ask questions much more than to find answers. They come searching, not knowing exactly for what.

This is what being a pilgrim means. We need to seek an encounter with God in a physical way, so that our spiritual and inner selves will be touched and grow. And Mary is there to show us the way.

The Least You Need to Know

◆ Mary is our mediatrix in that she intercedes to God on our behalf.

◆ Intercessory prayers have a long-standing tradition in the Jewish and Christian faiths.

◆ Visiting a pilgrimage site reminds us of God's constant presence through the story that it represents.

◆ Marian shrines offer a unique invitation to connect with Mary as Christian example, and as intercessor.

Chapter 21

Common Devotions

In This Chapter

◆ Praying the Rosary

◆ The Hail Mary

◆ Celebrating feast days

◆ Processions and public celebrations

There are many devotions or prayer traditions that have become either officially a part of church practice, like the Rosary, or that are cultural expressions of the faith, like ethnic festivals and feast days. These practices are not just "religious," as in belonging to one Christian denomination. They can be, and indeed are intended to be, vibrant expressions of the faith, and an invitation to personal and community renewal.

In this chapter, we will look at some of those traditions, and we will begin with the Way of the Cross (popularly called "Stations" of the Cross) because of its spiritual importance.

Walking the Passion with Jesus

During the first persecution against the young Christian church, begun by Emperor Nero after the burning of Rome in 64 A.D., many Christians were tortured and slain. The Roman historian Gaius Cornelius Tacitus recorded these events in his Annals, and so did Clement, the Bishop of Rome, in his letter to the Corinthians. The liturgical church still celebrates the feast of the First Holy Martyrs yearly on June 30.

Lord Knows

The great fire of Rome burned for a week. When the confused population looked for an offender, rumors quickly surfaced that Nero was responsible.

In the words of Roman historian Tacitus: "And so, to get rid of this rumor, Nero set up as the culprits and punished with the utmost refinement of cruelty a class hated for their abominations, who are commonly called Christians. Nero's scapegoats (the Christians) were the perfect choice because it temporarily relieved pressure of the various rumors going around Rome." This began an enormous swell of Christian persecution.

It was not surprising that this persecuted Christian church, whose members were martyred so early on for declaring their faith, found it hopeful to turn to and encounter the glory of the cross—and to look to Mary for strength and courage.

As with many ancient things, it's hard to track down exactly when the practice of "walking" the Way of the Cross by meditating on the passion began. But we know that it's an ancient practice, and that the actual name, "Via Crucis" has been used since at least the sixteenth century.

The Way of the Cross

Because the heart of the Christian faith rests on the experience and the reality of the cross, Christian prayers and devotions that help Christians remember Jesus' passion have been a long-standing tradition in the church.

We already discussed in Chapter 10 the historical development of the Stations of the Cross or the Way of the Cross, and how they evolved as a substitute for physically walking in Jerusalem where Jesus walked on his way to the cross. And in the same chapter, we also identified the fourteen traditional "stations" or markers describing each place.

But the point I want to emphasize here is this: as meaningful as physical pilgrimages can be, the Way of the Cross as a prayer form is not about the place or about specific streets or buildings in Jerusalem.

The Way of the Cross is a way of meditating on specific moments in those final twelve hours before Jesus died—with the purpose of helping the individual Christian grow in understanding not only the passion of the Lord, but his message of salvation.

Mary has always been at the center of this journey. She was central to the experience of the passion because she was there every step of the way, walking with her son, standing by the cross, being present to Jesus until his last breath as only a mother could.

But she is also central because in a spiritual sense she shows us what it means to be present to one another in the inevitable passion and death that most of us will experience during our lifetime. Sometimes the suffering will be physical. Other times the passion experience will be mental or spiritual.

We will experience many deaths in our lifetime. And Mary, who stood in solidarity with her dying son, can show us how to be present to someone we love who suffers.

The *Via Dolorosa* in Your Own Backyard

The object of the way of the cross is to help us make a pilgrimage, in spirit, to a key moment in the life of Jesus—and in the life of each Christian. Because of their value as a prayer tool, there are Way of the Cross (in Latin, *Via Crucis* or *Via Dolorosa*) displays set up at most retreat houses, churches, and prayer centers.

But sometimes you can even find them in people's backyards!

Just like the elaborate and decorative art paintings or sculptures, homemade Way of the Cross images can be as simple or as complicated as you want to make them. They can be a complex illustration, or a single word or image. They can be anything you want them to be!

Holy Mother

I told her, Fix me, please fix me. Help me know what to do. Forgive me … Help me stop lying. Make the world better. Take the meanness out of people's hearts.

I moved closer, so now I could see the heart on her chest … I saw August and me with our ears against the hive. I remembered her voice the first time she told the story of Our Lady of Chains. Send them rescue, send them consolation, send them freedom.

I reached out and traced black Mary's heart with my finger. I stood with the petals on my toes and pressed my palm flat and hard against her heart.

I live in a hive of darkness, and you are my mother, I told her. You are the mother of thousands.

—Sue Monk Kidd, *The Secret Life of Bees* (Penguin, 2002)

Because the Way of the Cross is meant to symbolize the actual walking that Jesus did, most of the time "stations" of the cross are set up a small distance from each other within a confined area so that the people can walk a little way from one image to the next. This would be easy to do if you are doing it at home or, literally, in your backyard!

The traditional prayer said as you arrive at each station is as follows:

> We adore you, O Christ, and we bless you,
> because by your holy cross,
> you have redeemed the world.

To pray the Stations or the Way of the Cross requires only that you meditate before each of the 14 stations on that particular moment of the Passion (See Chapter 10 for a list of the stations). It also invites you to reflect on what that particular moment in the Passion means for you and for your life.

If you are creating your own Way of the Cross, it's not difficult to find resources on the Internet or in prayer books to help you with reflections. Or better yet, you can write your own reflection for each station, bringing in your family's details.

For example, for the fourth station—"Jesus meets his mother"—your reflection could focus on moments when someone in your life has made it a point to walk with you through a difficult situation. Or it can lead you to ask the question, how is our family present to those in need in our community? How am I?

On the Road to Amarillo

My friend Judy and I have the good habit of keeping an eye out for unusual and often atypical places of interest that we can explore as we travel together on road trips. But this "find" would have been hard to ignore!

The first thing that catches your attention as you head west on I-40 after you pass the city of Amarillo, near the town of Groom, is a giant white 192-foot cross by the highway, the largest in the northern hemisphere!

The next feature you notice, however, is perhaps even more moving. Delicately placed around the striking cross is a reflective path with a series of life-size bronze sculptures depicting the Stations or Way of the Cross. See the first station in the image that follows, Jesus is condemned to death.

Bronze sculpture by Mickey Wells of the first station, Jesus stands before Pilate and is condemned to death.

© María Ruiz Scaperlanda

This "place" is not attached to any church or denomination, and there are no shops or other businesses associated with the site. It is the dream of Steve Thomas, who wanted to find a way of showing his gratitude to God by creating some sort of public symbol of faith.

The impressive statutes are the prayerful work of Mickey Wells (see www.mickeywellsartist. com), who crafted and molded each piece at his own foundry, Southwest Bronze Studio, in Amarillo, Texas.

> **Lord Knows**
>
> *Rosary* refers both to the type of prayer form of reciting prayers while following a string of beads or a knotted cord and to the string of beads itself.

On that spring morning, two stations touched me the deepest. First, the ninth station, Jesus falls for the third time.

I don't think that I had ever seen a life-size sculpture depiction of the Stations of the Cross before, and the image of Jesus on the ground struggling to catch himself as the weight of the cross propelled down on him brought tears to my eyes.

I was also deeply moved by the image of the *Pietà* that the artist added near the site where the crosses stand. Like the ones I've seen at St. Peter's Basilica in Rome, at Notre Dame Cathedral in Paris, and in other churches, seeing Mother Mary holding in her arms the limp body of her son is both disturbing and deeply touching.

*Bronze sculpture by Mickey
Wells of the ninth station,
Jesus falls for the third time.*

© *María Ruiz Scaperlanda*

Judy and I didn't need a formal written guide to tell us what station we were seeing (although they were marked). Nor did we need a suggested reflection or official prayers. We simply walked the path and silently stood, sometimes spontaneously knelt, before each image—and experienced exactly what the Way of the Cross is supposed to be, a mini-pilgrimage on the passion of Jesus.

The Rosary

No doubt you have seen rosaries in all sorts of interesting places. Sometimes people hang them from their car's rearview mirrors, and some entertainers have been known to wear them around their necks.

Rosaries are prayer beads. This type of prayer form of reciting prayers while following a string of beads or a knotted cord is widespread among major religious groups— Hinduism, Buddhism, and Islam. In Christianity the practice apparently dates back to the early days of the church and to early monks and hermits who used a piece of heavy cord knotted at intervals as an aid in reciting their shorter prayers.

The purpose of the Rosary is to bring to memory certain principal events—which are referred to as mysteries—in the life of Jesus and therefore, in the history of our salvation.

There are twenty mysteries or events reflected upon in the Rosary, which are divided into five Joyful Mysteries, five Luminous Mysteries, five Sorrowful Mysteries, and five Glorious Mysteries.

Which set of mysteries you do is no great mystery! Traditionally, each set is associated with a day of the week. For example, if you're praying the Rosary on a Friday, you would reflect on the five sorrowful mysteries because that's the day that Jesus died. And if you were praying it on a Sunday, you would meditate on the Glorious Mysteries, which begin with the Resurrection of Jesus.

But the main gist of it is that you name the mystery (or scene from the life of Jesus or Mary) that you are going to meditate on; for example, "the resurrection of the Lord." And for every mystery you begin by saying the Our Father, followed by a decade of (ten) Hail Marys.

> **Lord Knows**
>
> There are many online sources detailing the specifics of how to pray the Rosary. For example, see www.Rosary-center.org/howto.htm.

In my adult life, the Rosary has become not only a prayer tool, but also a form of intercessory prayer as I offer each decade in prayer for someone (or a specific situation) who comes to my mind. Sometimes a decade is all I have time for as I drive, using my fingers as prayer "beads." But whether or not I say the full Rosary or do it "properly," I see it as an opportunity to call God into my moment and my consciousness and to offer those prayers for that person.

At many of Mary's apparitions she has asked the seer(s) to say the Rosary and to invite others to pray through the Rosary. It is a simple and informal way of praying that also offers guidance, especially for those many moments in crisis when we are left speechless and don't know what to say.

> **Lord Knows**
>
> The transfiguration refers to the sudden appearance of Jesus in radiant glory that took place on the mountain, as recorded in Mark 9:2–13, Luke 9:28–36, and Matthew 17:1–3, and witnessed by some of his disciples.

As you will see in the sections that follow, many of the mysteries of the Rosary are associated with Mary's life. And by repeating the Hail Mary, we are invoking her prayers of intercession.

The Mysteries

The mysteries in the Rosary are divided in the following way. The Scripture verses listed here are usually read at the beginning of each decade.

The Joyful Mysteries

The Annunciation: "Upon arriving, the angel said to her: "Rejoice, O highly favored daughter! The Lord is with you. Blessed are you among women." (Luke 1:28)

The Visitation: "Elizabeth was filled with the Holy Spirit and cried out in a loud voice: 'Blest are you among women and blest is the fruit of your womb'." (Luke 1:41–42)

The Nativity of Jesus: "She gave birth to her first-born son and wrapped him in swaddling clothes and laid him in a manger, because there was no room for them in the place where travelers lodged." (Luke 2:7)

The Presentation of Jesus in the Temple: "When the day came to purify them according to the law of Moses, the couple brought him up to Jerusalem so that he could be presented to the Lord, for it is written in the law of the Lord, 'Every first-born male shall be consecrated to the Lord'." (Luke 2:22–23)

Finding the Child Jesus in the Temple: "On the third day they came upon him in the temple sitting in the midst of the teachers, listening to them and asking them questions." (Luke 2:46)

The Sorrowful Mysteries

The Agony in the Garden: "In his anguish he prayed with all the greater intensity, and his sweat became like drops of blood falling to the ground. Then he rose from prayer and came to his disciples, only to find them asleep, exhausted with grief." (Luke 22:44–45)

The Scourging at the Pillar: "Pilate's next move was to take Jesus and have him scourged." (John 19:1)

The Crowning with Thorns: "They stripped off his clothes and wrapped him in a scarlet military cloak. Weaving a crown out of thorns they fixed it on his head, and stuck a reed in his right hand." (Matthew 27:28–29)

The Carrying of the Cross: "Jesus was led away, and carrying the cross by himself, went out to what is called the Place of the Skull (in Hebrew, *Golgotha*)." (John 19:16–17)

The Crucifixion: "Jesus uttered a loud cry and said, "Father, into your hands, I commend my spirit." After he said this, he expired." (Luke 23:46)

The Glorious Mysteries

The Resurrection: "You need not be amazed! You are looking for Jesus of Nazareth, the one who was crucified. He has been raised up; he is not here. See the place where they laid him." (Mark 16:6)

The Ascension of Jesus: "No sooner had he said this than he was lifted up before their eyes in a cloud which took him from their sight." (Acts of the Apostles 1:9)

The Descent of the Holy Spirit upon the Apostles: "All were filled with the Holy Spirit. They began to express themselves in foreign tongues and make bold proclamation as the Spirit prompted them." (Acts of the Apostles 2:4)

The Assumption of Mary into Heaven: "A great sign appeared in the sky, a woman clothed with the sun, with the moon under her feet, and on her head a crown of twelve stars." (Revelation 12:1)

The Coronation of the Blessed Virgin Mary: "You are the glory of Jerusalem,
the surpassing joy of Israel;
You are the splendid boast of our people ....
God is pleased with what you have wrought.
May you be blessed by the Lord Almighty
forever and ever!" (Judith 15:9–10)

The Luminous Mysteries

The Baptism of Jesus in the River Jordan: "With that, a voice from the heavens said, "'This is my beloved Son. My favor rests on him.'" (Matthew 3:17)

The Wedding at Cana: "Jesus performed this first of his signs at Cana in Galilee. Thus did he reveal his glory, and his disciples believed in him." (John 2:11)

The Proclamation of the Kingdom of God: "Jesus appeared in Galilee proclaiming the good news of God: 'This is the time of fulfillment. The reign of God is at hand!'" (Mark 1:14–15)

The Transfiguration of Jesus: "He was transfigured before their eyes. His face became as dazzling as the sun, his clothes as radiant as light." (Matthew 17:2)

The Last Supper, the Holy Eucharist: "During the meal Jesus took bread, blessed it, broke it, and gave it to his disciples. 'Take this and eat it,' he said, 'this is my body.'" (Matthew 26:26)

The Hail Mary

Even those of us who are not radical football fans have heard the term "Hail Mary pass" used by TV announcers to describe a desperate throw into the end zone by a quarterback hoping for a score.

The typical Hail Mary is a very long pass thrown at the end of a game when there are no possibilities for any other play to work, and it has a very low rate of completion. Yet every playbook at the professional and college levels includes it as a standard play. From football, the term has spread to other areas of life to describe acts or situations where there is such a small chance of success that it would require divine intervention!

But of course the term comes directly from the opening words of the ancient prayer to the Virgin Mary called the Hail Mary, or *Ave Maria* in Latin.

Lord Knows
The term "Hail Mary pass" was coined by Dallas Cowboys quarterback Roger Staubach. Staubach told reporters on December 28, 1975, after his game-winning last-minute touchdown pass that he closed his eyes, threw the ball as hard as he could, and said a Hail Mary prayer. His desperate pass to receiver Drew Pearson was caught, and Pearson ran into the end zone for the touchdown.

The words to the first part of the Hail Mary come straight out of Luke's infancy narrative, and it has appeared in liturgies as early as the sixth century. They are the words said by the archangel Gabriel to Mary at the Annunciation.

> Hail Mary,
> full of grace,
> the Lord is with you. (Luke 1:28)

The next phrase comes from the words spoken by Elizabeth at the Visitation:

> Blessed are you among women,
> and blessed is the fruit of your womb, [Jesus]. (Luke 1:42)

The only addition to these two Scripture verses is the names of Jesus and Mary, to make clear to whom one is referring!

In the third and final part, we ask for Mary's intercession using a familiar term, which we've already discussed, Mother of God:

Holy Mary, Mother of God,
pray for us sinners
now and at the hour of our death. Amen.

Prayers to the Queen of Heaven

In the same spirit as liturgical celebrations, formal, set prayers that could be learned by entire communities and recited together became a popular way for Christians to pray.

Because she was a familiar and everyday part of the faith, prayers in honor of Mary are some of the oldest prayers in the Christian Church.

Queen of Heaven or *Regina Coeli*

A beautiful prayer that has been a part of the church for centuries is the "Regina Coeli" or "Queen of Heaven."

As a simple anthem to Mary, the prayer has often been set to music, and by many composers.

We do not know who authored the prayer, but it has been traced back at least to the twelfth century—and it is still recited as part of the church liturgy during the Easter season.

The words are:

Queen of Heaven rejoice,
alleluia:
For He whom you merited to bear,
alleluia,
Has risen as He said,
alleluia.
Pray for us to God,
alleluia.

There is a legend that says that it was Gregory the Great (d. 604) who heard the first three lines chanted by angels on a particular Easter morning in Rome while he walked barefoot in a great religious procession. According to the legend, it was that great saint who added the fourth line: "Ora pro nobis Deum. Alleluia," or pray for us.

Hail Holy Queen or *Salve Regina*

Still recited as an antiphon at daily compline since the early 1200s, the Hail Holy Queen prayer was first used as a daily processional chant. And like the "Queen of Heaven," it can be recited or sung.

The words are:

> Hail holy Queen,
> Mother of mercy,
> our life, our sweetness, and our hope.
> To thee do we cry, poor banished children of Eve.
> To thee do we send up our sighs,
> mourning and weeping in this valley of tears.
> Turn then, most gracious Advocate,
> thine eyes of mercy toward us.
> And after this our exile show unto us
> the blessed fruit of thy womb, Jesus.
> O clement, O loving, O sweet Virgin Mary. Amen.
> Pray for us, O Holy Mother of God.
> That we may be made worthy of the promises of Christ.

Litany of Loreto

A litany is a specific type of liturgical prayer that became popular in the Middle Ages. A litany consists of a series of petitions recited by a single leader, with alternating responses by the congregation.

The origins of the Litany of Loreto, like many ancient devotions in the church, are disputed.

What this basically means is that we don't know exactly where it came from! Some claim its origin dates back to the fifth century, but it was probably composed around the end of the fifteenth century.

Many Marian litanies began to appear in the twelfth century as a devotional practice—and litanies grew in popularity over the next few centuries. But the Loreto Litany had the good fortune of being adopted by a famous shrine in Loreto, Italy. This meant that pilgrims who visited the shrine took the text and their knowledge back home when returning to their various countries around the world.

Pay attention to the many "names" given to Mary here. They are beautiful! And each can be a source of meditation not only on Mary, but also on how you live that quality in your life now.

The text of the Litany of Loreto:

> Lord, have mercy.
> Christ, have mercy.
> Lord, have mercy.
> Christ, hear us.
> Christ, graciously hear us.
> God, the Father of heaven,
> have mercy on us.
> God the Son, Redeemer of the world,
> have mercy on us.
> God the Holy Spirit,
> have mercy on us.
> Holy Trinity, one God.
> have mercy on us.
> Holy Mary, pray for us.

> [*from here on, "Pray for us" is repeated after each invocation]

Holy Mother of God,
Holy Virgin of virgins,
Mother of Christ,
Mother of the Church,
Mother of divine grace,
Mother most pure,
Mother most chaste,
Mother inviolate,
Mother undefiled,
Mother most amiable,
Mother most admirable,
Mother of good counsel,
Mother of our Creator,
Mother of our Savior,
Virgin most prudent,
Virgin most venerable,
Virgin most renowned,

Virgin most powerful,
Virgin most merciful,
Virgin most faithful,
Mirror of justice,
Seat of wisdom,
Cause of our joy,
Spiritual vessel,
Vessel of honor,
Singular vessel of devotion,
Mystical rose,
Tower of David,
Tower of ivory,
House of gold,
Ark of the covenant,
Gate of heaven,
Morning star,
Health of the sick,
Refuge of sinners,
Comforter of the afflicted,
Help of Christians,
Queen of angels,
Queen of patriarchs,
Queen of prophets,
Queen of apostles,
Queen of martyrs,
Queen of confessors,
Queen of virgins,
Queen of all saints,
Queen conceived without original sin,
Queen assumed into heaven,
Queen of the most holy Rosary,
Queen of families
Queen of peace.
Lamb of God, You take away
the sins of the world;
spare us, O Lord.

Lamb of God, You take away
the sins of the world;
graciously hear us, O Lord.
Lamb of God, You take away
the sins of the world;
have mercy on us.
V. Pray for us, O Holy Mother of God.
R. That we may be made worthy
of the promises of Christ.
Let us pray.
Grant, we beg you, O Lord God,
that we your servants may enjoy lasting health of mind and body, and by the
glorious intercession of the Blessed Mary, ever Virgin, be delivered from present
sorrow and enter into the joy of eternal happiness. Through Christ our Lord.
Amen.

Celebrating Her Feast Days

Feast days dedicated to Mary are exactly that, days when the people of a town feast
and celebrate Mother Mary's care for them as her children. The official liturgical
feast days of Mary are celebrated as national holidays in traditionally Catholic countries, and often include processions, special masses, and a festival celebration for one
or several days.

Sometimes feast days are connected to a particular name given to Mary. For example, the city
of Zaragosa in Spain claims the patronage of
Nuestra Señora del Pilar, Our Lady of the Pillar,
so called because of a legend of a miraculous
apparition on a pillar in Zaragosa.

For her feast day, October 12, and for other
religious festivals, the people organize processions (similar to a parade, but with a religious
theme) carrying banners and the image of Mary.

> **Holy Mother**
>
> A hermit had on a certain night
> for many years heard music in
> the heavens. When he asked the
> cause an angel answered, 'The
> Virgin was born this night, and
> what is ignored on earth is being
> celebrated by angels."
>
> —Legends of Mary (thirteenth
> century)

The people of Zaragosa celebrate feast days of Mary
with public processions
through the city streets carrying banners and images of
Mary.

© Phillip Reilly

Festivals

On my first visit to Spain to meet relatives related to my grandfather, I was delighted
to participate in several town and parish festivals celebrating either a local saint or a
Marian feast. It somehow felt like it was a nightly event to decide which of the small-
town festivals we were going to go to!

The festivals often involve public displays through the town, as we've already discussed,
and always involve the local church or parish. One favorite aspect of these festive celebrations is that children and adults dress in local ethnic clothing typical of that particular region. See the following example from a big-city procession in Zaragosa, Spain.

The people of Zaragosa celebrate a Marian feast by
dressing in ethnic clothing
for a procession through the
city streets.

© Phillip Reilly

Ethnic Celebrations

Every August 29, the residents of the southern Italian village of Palmi pull a 20-ton wooden structure with a 16-meter high obelisk, called a *Varia*, during a religious festival in honor of the Virgin Mary.

On top of the obelisk sits a young girl playing the part of the Virgin Mary, a man playing the role of God, and dozens of young girls dressed as angels. The traditional festival started five centuries ago, after the end of a cholera epidemic in the region.

Individual people have been calling on Mary for assistance in time of crisis from the beginning of the church. But sometimes, entire communities gathered in the local church asking for her intercession.

As we've already discussed, Mary has often been given a special and unique name by individual cities, countries, even continents, claiming her as patron—as their defender!

> **Lord Knows**
>
> Check out this listing of names given to Mary as patron of different countries: www.udayton.edu/mary/resources/flash/patronages.swf. You can search the whole world!

The Least You Need to Know

- Mary is a central character in the Way of the Cross devotion.
- Groom, Texas, has an impressive and powerful life-size sculpture garden or meditation path featuring a Pietà and the Way of the Cross.
- The purpose of the Rosary is to bring to memory certain principal events— mysteries—in the life of Jesus and Mary.
- Feast days dedicated to Mary are days when the people of a town celebrate Mother Mary's care for them as her children.

Chapter 22

Nonverbal Praying

In This Chapter

- ◆ Poetry as nonverbal prayer
- ◆ Iconography
- ◆ Monks and monasticism
- ◆ Meditation

Conversing with God does not require words. Anyone who has sat still at the edge of the ocean or by a waterfall for five minutes will testify to knowing a powerful experience of divine presence that transcends words.

We've talked about many forms of prayer related to Mary already. But in this section we will reflect on some prayer forms that are based on non-verbal communication.

I realize it might sound odd to begin with poetry, because obviously, poetry uses words. But I will explain the reason for poetry's inclusion in this chapter.

Reflecting on Mary in Poetry

Yes, in order to create poetry, you must use words. So what is this prayer form doing in a chapter on nonverbal praying?

I have a theory about poetry that is totally personal and not based on the thought of any great expert. It goes like this. Although poetry uses letters and words to exist, to be, poetry as an expression of art belongs next to visual art and not literature.

Poetry expresses truth by allowing words to create images. The words in poetry are really superfluous, almost like the brush used by the painter as she visualizes a picture.

It is the image that the words give birth to in a poem that actually "speaks" the truth being expressed.

And in fact, unless the image is crafted in the reader, the poem is, well, worthless!

Sometimes poetry is very much like a prose essay. Other times it's a short, sharp paragraph. But the words are not the end. It is the ideas that matter.

To make my point, I would like to offer two poems by contemporary writers. Both writers begin with a Marian theme and build a contemporary idea around it to give the reader an image.

I will not comment on either poem, but instead allow the poet to tell you in his or her own voice the truth they experienced and wanted to share with you, the reader.

Blessed Are They Among Women

Christmas is the time
for remembering
an ancient story
of a young girl
who learned from an angel
that she was to become a mother.
The girl, Mary of Galilee,
despite difficulties,
accepted pregnancy
with grace:
"Be it done unto me
according to Thy Word!"
From this acceptance
was born the Holy Babe,
Jesus Christ,
Son of God,
foundation
of Christian faith.
Now other unwed women
in diverse, dissimilar
circumstances also learn
they are expectant;
but modern options
often kill
creative will.
Many do not accept maternity,
do not nurture a life,
do not allow a new soul
a place in God's world.
Blessed are they among women
who, like Mary of Galilee,
choose to bear
the fruit of their wombs.
Their decisions
dignify life
and complement
selfless love:
the very essence
of Christmas.

© Shirley Vogler Meister

The Original Luminous Candy-Flaked Dream Machine

September 6, 2001

Moonlight on river
shimmers, shines, even delights.
It fascinates me.
Diced and chopped river
breaks the light up and creates
shining silver path
from me to the moon.
Near me the image is small,
broadens as it moves
across the river
toward this cool burning night light.
It's no wonder we've
compared Mary to
this reflection of the sun
that guides us by night.
My wife's students
have made the observation,
matter of factly,
that God gave us moon
as light for the evening.
Peasant immigrants,
they've not forgotten
what we, "the civilized"
never even learned.
Our harsh city lights
have made us quite ignorant
of natural things,
even most basic
causes for our gratitude
remain mysteries.
Blinded by the light
of the work of our own hands
we miss brighter orbs.

© Jeff Hensley

Iconography

The dictionary must be wrong. Iconography is much more than simply "the pictorial illustration of a religious figure."

The word *iconography* describes a particular style of two-dimensional church art which grew out of the culture of the Byzantine (Constantinople) Empire. Iconography portrays only religious themes: the Trinity, angels, Mary the Mother of God (Theotokos), sacred events, saints, and of course Jesus.

Icons—from the Greek word for "image"—are found in churches, wayside shrines, and homes, and they are a prayer tool for both liturgy and private devotion. Although there is evidence of icons existing in the second century, iconography became most developed in Constantinople (Eastern Christian Church) in the early Christian era.

Icons are also unique as an art form because they are not meant to be expressions of an artist's views or personal style. The icon expresses traditions, describes Scripture, and tells tales of the historical church. Its symbols are repeated throughout the centuries and are part of the liturgical expression.

There are strict rules on subject and technique in iconography that ensure a universal quality to the scenes and the people being portrayed.

For example, the way that the fingers and the hands are positioned tells a part of the story. And the way the particular people are depicted have been traditionally so similar that iconographers today can distinguish between St. Paul and St. Peter, for instance, because each saint has a fixed way of being presented.

For example, by the sixth century, halos were used to identify saints and angels in addition to Jesus. The type of tunic that the icon wears can identify the saint specifically as an apostle. Based on descriptions by Eusebius of Caesarea from the third or fourth century, Saint Peter is depicted with short, curly hair, a short beard and wrinkles, because he was an older apostle. Peter is also the only one shown with keys (usually holding keys in one of his hands), because he is said to hold the keys to heaven (or Paradise).

Icons of Mary affirm her status as Theotokos, Mother of God. She is always depicted with her hair and shoulders covered. And the three stars on her garments represent that she was a Virgin before, during, and after the birth of Christ.

Icons in Eastern Spirituality

Icons are intrinsic to Eastern Christian spirituality.

They are made by the artist and used by the community in an atmosphere of prayer. An icon image is meant to bring the people of God into a wordless encounter with God's presence.

Iconography is the study of God in images, much like theology is the study of God using language. And so icons are a visual Gospel!

Russia has been the center of iconography since the tenth century when the country became Christian. The figure that follows is an example of a Russian icon.

Icon of Mary the Mother of God from the Novodevichy Convent in Moscow.

© *Brian J. McMorrow*

There is a legend that says that it was Jesus who produced the first icon. When the king of Edessa, a leper, heard of Jesus' healings and miracles, he sent an envoy to bring back Jesus to heal him. But along with a letter explaining why he couldn't come, Jesus sent a *mandilion*—a cloth bearing the image of Jesus—and through this icon, the king was cured.

Another legend credits Luke with creating the second icon. According to that story, the apostle and Gospel writer portrayed Mary the Mother of God, holding her son Jesus. But this icon was made by using Mary as a model and not from Luke's imagination, so it is an actual image of Mary and Jesus. There even exist icons telling this story, showing Luke painting Mary and Jesus!

Lord Knows

The **mandilion** (a word that just means mantel or cloth) is the icon image of Jesus "not made by human hands," but by Christ himself. According to the legend, the image on the cloth was the true appearance of Jesus sent to King Abgar V of Edessa after the king prayed that Jesus would come and heal him. Although Jesus did not come, the icon he sent the king did heal him.

Not Church Decoration: Nonverbal Worship

The Christian church has always employed the arts as a means of instruction, a way of professing and explaining the culture and the details of the Christian faith. Look at the walls of the catacombs from those first centuries, for instance, decorated with many paintings and mosaics of Jesus, Mary, and popular Scripture stories.

Later on, every aspect of church buildings has been used to tell the stories from the Hebrew and Christian Scriptures and from the lives of the saints: the walls, ceilings, windows, altars, furniture, books, even the objects and clothing used in liturgy!

The image that follows is an example of an icon found in the ceiling of the Smolensk Cathedral in Moscow.

Icons are clearly not just decorations. As liturgical art, they provide a visual aid for worship. But they are also part of the liturgy itself. In fact, the images become liturgy.

Because the entire purpose of the art form is to portray the truths of the faith, an iconographer is by definition a Christian.

An iconographer is said to "write" an icon because he is telling a story of faith through the image. But an icon artist is never reproducing what he sees or imagines. He is "writing" what he understands about God, and this understanding comes through a life of prayer.

Image of two angels holding an icon of Mary, the Mother of God, with Jesus in her arms, from the Smolensk Cathedral in Moscow.

© Brian J. McMorrow

Because in this art form the artist is regarded not as creator, but as an instrument inspired and guided by God, icons are not signed by the iconographer. God is considered the real artist of the icon.

Symbolism

When praying with an icon, every detail matters. Who is in the picture? Which way are the people or entities facing? How are the bodies positioned? The positioning and gestures of the hands and faces are especially important.

Icons are rich in symbolism because every aspect of the image is part of the story. It tells the story. An open hand, and a hand lifted up, are making a gesture of prayerful intercession. Both hands raised means praise as well as intercession.

Holy Mother

The Memorare

Remember, O most gracious Virgin Mary that never was it known
that anyone who fled to your protection,
implored your help,
or sought your intercession
was left unaided.
Inspired by this confidence,
we fly unto you,
O Virgin of virgins, our Mother.
To you we come, before you we stand,
sinful and sorrowful.
O Mother of the Word Incarnate,
despise not our petitions,
but in your mercy hear and answer us.

—Twelfth-century prayer attributed to Bernard of Clairvaux (d. 1153)

In an image of Christ the *Pantokrator*—the All-Ruler—the individuals and angels within the icon converge toward the throne, imploring or pleading in prayer, but also glorifying God.

Angels placed near Mary are often seen looking toward the viewers, inviting and engaging them to contemplate the Mother of God.

The different colors of the robes and the images are important. Red signifies royalty, but also the vitality or intensity of the color speaks of the figure's significance.

Contemplation, Relaxation, and Self-Help

Meditation and contemplation are long-standing prayer traditions in the Christian church.

Contemplation is not a relaxation exercise. It is not yoga. It might bring relaxation, but that's a side effect of its practice.

Contemplation is about relationship, and as such it's not so much a technique as it is an actual prayer!

Contemplation is also not focused on the self. It might bring about self-awareness and growth, but again, that's a side effect, not its intention.

Contemplative prayer is resting in the spirit of God; very much in the way that Mary pondered in her heart all the events of her life. (See Luke 2:19, 51)

It is both an intentional time set aside to be open to hearing God in the quiet of our beings and an attitude toward life. That is the openness that we've already seen in so many moments in Mary's life!

Monasticism

People who live a mode of life that is dedicated to prayer, work, and contemplation are called monastics.

And even though the word *monasticism* literally means the act of "dwelling alone," *monasticism* is commonly used to describe a particular lifestyle: living in seclusion from the world, under religious vows, and subject to a fixed rule. This describes, of course, monks, friars, nuns, or in general those who have taken religious vows (usually to poverty, chastity, and obedience) and who live in community.

Lord Knows

Although the word *Catholic* is commonly used to refer to Christians who are of the Roman Catholic tradition, the word *catholic* actually means "universal." It was used to describe the church by Ignatius of Antioch in approximately 107 A.D. "Whenever the Bishop shall appear, there let the people be, even as where Jesus is, there is the Catholic Church."

Monasticism can be found in every religious system that has attained a high degree of ethical and spiritual development, such as the Buddhist, Jewish, Christian, and Muslim religions.

In the Christian world, Marian prayers and meditating on Mary are an intricate part of the monastic prayer life.

The Carmelite Order, for example, a contemplative order of men and women, see Mary as their supreme example in prayer, contemplation, and solitude. For Carmelites, Mary is remembered under the name of Our Lady of Mount Carmel. She is the handmaid of the Lord, who models in the best of ways how to live out simplicity, faithfulness, and trust in a prayerful life.

Every once in a while, elements from this "other world" of contemplation cross with popular culture and remind us of its existence.

A few years ago, award-winning writer and poet Kathleen Norris published a book called *The Cloister Walk*, which rapidly exposed people to language and prayer forms they had never heard of.

Norris wrote about things like monastic liturgy, obedience, monastic rule, and saints' feast days. Even the name of the book was instructive. The cloister walk refers to the connecting arched passageway that links the monastery to the church and which the monks walk seven times a day, every day, on their way to community prayer.

Monks and the monastic tradition have even been at the forefront of fiction recently, including providing the main setting for the latest Sue Monk Kidd novel, *The Mermaid Chair*.

But leaving aside curiosity and novelty, what's important to remember is that the monastic tradition has been a part of the Christian faith for as long as Christianity has existed.

Monasteries, Convents, and Other Contemplative Structures

Modern architecture has often focused more on the practical aspects of a church than on its ascetic quality, but the truth is that beauty does invite us to experience the spiritual and to get in touch with the divine.

Centuries ago, when the majority of people were illiterate, it was very important in terms of passing on the faith that everything about a church building spoke of God, including it's beauty!

Look at some of the major cathedrals named after Mary for a good example of this. Millions of pilgrims don't visit the Cathedral of Notre Dame merely because of its history. They go because everything about it—including its unique design and structure—invite the visitor into a worship experience that goes beyond themselves.

They come because its entire "being" is meant to honor Notre Dame, Our Lady! They come because it is a quiet, prayerful atmosphere that draws the visitor into relationship with God.

Monasteries and convents, like churches, are structures meant to praise God. Like iconography, they model set rules in how they live, in how they pray, even in how the buildings are designed. These common elements allow them to be places that in essence transcend differences in cultures and even history.

Even the grounds of a monastery encourage and invite visitors to come away from the world and be still.

Holy Mother

Mary was alone at the annunciation. She had to be; each human must make alone those personal choices that confirm the deep structures of a unique human life. She made her choices alone, each of which turned out to be a generous self-donation, first to God, then to the One to come, and in the end to all with whom she shares humanness.

—Joseph A. Tetlow (twentieth century)

Part of the design of a monastery includes outdoor places to pray, such as the Way of the Cross, or even a garden bench, as well as places to sit and contemplate a visual sculpture or image, such as the following garden shrine to Mary from a Carmelite monastery in Ghent, Belgium.

In a very real way, monasteries and convents around the globe are oases of peace that exist with the world, and yet are not of the world. While remaining plugged in to the world, monks devote their entire lives to prayer.

This garden shrine to Mary is a quiet place in the grounds of the Carmelite Monastery in Ghent, Belgium.

© María Ruiz Scaperlanda

Don't get the wrong idea, however. Monasteries are not places you go to get away from the world. They are places you go to come home, in a spiritual sense, to God.

Many of the nuns and monks that I know are more aware of news events than most of us! They need to be, after all; their vocation is to pray for the world, and that means they have to be aware of what's going on in the world in order to pray for it!

The Least You Need to Know

- ◆ Iconography describes a particular style of two-dimensional church art that grew out of the culture of the Byzantine Empire.

- ◆ Iconography is the study of God in images, much like theology is the study of God using language.

- ◆ Contemplative prayer is resting in the spirit of God, very much in the way that Mary "pondered" things in her heart.

- ◆ Marian prayers and meditating on Mary are an intricate part of the monastic prayer life.

Chapter 23

Tradition! Mary Through the Centuries

In This Chapter

- ◆ Keeping Mary in memory
- ◆ Music, art, and literature
- ◆ The Guadalupe story
- ◆ Storytelling

As a Cuban-American, the importance of honoring and remembering tradition has been ingrained in me by my refugee parents. I think of this often with regard to Mary and how the Christian church has experienced and grown to know her through the centuries.

Tradition is much more than knowing facts or memorizing dates and names. Like iconography, tradition is a living and breathing experience based on understanding, not knowledge.

Mary has been honored and remembered in church tradition through feasts, prayers, and Scripture stories. But she has also been experienced through literature, art, and music. And it is here that we get in touch with how the Christian body of believers has understood Mary. In this chapter, we will also take a moment to look at oral tradition and the art of storytelling and how this part of tradition has promoted our understanding of Mary.

Making Memories

Images and references to Mary are not confined to any one particular culture or country, language, period of history, or even to Christianity.

Mary is beyond borders!

A good way to experience a taste of this aspect of Mary is to look at examples of how Mary has been experienced in music, literature, and other forms of art.

Obviously, this is a mere sampling, and a small one at that. But it is important to include it as part of our understanding of Mary. These expressions are birthed from the heart of the people.

Perhaps Mary's constant love and faithfulness for her adopted children is her most endearing quality, across languages, ethnic cultures, or nationalities.

Lord Knows

Saint Benedict, the founder of what is known as the Benedictine Order, was born around the year 480 in Nursia, high in the mountains northeast of Rome. Even as a young man, Benedict desired monasticism, the simple and austere prayer life of being a monk.

He established the first monastery of his growing community in Monte Cassino, about 80 miles southeast of Rome. It was there that Benedict wrote the Rule of Benedict, guidelines that are still used in monasteries and convents across the world today.

But how this love is experienced—and the art it creates within and from the artist's hands—is as varied and unique as each flake of snow.

It's impossible to list the thousands of renditions of Mary in art over the past two thousand years, or the way her image pervades even a Protestant culture like that of the United States.

You can spot her on book covers of all kinds (she sells books!), and as a small figure in people's gardens. She is disguised as a nameless "Madonna" figure in a restaurant's wall, and her name is thrown about "randomly" in modern song lyrics.

Mary is inviting. She is real. We portray Mary in all kinds of unconventional ways because we remember her. And regardless of your faith tradition, you have to acknowledge that she is an intrinsic part of the greatest story every told.

Of course we continue to bring her visually and audibly to our consciousness!

Mary in Music

Pat and I walked in early enough to assure us the opportunity to wander through the large nave of the church without attracting attention, and to silently examine the images on both sides of the large stone building in the town of Santo Domingo de Silos in Spain.

Like John within Elizabeth's womb, our spirits jumped, recognizing that we were in the presence of holiness.

This particular church structure in Santo Domingo de Silos is "only" roughly 300 years old. But the hermit tradition of monasticism found here dates back to the beginning of the seventh century when a group of monks lived in this small valley north of the city of Burgos in northern Spain.

The small town of red-tiled roofs and stone structures literally grew around the community of hermits that eventually gathered under one roof to follow the Benedictine Rule as monks in the monastery of Santo Domingo de Silos.

Like many pilgrims who come to this out-of-the-way place, Pat and I went to Santo Domingo de Silos specifically to pray by listening to the monks sing Evening Prayer in Gregorian chant.

Gregorian chant has been around since the 800s, but the monks of Santo Domingo de Silos brought this monophonic prayer to the forefront of modern culture when their "Chant" album broke into the pop charts in the 1990s in the United States.

As we listened to the sung psalms that night and to the final prayer dedicated to Mary, I was reminded and aware that Mary has held believers together for centuries through her faith and her example.

Music has been one of the most powerful ways that master composers and native musicians have tried to give voice and sound to this amazing reality. Sometimes they simply took the liturgical prayers of the church and put them to music, like the monks at Santo Domingo de Silos. Other times they were inspired by an image of Mary or a particular attribute that moved them.

Bach's *Magnificat*. Verdi's *Laudi alla Vergine Maria*. Grieg's *Ave Maris Stella*. So many famous names have written masterpieces in honor of Mary over the centuries that it is literally impossible to list them.

The *Ave Maria* alone has renditions by countless composers, including Mozart, Verdi, Arcadelt, Bach, Brahms, Rachmaninoff, Bruckner, De Victoria, Stravinsky, Holst, and Franck.

Most of us have been lucky enough to hear Schubert's *Ave Maria* sung at a wedding, or perhaps have heard jazz and pop singer Aaron Neville's modern rendition of it in one of his albums!

And some of us wonder whether, despite his purported denial, Paul McCartney was writing at least partially about Mother Mary, the Mother of Wisdom, in The Beatles' hit song "Let It Be."

Mary in Visual Art

Mary portrayed as a wealthy Renaissance woman was a popular image in the Renaissance.

> **Holy Mother**
>
> God of power and mercy,
> you blessed the Americas at Tepeyac
> with the presence of the Virgin Mary of
> Guadalupe.
> May her prayers help men and women
> to accept each other as brothers and
> sisters.
> Through your justice present in our hearts
> may your peace reign in the world.
> We ask this through our Lord Jesus Christ,
> your Son,
> who lives and reigns with you and the
> Holy Spirit,
> one God for ever and ever.
> Amen.
>
> —Opening prayer of the memorial of
> Our Lady of Guadalupe, Roman
> Catholic liturgy

All the great masters—Raphael, Leonardo da Vinci, Sandro Botticelli, El Greco—painted the Virgin Mary often and proficiently, and they often placed her image within their own environment and atmosphere!

Raphael in particular is famous for the many pictures he did of Mary, so many in fact that historians trace his biography as a painter by them.

When I consider my favorite images of Mary in fine art, whether a portrait or one representing a scene from her life, I don't think of classics like Rubens' *Madonna and Child* or van Eyck's *Enthronement of Saint Mary*.

What comes to mind instead is an image that could be described as realistic, quotidian, and even earthy.

Traveling through Spain I saw many renditions of Mary as mother, but my all-time favorite portraits were when Mary was portrayed as a real woman and a real mother—breastfeeding an infant Jesus cradled in her arms, for example, or holding a baby Jesus whose small but persistent hand is digging into his mother's shirt—much as my own children did to me when they were infants!

Mary has been depicted in many ways, in many acts, and indeed, even in many colors. There are some 200 examples of Black Madonna images throughout Western Europe, many of which have become pilgrimage sites for believers. And of course, we've already discussed how individual countries also have adopted particular images of Mary, always serving as reminders of Mary's motherly presence to their people.

As the description of a recent exhibit at the University of Dayton on "Polish Madonnas in Art and Poetry" notes, in these paintings, "Mother Mary worries about her child and, by the same token she suffers with the Polish nation. There is no chasm between this world and the life to come," explained Rev. Johann Roten. "They are both filled to the brim with the vivid colors of the Polish character and daily life, and permeated with holy enthusiasm and gentle grace."

Featuring fifty paintings by contemporary Polish artist Wislawa Kwiatkowska, the images tell the beautiful love story between the Polish people and the Bogarodzica, the Polish "Mother of God."

Each painting overflows with color and symbolism, blending natural images such as a flower, with the cape of the Virgin or with the Madonna herself.

Just as with Kwiatkowska's paintings there exists no boundary between picture and frame, in these images there is no gap between this world and the divine.

This is a beautiful illustration of symbolism for describing how Mary "functions" for Christian believers!

Mary blends the earthy with the divine, reminding us constantly of the truth of the Incarnation—God is here, one with us, and not some distant and unreachable deity.

The following are two examples of Mexican folk art from New Mexico called *retablos*.

Retablos, referred to as *laminas* in Mexico, are small paintings on tin, zinc, wood, or copper that venerate a multiplicity of Catholic saints in one piece of art. The literal translation for *retablo* is "behind the altar."

This first *retablo*, or altar art, dates back to the nineteenth century and it features not only official church saints, but many local saints from the artist's small rural town.

The second *retablo* is a twentieth-century piece from Santa Fe, New Mexico, featuring Our Lady of Guadalupe in the top center as well as other saints.

This nineteenth-century retablo, *or altar art, from a small town in New Mexico features both official and local "saints" or holy men and women.*

© *María Ruiz Scaperlanda*

This twentieth-century retablo, *or altar art, from Santa Fe, New Mexico, has Our Lady of Guadalupe prominently featured in the middle at the top.*

© *María Ruiz Scaperlanda*

Mary in Literature

The paintings in the exhibit of Polish Madonnas by Wislawa Kwiatkowska were inspired by poetry written by modern Polish authors.

The themes of both poems and paintings emphasize the presence of Mary in the ordinary and daily settings of Polish life—holy shrines, a forest with mushrooms, flower gardens.

Polish literature from its earliest beginning has always been inspired by Mary. One of the earliest examples of the written Polish language—and the earliest existing document of Polish poetry—is *Bogarodzica* or Mother of God.

As the exhibit notes explain, this fifteenth-century hymn illuminates the devotion of the Polish people to the Holy Mother and portrays the Polish understanding of Mary's role as mediatrix. "Sung by the knights in the Battle of Grunwald in 1410, Bogarodzica had become 'carmen patrium,' (the hymn of the motherland), and has been a sign of Polish national identity through the centuries. It illustrates the Polish belief that human freedom and prosperity are connected to Mary's intercession with her Son," explained Stefan Ceglowski, director of the Diocesan Museum of Plock.

The Poland story is only one example of how intrinsic Mary the Mother of God has been to the national and cultural understanding of many Christian countries.

Lord Knows

Unaccompanied singing, known as *a cappella*, has been a part of the liturgy of the Christian church since its beginnings. It was probably inherited from Jewish practices in the Temple, and later from synagogue services.

Gregorian chant, also called plainchant or plainsong, refers to any monophonic liturgical music without strict meter and sung without accompaniment.

In literature, references to Mary in poetry and fiction are abundant and have been throughout recorded history. One of the most imaginative examples is a recent novel answering what one of my friends describes as her childhood question: What would I do if Mary came to see me for a visit?

On an ordinary Monday in April, a nondescript woman wearing Nikes and a blue trench coat suddenly appeared in a woman's living room apartment. She called herself "Mary, Mother of God." To the narrator's greatest surprise, however, this Nike-wearing Mary asked to stay with her for a week to rest up and prepare for the challenging and eminent month of May, long ago dedicated to her by the Christian church.

The rest of the story in Diane Schoenperlen's novel *Our Lady of the Lost and Found* is basically about the two women and how they spend the week: talking, shopping, cooking, and sharing secrets with one another. Mary even tells the narrator about some of her miracles throughout the ages—or so this story goes.

This might be an unconventional, fictional narrative, but it also serves as an example of how embedded Mary is to contemporary cultural psyche—to the mind of the culture, if you will.

The Art of Storytelling

Last year I went with my friend Judy to an evening of storytelling at a local theatre, part of a storytelling festival. We watched and listened to four different storytellers, each with his or her own style (one even danced as she told her story!), each with his or her own objective.

Some were serious. Some were hilarious. One was clearly enjoying weaving together random stories about animal tales!

Besides its obvious entertainment factor, storytelling could be described as the most ancient form of history.

Storytelling has been part of many cultures. According to Anne Pellowski's *The World of Storytelling*, records documenting storytelling have been found in many languages, including Old German, Latin, Greek, Chinese, Sanskrit, Icelandic, and Old Slavonic.

But the origins of storytelling are even older. Perhaps the oldest surviving record of storytelling in an ancient civilization is an Egyptian papyrus detailing how the sons of Cheops (the pyramid builder) used to entertain their father with stories.

Storytelling and Religion

One more note about storytelling.

Storytelling has been a part of many world religions as a teaching tool, such as in *Buddhism*. In *Hinduism*, Hindu storytellers have used story clothes to illustrate their narratives.

Hasidic Jews used storytelling to introduce rituals and faith beliefs to young children.

Sunday School

Followers of **Buddhism** venerate Buddha's doctrine that enlightenment obtained through right conduct, wisdom, and meditation releases one from desire, suffering, and rebirth. It is especially prominent in Asia.

Hinduism is the predominant religion of India. It is characterized by a caste system and its belief in reincarnation and a supreme being of many forms and natures.

And of course, Jesus used many stories in the form of parables in his teachings. Although storytelling remains a popular way of introducing the Bible in Christian services to young children, Jesus used storytelling for everyone, especially adults!

Some stories truly are better told orally, like the story of Mary's first recorded appearance in the continent of the Americas.

The Mexico Story

Perhaps in no other Marian story is storytelling as important to its memory as in the Guadalupe story.

We've already told the story of Juan Diego Cuautlatoatzin, the Aztec Indian to whom Mary appeared in 1531. And you have probably seen the image of Our Lady of Guadalupe, as I have, in all kinds of unusual places, including hanging on the wall of a local Mexican restaurant. Perhaps you have seen it on the back window of a truck, or tattooed on the arm of a Mexican American teenager.

Many people have written about the image of Our Lady of Guadalupe and its significance as a symbol of ethnic pride for the Mexican people.

But I think this particular image of Mary is so much more than a symbol. She embodies in her brown skin her oneness with the poorest of the poor, those of a mixed race, who are often disregarded and forgotten in society.

And it's important to note that it was the strong oral tradition of the Aztec and colonial Spanish communities in Mexico that allowed the Guadalupe story to not only survive, but to flourish!

Grandparents who told the story to their children and grandchildren preserved the history of Juan Diego and Mary, under the title of Our Lady of Guadalupe.

In fact, when the time came to officially study the Guadalupe apparition and examine the historical data available about Juan Diego, it was the written accounts of people's testimonies, their oral history, that pieced the story together.

The Importance of Guadalupe

Virtually unknown 100 years ago in the United States, except in the Hispanic southwest, the familiar image of Juan Diego humbly kneeling before Our Lady of Guadalupe remains today a powerful symbol of hope, a living sign of God's message of love for all his children.

Our Lady of Guadalupe, sometimes endearingly called *la morenita*, or "the dark-skinned Lady," by Latinos, is especially dear to Mexicans, for whom Guadalupe is truly a national symbol of pride.

Much like the Incarnation, the Guadalupe story represents a scandalous idea: the Mother of God appeared to a working class, 57-year-old Nahuatl Indian, and she asked for his help!

Think about it. The year was 1531, a mere 10 years after the Aztec capital of Tenoch-titlan fell to Hernán Cortés—and 89 years before the Mayflower set sail across the Atlantic Ocean for North America.

And Mary chose to appear to an ordinary Indian. She called Juan Diego her son. She spoke to him in his native language. She told him that she was his "compassionate Mother" and "the Mother of the True God." And she commissioned him to go visit the local bishop and give him a message: Mary the Mother of God wants a church built on that particular hill.

Holy Mother

My whole image of Mary was challenged and changed on a hot day in 1975, when some other Sisters and I joined Cesar Chavez and his walk for farmworker justice and the new California Agricultural Labor Relations Act.

She was always chosen, in the form of her banner, to precede marches and liturgies, and hanging in Cesar's office. Through the farmworkers, and subsequently through my knowledge of the Guadalupe story, her role in the Mexican struggle for independence, I came to know Mary not as a remote pink figure on a pedestal, who was removed from the confusions of young women and teenagers or from professional women and homemakers—but as someone who was human.

—Marie Tess Browne (twentieth century)

It's not unusual for Mary to choose unlikely messengers. She did so at Lourdes and Fátima, too. The lowly. The uneducated. The poor and simple. The disfranchised—too old or too young.

So it is no surprise that a colonized people would identify themselves with, and admire with heartfelt loyalty, the dark-skinned Mary of Tepeyac, the one who came with a personal message of love and compassion.

The Rest of the Story

In addition to honoring her and her role as mother of their Messiah, early Christian believers could relate to Mary because she was a human mother, a person, very much like them.

They heard the stories and the manuscripts describing Mary's ordinary, even mundane, life in an unremarkable country town in Palestine.

Indeed, like the character wearing Nikes in *Our Lady of the Lost and Found*, Mary and her life was so ordinary she could be sitting in your living room today!

Yet in many ways she has been remembered for the past two thousand years exactly because of this scandalous bringing together of the ordinary and the divine.

I found this representation of the Crucifixion scene with Mary at the cross in Santiago de Chile. But the image was brought over to Chile from Germany by a Marian group called Schoenstatt.

This unique representation of Mary at the foot of the cross places Mary within the image of the cross.

© *Beverly Bradley*

As artists, composers, and authors have done, believers continue to remember Mary in a mystical sense because in doing so they re-member, bring together, the ordinary woman who humbly and completely gave herself to God. She allowed the human and the divine to become one within her own body. And in doing so, God did great things in her!

With her life and through her story we bring together, re-member, Mary so that she can show us the way to God.

The Least You Need to Know

◆ The experience of Mary is not confined to any one culture, country, language, period of history, or even to Christianity.

◆ Gregorian chant is an ancient form of prayer through music.

◆ As languages were created and developed, Marian prayers, poetry, and hymns became some of the first written pieces of literature.

◆ The oral testimony of Christian believers ensured the survival of the story of Our Lady of Guadalupe.

Chapter 24

To Be or Not to Be: Mary Today

In This Chapter

- ◆ Making the cover
- ◆ Not just for Catholics
- ◆ Mary's Magnificat
- ◆ Thérèse of Lisieux

Improbable. That would be the gentlest way to describe the idea that anyone would remember, let alone be talking about, a young Jewish woman from a nameless town in the Middle East.

Yet here she is, this Mary of Nazareth, still making the news after two thousand years.

Obviously, the first and foremost reason for this is due to whose mother she was. But it's more than that. In this chapter we will see why Mary remains a vibrant part of Christianity today, mothering those who have chosen the path to follow her son, Jesus.

The Cover Story

You don't have to be a journalist to recognize the level of importance attributed to a subject when it becomes "the cover story," the central piece in a publication, or the top news item in a newscast.

At last count, Mary the mother of Jesus had made the coveted cover of *Time* magazine (at least) eleven times—more than any other woman in history, and more frequently than any other image.

Time Magazine's Most Prevalent Art Subject

As *Time* declared in its December 30, 1991, article, "Handmaid or Feminist," "Among all the women who have ever lived, the mother of Jesus Christ is the most celebrated, the most venerated, the most portrayed, the most honored in the naming of girl babies and churches. Even the Koran praises her chastity and faith."

That's quite a number of superlatives for a simple woman of such humble upbringing!

Why is this so?

Surely part of the media fascination with Mary includes controversy. That always sells good copy.

If one Christian tradition makes a declaration or statement of faith about Mary, that proclamation can, and usually does, offend and affect another group of Christians. And media coverage often focuses on the ideas or beliefs about Mary that divide Christian traditions.

But we can't blame the media alone. There have been many periods and movements in the Christian faith when Mary has been treated like a trophy that is either lusted after or completely discarded.

In this sort of tug-of-war theology, for example, if Catholics are giving her a prominent role in their faith traditions, then obviously, Protestants should not. Or so the old thinking would go.

But this misses altogether the essence of Mary's importance.

Still Popular After All These Years

Debating over Mary as if she was an interchangeable tenet of faith or a bendable thesis of dogma dismisses her reality.

Mary was a real person. Mary was the mother of Jesus, the Messiah, as proclaimed by Christians. From the moment that she became a mother, Mary lived and proclaimed that she believed this reality throughout all of her life. She was there throughout Jesus' public moments—and she was there as a faithful disciple all the way to the cross. Mary remained a vibrant presence in the early Christian church after her son's ascension to heaven.

She was honored and respected as Jesus' mother and as his believer from the beginning of Christianity. And she remains an example of what it means to make Jesus first in your life.

Controversial topics on Mary might sell copies, but it is Mary's place in the community of believers that has kept her "alive" and central to Christianity for over two thousand years.

> **Holy Mother**
>
> O Mary, immensity of heaven,
> foundation of the earth,
> depth of the sea, light of the sun,
> beauty of the moon,
> splendor of the stars in the heavens.
> You are greater than the cherubim,
> more eminent than the seraphim,
> more glorious than the chariots of fire.
> Your womb bore God,
> before whose majesty mortals stand in awe.
> Your lap held the glowing coal.
> Your knees supported the lion,
> whose majesty is fearful.
> Your hands touched
> the One who is untouchable,
> and the fire of the Divinity which is in him …
> O Mary, who nurtured in your womb
> the fruit of oblation,
> we children of this sanctuary
> pray to you with perseverance
> to guard us from the adversary which ensnares us;
> and as the measure of water
> cannot be parted from the wine,
> so let us not be separated from you and your son,
> the Lamb of salvation.
>
> —Ethiopian anaphora (eighth century)

Not Just for Catholics

In the recently published book *God Called a Girl: How Mary Changed Her World and You Can Too* (Bethany House Publishers, 2005), the book's author (Shannon Kubiak) draws parallels for young women from the life of Mary, suggesting how Mary's choices can model the way for contemporary young women striving to grow in character and faith.

This is not an extremely provocative idea until you consider the fact that both the author and the book's publisher are of the evangelical Christian tradition!

I shouldn't be surprised, but I do love hearing stories from my non-Catholic friends about how and when they "discovered" Mary.

For my friend Sue, Mary simply "made sense" as a woman who survived tremendous suffering, someone who could understand the grief and loss she felt after her husband died.

Scott also turned to the Passion Narratives to discover Mary. But to him, Mary became the model of what it means to remain with Jesus when events in life make no sense, and even when all other believers leave—as it was at the crucifixion.

Beverly, an Episcopal pastor, fell in love with Mary as she allowed herself to talk in prayer with this devoted mother. As she told me, "Who makes a better mother to think and preach about on Mother's Day?"

Aside from her son Jesus, the main reason for Mary's enduring involvement in Christianity is clearly because there is so much that she still has to teach us and share with us regarding what it means to be a Christian, a follower of Jesus, a woman, a parent, a mother.

For some, this means interpreting Mary as a strong and radical feminist. Others see Mary as a crusader for the poor and the oppressed. For the myriad immigrant and refugee communities in the United States, but especially for Hispanics and Vietnamese—Mary, Joseph, and Jesus are not just a symbol called the holy family. They, too, were refugees in a foreign country.

And if these activist-implicated angles don't speak to you, there are more traditional ones.

Lord Knows

The Magnificat is the canticle of the Virgin Mary from Luke 1:46. It's name comes from its beginning in Latin: *Magnificat anima mea Dominum, My soul magnifies the Lord.*

But the word *magnificat* has also come to mean in popular culture a song of praise and thanksgiving! As in, she got to the top of the mountain and said a *magnificat*.

Consider Mary, the selfless, devoted mother. And don't forget Mary the committed, prayerful woman who completely entrusted every unpredictable and unforeseen moment in her life to a loving God who was and remains in charge of all creation.

Across cultural, religious, and ethnic boundaries, the world continues to cry out for and demand many things from Mary—and continues to receive them.

And although Mary has always been intertwined with the culture and faith for Catholics and Orthodox across the world, Mary has no boundaries.

Mary of Nazareth is not one of these roles and ideologies; she is all of them combined. No one can argue that she is not a woman of strength. She experienced poverty and what it felt like to be a single, pregnant mother. She struggled with her husband and her son as a refugee and knew what it meant to be an exile. And yes, Mary as a mother understood pain and lived through profound suffering.

As a Protestant father recently suggested in the latest *Time* magazine article on Mary, there should be a movement of bracelets that read HOW WOULD MARY REACT, just like the now famous WHAT WOULD JESUS DO wristbands.

In a nutshell, that's why we can claim Mary in so very many ways: because she truly lived a life that incorporated all these aspects, all these experiences. Mary understands because Mary lived it all—at least all the major events of human trauma that we live with in our world today.

Like the image in the photo that follows, Mary's arms are open, ready, waiting, and ever protecting her children.

From the top of a hill, Mary's image overlooks the capital city of Santiago de Chile.

© María Ruiz Scaperlanda

A Powerful Witness

Mary's response to her kinswoman Elizabeth and to Elizabeth's greeting is often called Mary's hymn, or her Magnificat (its Latin title) because of it's beginning: "My soul magnifies the Lord," or as my Bible translation reads "My being proclaims the greatness of the Lord."

I have waited until the end of this book to discuss Mary's canticle, her Magnificat, because above everything else, it is what describes Mary best. And following the spirit of the wedding at Cana, I wanted to save the best for last!

Mary's Magnificat

There are many things that make the Magnificat a remarkable and compelling canticle of praise, including its spirit of thanksgiving.

As Scripture scholars point out, in its style and its themes, this canticle is reminiscent of Hannah (1 Samuel 2:1–10), the mother of Samuel, and of many other canticle passages in the Hebrew Scriptures that offer poetic *praise* to God in thanks for His gifts.

But I want to call attention to two specifics about Mary's hymn as found in this first chapter of the Gospel of Luke that make it a deep and moving illustration of Mary's unique spirituality: its prediction and its vision of God.

In the first half of this lovely canticle, Mary herself acknowledges the gift of salvation growing within her as she predicts all ages to come shall call her blessed.

> **Sunday School**
>
> To **praise** is more than to express approval or support. It is to offer words of reverence and veneration as an act of worship.

Although this might sound like an awkward thing for anyone to say, coming from Mary's humble voice this statement is above all a proclamation of an unthinkable and wonderful reality about God: in his great love, God chose to become one with humanity.

And God chose a woman as his vessel to come into the world!

What an amazing thing to say about the Creator of the universe. The Holy One, the Mighty God, chose to become fully human out of love for his people.

No wonder Mary begins her hymn by proclaiming the greatness of the Lord! Her spirit is truly in awe pondering what this reality means, and she humbly responds that, for all time, she will be seen as richly blessed by God.

In Praise of God's Mercy

The second aspect of the Magnificat that I want to call attention to is the powerful vision of a merciful and loving God that Mary describes.

With each poetic line, Mary reminds us of God's great love and of his abundant mercy for his people. This is a strong God, yes, with a mighty arm!

But above all, the God that Mary sings to is a merciful and generous God who loves and protects his people. He protects the hungry. He defends and sustains his people Israel with his mercy.

And he has fulfilled and remembered his promise to Abraham and all of Abraham's descendants with the child growing within her womb.

It is with all her heart that Mary therefore sings *Holy is God's name!*

Song of Praise and Thanksgiving

Like the prophets from Hebrew Scripture, Mary's voice in this canticle of praise is that of a prophet admiring God's abundant mercy for his people.

Twice in this personal poem, Mary notes God's mercy—and it fills her spirit and her heart with thanksgiving!

What a beautiful model for our daily walk.

Queen, Yes, but Mother First

One of my favorite quotes about Mary is by a nineteenth-century Frenchwoman named Thérèse of Lisieux (d. 1897).

For Thérèse, Mary was a real and accessible mother to all of us.

"The Blessed Virgin is the Queen of heaven and earth, quite true," Thérèse said, "but she is more mother than queen."

More mother than queen! Now there's something I can relate to—and a sensible place to begin to get to know in a personal way the mother of Jesus.

The following image is a stained glass rendition of a young Mary as our heavenly mother, created only 22 years after Thérèse's death.

Image of Mary as heavenly mother, a stained glass window from the Cathedral of Our Lady of Perpetual Help in Oklahoma City.

© Anamaría Scaperlanda-Ruiz

Thérèse of Lisieux

Much has been written about this Frenchwoman from the town of Lisieux named Thérèse. This in itself is remarkable, considering this uneducated country girl died at the young age of 24 and hardly traveled outside her home country.

She is popularly known as Thérèse of Lisieux, Thérèse of the Little Flower, or simply the Little Flower.

Born to a middle-class family whose father, Louis, was a watchmaker, Thérèse Martin had a simple yet deep awareness of God's spirit in the world and in her. Her understanding of the love and trust in God led her to become a Carmelite nun at the amazingly young age of fifteen.

Perhaps because she lost her own mother to cancer when she was only four years old, Thérèse saw and sought in Mary a loving companion.

We might never have heard about Thérèse if it hadn't been for her spiritual director who, against her wishes, asked Thérèse to dictate her famed autobiography, published eventually under the title *Story of a Soul*.

Her spiritual awareness, her understanding of how to recognize God in the world, is popularly described as "the little way," because it focused on seeing God in the smallest and most mundane aspects of our life. For instance, Thérèse's little way of love means learning to love and accept the woman in my office who drives me nuts with her annoying habit of clicking a pen!

Thérèse has a lot to teach us about how to live a life of faith. She was practical and had great common sense. Prayer, for example, was a simple look toward heaven. And spiritual perfection, explained Thérèse, consisted simply in "being what God wants us to be."

> **Holy Mother**
>
> The definition of the Assumption proclaims again the doctrine of our Resurrection, the eternal destiny of each human body, and again it is the history of Mary that maintains the doctrine in its clarity. The Resurrection of Christ can be regarded as the Resurrection of God, but the Resurrection of Mary foreshadows the Resurrection of each one of us.
>
> —Novelist Graham Greene (d. 1991)

This understanding of "perfection," therefore, is intricately connected to the small and the ordinary and does not require that we achieve great successes, at least not as the world measures success.

Thérèse of Lisieux was declared a saint by the Catholic Church a mere 28 years after her death on September 30, 1897, in Lisieux, France, from tuberculosis. She is also considered a Doctor of the Church by the Catholic Church.

A Mother Like No Other

The Blessed Virgin never failed to protect her, Thérèse said. "In my troubles and anxieties I very quickly turn towards her and, like the most tender of mothers, she always takes care of my interests."

It was disappointing to Thérèse that Mary was often presented as a distant and unapproachable character in a book.

She saw Mary's life as "quite ordinary," in the sense that everything that took place for Mary also takes place in our own lives. This is what makes it possible for us to imitate Mary, said Thérèse, by practicing what she called Mary's "hidden virtues."

Like Thérèse, we are invited to turn to Mother Mary as our heavenly mother who never fails to protect us.

And like Mary of Nazareth, we are invited to acknowledge and to praise God's great mercy and love, in our lives and in our world.

The Least You Need to Know

- ◆ Mary is waiting to be discovered as the Mother of the Church, not just by Catholics, but by all Christians.

- ◆ The Magnificat is Mary's canticle of praise and thanksgiving for God's mercy.

- ◆ In spirit and deed, Mary's soul magnified the Lord.

- ◆ Mary is always a mother first!

Glossary

Acts of the Apostles   The fifth book in the New Testament.

angels   Spiritual, immortal creatures that glorify God without ceasing, assist in the divine plan, and serve God as messengers.

Annunciation   The name given to the moment when Mary of Nazareth learned that she had been chosen to give birth to the son of God.

apocrypha   Literally means "hidden." It has several meanings with relation to Scripture. It is used by Protestants to refer to the books accepted in the Catholic and Orthodox canon, but considered noncanonical by Protestants. It is also used in reference to early Christian writings proposed as additions to the New Testament but rejected by the major canons. Finally, it means writings or statements of questionable authenticity.

Bible   The name given in the fifth century to the entire collection of sacred books, or the *Library of Divine Revelation*. Sometimes called the sacred scriptures, Bible is the classical name for both the Hebrew Bible of Judaism as well as the combination of the Hebrew Scriptures and New Testament of Christianity.

bishop   From the Greek word meaning "overseer." In the modern church, a bishop has spiritual and administrative authority over a group of priests or ministers and the churches in a certain region. They are considered the successors of the apostles by divine institution.

Buddhism   Religion venerating Buddha's doctrine that enlightenment obtained through right conduct, wisdom, and meditation releases one from desire, suffering, and rebirth.

circumcision   A religious rite consisting of the removal of the foreskin of males, traditionally done on boys eight days after birth in both the Jewish and Muslim traditions. Circumcision was considered a sign of the Jewish people's consecration to God, a special badge that set them apart from others.

Compline   The final of the seven times a day at which canon law prescribes that certain prayers are to be said—by monastic communities throughout the world.

creed   From the Latin *credo*, meaning "I believe." A creed is a brief summary statement or profession of Christian faith.

deuterocanonical   There are seven deuterocanonical books: Tobias, Judith, Wisdom, Ecclesiasticus, Baruch, I and II Maccabees, and portions of Esther and Daniel. They are classed by Protestants as "apocrypha" and not included in the Protestant Bible.

devotion   An act of religious observance or prayer, especially when private, but it can also be a public observance.

disciple   Those who accepted Jesus' message to follow him are called his disciples. The word *disciple* comes from the Latin *discipulus*, or "pupil," from *discere*, "to learn."

epistle   A letter or a formal writing directed or sent to a person or group of persons. The letters from Paul and the apostles to Christian communities that make up the New Testament are often referred to as epistles.

fasting   A religious discipline that can be both a public and a private practice. Although it has also been used as an expression of mourning, as a spiritual rite, fasting can be understood as a humbling of oneself before God, as well as a discipline for opening the self to God in prayer.

heresy   A religious doctrine that develops contrary to the doctrines of Christianity. From the Greek *hairesis*, the word can mean either a choice of beliefs or a group of dissident believers.

Hinduism   The predominant religion of India. It is characterized by a caste system, its belief in reincarnation, and a supreme being of many forms and natures.

iconography   A particular style of two-dimensional church art that grew out of the culture of the Byzantine Empire.

Incarnation   The belief that the son of God was conceived in the womb of Mary of Nazareth, and that Jesus is, therefore, true God and true man.

Kabbalah (or *Kabala*, *Kabalah* and other variations)   A body of mystical teachings, rabbinical in origin, that are based on a mysterious interpretation of the Hebrew Scriptures.

liturgy   A prescribed form for public religious worship. In Christianity, the word *liturgy* also means the celebration of the Eucharist, also called the Lord's Supper or the Holy Eucharist.

manger   The container (usually in a barn or stable) that holds the food for cattle or horses.

mediatrix   A woman who acts as a mediator, who intercedes.

ministry   From the Latin meaning *servant*. It has come to mean an act or activity that involves serving, as well as the profession, duties, and services of a minister or Christian clergy.

monks   Members of a community who live in a cloister and devote themselves to a discipline of contemplation, prayer, and work. Monks can be men or women, but it has traditionally been used for male communities.

mystery   Anything that baffles understanding and cannot be explained. Also a religious truth that is ultimately incomprehensible to reason, knowable only through divine revelation.

Passover   Also known as *Pesach* or *Pesah*, is a Holy Day observed by several religions, beginning on the evening of the fourteenth day of the Jewish month of Nissan and lasting for seven days. It commemorates the exodus and freedom of the Israelites from Egypt.

patron   Someone who supports, protects, or champions someone or something. In church language, a patron saint is a holy man or woman who is venerated as a special intercessor before God.

Pentecost   The day on which the Holy Spirit descended upon the apostles, and on which, under Peter's preaching, many thousands were converted in Jerusalem. (Acts 2)

pilgrim   A person on a journey to some sacred place as an act of religious devotion.

pilgrimage   A journey taken as a spiritual quest.

praise   To offer words of reverence and veneration as an act of worship.

prayer   Lifting the mind and heart to God in praise, in petition, in thanksgiving, or in intercession on behalf of others before God. In the words of Saint Augustine, "Prayer is communication with God."

prophecies   Revelations about events in the future, often about a particular period or about a certain group of people. A prediction made by divine inspiration.

rabbi   A person trained in Jewish law, ritual, and tradition, and ordained as chief religious official of a synagogue. A scholar qualified to interpret Jewish law.

Reformation (and reformers)   A sixteenth-century religious movement throughout Western Europe that aimed at reforming and reorganizing specific doctrines and practices of the Christian church. It ended in division and the establishment of new religious institutions, such as Lutheranism, Anabaptists, and the Reformed churches. It also led to what is known as the Counter-Reformation within the Roman Catholic Church.

refugee   Someone who has left his or her native country and who is unable to return to it because of persecution or fear of persecution.

Rosary   Refers both to the prayer method where the Lord's Prayer and the Hail Mary are repeated in a designated pattern—and to the actual string of beads that is used for counting during the prayer.

sanctuary   A sacred place, such as a church, temple, or mosque. Also, a consecrated area where sacred objects are kept, often the holiest part of a sacred space.

Synoptic   The first three Gospels of the New Testament (Matthew, Mark, and Luke), which share content, style, and order of events—and which differ largely from John.

Talmud   A collection of ancient Rabbinic writings considered the basis of religious authority in Orthodox Judaism.

Transfiguration   The sudden appearance of Jesus in radiant glory that took place on the mountain, as recorded in Mark 9:2–13; Luke 9:28–36; and Matthew 17:1–3, and witnessed by some of his disciples.

Trinity   The central doctrine of the Christian faith that declares that there are three distinct persons in one God: God the Father, God the Son (Jesus), and God the Holy Spirit.

virtue   The quality of doing what is right and avoiding what is wrong. Virtue is moral excellence, goodness, and righteousness. It is also a particularly effective quality, such as the virtue of patience.

Appendix B

Sources for Further Reading

If you're interested in learning more about Mary of Nazareth, you will find these books very helpful.

Azzarello, Marie. *Mary the First Disciple*. Ottawa: Novalis, 2004.

Baker, J. Robert and Barbara Budde. *A Sourcebook about Mary*. Chicago: Liturgical Training Press, 2002.

Ball, Ann. *A Litany of Mary*. Huntington, IN: Our Sunday Visitor, 1988.

——— *The Other Faces of Mary*. New York: Crossroads, 2004.

——— *Stations of the Cross/Stations of Light*. Huntington, IN: Our Sunday Visitor, 2004.

Brown, Raymond E., Joseph A. Fitzmeyer, and Roland E. Murphy. *The New Jerome Biblical Commentary*. Englewood Cliffs, NJ: Prentice Hall, 1989.

Buby, Bertrand. *Mary of Galilee, Vol. 1, 2, 3*. New York: Alba House, 1994, 1995, 1997.

Cantalamessa, O.F.M. Cap., Raniero. *Mary: Mirror of the Church*. Collegeville, MN: Liturgical Press, 1992.

Chiffolo, Anthony F. *100 Names of Mary: Stories & Prayers*. Cincinnati, OH: St. Anthony Messenger Press, 2002.

Cunneen, Sally. *In Search of Mary: The Woman and the Symbol*. New York: Ballantine Books, 1996.

Cunningham, Lawrence. *Mother of God*. San Francisco: Harper & Row, 1982.

Dickson, Charles. *A Protestant Pastor Looks at Mary*. Huntington, IN: Our Sunday Visitor, 1996.

Elizondo, Virgil. *Guadalupe: Mother of the New Creation*. Maryknoll, NY: Orbis, 1997.

Finley, Mitch. *Surprising Mary: Meditations and Prayers on the Mother of Jesus*. New York: Resurrection Press, 1997.

Florendo, Andrea Oliva. *Liturgy of Flowers in a Mary Garden—A Contemplation*. New York: Oliva and Florendo Publishers, 2004.

Flusser, David. *Mary: Images of the Mother of Jesus in Jewish and Christian Perspective*. Philadelphia, PA: Fortress, 1986.

Gangloff, Mary Francis. *Remarkable Women, Remarkable Wisdom: A Daybook of Reflections*. Cincinnati, OH: St. Anthony Messenger Press, 2001.

Gaventa, Beverly Roberts. *Mary: Glimpses of the Mother of Jesus (Personality of the New Testament)*. Minneapolis, MN: Augsburg Fortress Press, 1999.

Gaventa, Beverly Roberts, and Cynthia L. Rigby, ed. *Blessed One: Protestant Perspectives on Mary*. Louisville, KY: Westminster John Knox Press, 2002.

Johnson, Elizabeth A. *Truly Our Sister: A Theology of Mary in the Communion of Saints*. New York: Continuum, 2003.

Kelly, Liz. *The Rosary: A Path into Prayer*. Chicago: Loyola Press, 2004.

——— *May Crowning, Mass, and Merton*. Chicago: Loyola Press, 2006.

Koenig-Bricker. *365 Mary: A Daily Guide to Mary's Wisdom and Comfort*. San Francisco: Harper, 1997.

Krymow, Vincenzina. *Mary's Flowers: Gardens, Legends, and Meditations.* Cincinnati, OH: St. Anthony Messenger Press, 2002.

McGrath, Michael O'Neill, and Richard N. Fragomeni. *Blessed Art Thou: Mother, Lady, Mystic, Queen.* Franklin Park, IL: World Library Publications, 2004.

Norris, Kathleen. *The Quotidian Mysteries: Laundry, Liturgy and "Women's Work."* Mahwah, NJ: Paulist Press, 1998.

——— *Meditations on Mary.* New York: Penguin, 1999.

O'Carroll, Michael. *Theotokos: A Theological Encyclopedia of the Blessed Virgin Mary.* Collegeville, MN: Liturgical Press, 1990.

Orsini, Jacqueline Mary. *Images of the Holy Mother.* San Francisco: Chronicle Books, 2000.

Pelikan, Jaroslav. *Mary Through the Centuries: Her Place in the History of Culture.* New Haven: Yale University Press, 1998.

Pennington, M. Basil. *Mary Today: The Challenging Woman.* New York: Doubleday, 1987.

Ratzinger, Joseph Cardinal. *Seek That Which Is Above.* San Francisco: Ignatius, 1986.

Rupp, Joyce. *Your Sorrow Is My Sorrow.* New York: Crossroads, 1999.

Scaperlanda, María Ruiz. *The Seeker's Guide to Mary.* Chicago: Loyola Press, 2002.

Scaperlanda, María Ruiz, and Michael A. Scaperlanda. *The Journey: A Guide for the Modern Pilgrim.* Chicago: Loyola Press, 2004.

Streep, Peg. *Mary, Queen of Heaven.* New York: Quality Paper Back Book Club, 1997.

Trouvé, Marianne Lorraine, ed. *Mother of Christ, Mother of the Church: Documents on the Blessed Virgin Mary.* Boston: Pauline, 2001.

Appendix C

Internet Resources

The Mary Page

www.udayton.edu/mary

This is *the* definitive online source on anything Marian. By clicking **Contact Us**, you can get an answer to *any* and all questions about Mary. Operated by the International Marian Research Institute located at the University of Dayton, Ohio, an international center of study and research on Mary, the mother of Jesus Christ.

The Mariological Society of America

www.mariologicalsocietyofamerica.us

This academic agency with information on events and educational programs focuses on Mary and also publishes a journal called *Marian Studies*.

Marian Events

www.udayton.edu/mary/events.html

This page is dedicated to listing Marian events in the United States, Puerto Rico, Canada, and Mexico, with links to each. There is also an **International** option in the drop-down selection list for events in other countries.

Early Mariology Database

http://tsam.cecs.acu.edu.au

This is an ongoing, long-term project to collect all reliably dated Greek, Latin, and Syriac texts containing references to Mary up to the Council of Ephesus. Its growing database is available online.

Jewish Virtual Library

www.jewishvirtuallibrary.org/index.html

This library is a division of the American-Israeli Cooperative Enterprise. It has a wonderful "search engine" for anything related to Israel or the Jewish faith.

The Map Room of the Focus on Jerusalem

http://focusonjerusalem.com/maproom12.html

This website includes great area maps for different parts of Israel, including a helpful chart with distances between cities.

Bible Search Engine

www.biblegateway.com

At this website, you can search by book, topic, language, and even Bible version. (Note: This search engine does not include the deuterocanonical books in the Catholic Bible, which non-Catholics conventionally know as the *Apocrypha*.)

Books of the Bible

www.usccb.org/nab/bible/index.htm

This is an alphabetical listing (with links to the text) that includes all the books of the Bible, including the ones in the Catholic Bible.

The New Testament Gateway

www.ntgateway.com

The NT Gateway is a reliable directory of Internet resources on the New Testament, and includes a search engine.

Search Engine for the Catechism of the Catholic Church

www.scborromeo.org/ccc.htm

The NagHammadi Library

www.nag-hammadi.com

This is a guide to the ancient apocryphal texts discovered in 1945 in Egypt, including the gospels of Thomas, Philip, and the Egyptians.

Society of Biblical Literature

www.sbl-site.org

This is the official website of the Society of Biblical Literature, an academic association that supports the critical investigation of the Bible. One of the website's best offerings is its "resources" area and its helpful links.

Catholic Biblical Association of America

http://cba.cua.edu/default.cfm

This is the official website of the Catholic Biblical Association. Check out its links to current archeological digs, and its extensive and useful list of other links.

Wesley Center Online

http://wesley.nnu.edu/biblical_studies/noncanon/index.htm

This comprehensive collection of noncanonical literature provides full texts online.

Early Christian Writings
www.earlychristianwritings.com/index.html
This nonscholarly site includes full listing of all early writings, canonical and noncanonical, listed by the year it was written.

Church Fathers
www.newadvent.org/fathers
This website lists "Church Fathers" in the early Christian church by name and by dates, with links to individual texts on each one.

Catholic Encyclopedia
www.newadvent.org/cathen
The Catholic Encyclopedia is a good resource on people and topics, not just on Catholic subject matter. Check out its helpful "search engine."

Lourdes, France
www.lourdes-france.com/index.php?page=menu&texte=1&old=&langage=en
This is the official website of the shrine dedicated to Our Lady of Lourdes. It includes information on the apparitions.

Fátima, Portugal
www.santuario-fatima.pt/portal/index.php?lang=EN
This is the official website of the Santuario dedicated to Our Lady of Fátima. Under "history," it also provides information on the apparitions that took place there.

Basilica of Our Lady of Guadalupe, Mexico
www.virgendeguadalupe.org.mx/index.htm
This is the official website (in Spanish) of the sanctuary in Mexico City built at the site of the apparitions.

How to Pray the Rosary
www.medjugorje.org/rosary.htm
This website offers diagrams and easy-to-follow instructions (with illustrations) on how to pray the rosary.

The Way of the Cross
http://198.62.75.1/www1/jsc/TVCmenu.html
This site explains the prayer tradition of the Stations of the Cross based on the Jerusalem way of the cross, or Via Dolorosa, with pictures of the actual sites in Jerusalem.

Icons and Iconography
www.iconograms.org/
This site, sponsored by the Greek Orthodox Archdiocese of America, contains an extensive gallery of icons (including a description of the saint or feast depicted in the icon) listed by date or feast. The icons can also be sent as free e-cards!

Saint of the Day

www.americancatholic.org/Features/SaintofDay/default.asp

Much like the "Iconograms" website, this site features an illustration and information on a saint each day. But it also includes an option of links to saints by name, by patron saint, and by date.

Patron Saints Index

www.catholic-forum.com/saints/indexsnt.htm

This website includes a search engine (by topic or name) of official saints and their patronage.

Pilgrimages

www.pilgrimsprogress.org.uk/index.htm

This site is not associated with any group or business, but it is a good resource on pilgrimages around the world and on the value of making a pilgrimage.

Sacred Sites

www.sacredsites.com

This website has an excellent collection of essays and photography on pilgrimage sites around the world, including non-Christian ones.

Basic Historical Timeline, Including Key Marian Dates

This chronology of Christian history is compiled from several sources. The most helpful from a Marian perspective is the **Chronological Table of Marian Events** found at www.udayton.edu/mary/resources/Timetable.htm. Permission to reprint this article has been received from The Mary Page at: www.udayton.edu/mary of the Marian Library/International Marian Research Institute, University of Dayton, Dayton, Ohio, USA.

Entries taken directly from this source (without the use of quotation marks) are marked with an asterisk (*). Some entries, especially from the first centuries are approximations, with scholars debating the exact dates.

4 B.C.	The Birth of Jesus Christ in Bethlehem
	The Magi (the three kings) come from afar to pay homage to Jesus
	Jesus, Mary, and Joseph seek refuge in Egypt from Herod's wrath
8 A.D.	Mary and Joseph desperately look for Jesus, finding him in the Temple in Jerusalem
26 A.D.	Wedding at Cana
30 A.D.	Crucifixion, Resurrection, and Ascension of Jesus
30 A.D.	Descent of the Holy Spirit and Birth of the Church
32 A.D.	Stephen martyred
33 A.D.	Conversion of Paul
44 A.D.	James, brother of John, martyred
48 A.D.	Council of Jerusalem, First Church Council
54–60 A.D.	First allusion to Mary in Paul's *Letter to the Galatians* (4:4 "God sent his son born of a woman")*
65 A.D.	Mary mentioned twice in Mark's Gospel*
64–67 A.D.	Peter and Paul martyred in Rome
70 A.D.	Fall of Jerusalem
70–100 A.D.	Matthew's Gospel, Luke Acts, and John's Gospel show Mary's presence in the life of Jesus and the early Christian community*
90–100 A.D.	Mary and the Church are both symbolized in the image of the woman in the *Book of Revelation* (chapter 12)*
ca. 110 A.D.	Ignatius of Antioch makes references to Mary as Virgin and Mother*
150–165 A.D.	Justin Martyr brings the comparison between Eve and Mary*
150–202 A.D.	Irenaeus of Lyons points to Mary's role in redemption*
Late second century	Early paintings of Mary in the catacombs*
200–350 A.D.	Composition of the prayer *Sub tuum praesidium*—the oldest Marian prayer*
217 A.D.	Founding of [the church] Santa Maria in Trastevere, Rome*
300 A.D.	Introduction of the *Akathistos* Hymm in the East*
313 A.D.	Emperor Constantine issue edict establishing toleration of Christianity
330 A.D.	The original St. Peter's Basilica (built on the burial site of Peter on Vatican Hill/Rome) was dedicated by Constantine

306–373 A.D.	Ephrem of Syria, known for his poetic writings about Mary*
352–366 A.D.	Founding of [the basilica church] Saint Mary Major [in Rome] under Pope Liberius I*
370 A.D.	Earliest liturgy of Mary composed in Syria*
339–397 A.D.	Ambrose of Milan speaks of Mary as type of the Church*
354–430 A.D.	Augustine of Hippo speaks of Mary as most excellent member and type of the Church*
410 A.D.	The Visogoths sack Rome
432 A.D.	St. Patrick returns to convert Ireland
400–500 A.D.	Introduction of the Feast of the Commemoration of the Virgin throughout Europe, Feast of the Annunciation celebrated in Byzantium*
431 A.D.	Council of Ephesus proclaims Mary as *Theotokos**
440–461 A.D.	Introduction of the Marian reference in the Eucharistic prayer of the Leonine Sacramentary*
550 A.D.	Celebration of the Feasts of the Birth of Mary, the Presentation of Jesus, and the Dormition in Byzantium*
600–700 A.D.	Composition of the Marian antiphon *Ave Maris Stella*, Celebration of the Feast of the Purification (February 2), the Annunciation (March 25), the Assumption (August 15), and the Birth of Mary, in Rome*
625 A.D.	Muhammad begins to dictate the Koran (Qu´ran)
649 A.D.	Council of Lateran declares the perpetual virginity of Mary*
680–681 A.D.	The Third Council of Constantinople reaffirms Mary's Divine Motherhood*
787 A.D.	The Second Council of Nicaea defines regulations for the veneration rendered to images of Mary*
ca. 802 A.D.	Alcuin composes Masses in honor of Our Lady on Saturday, which become part of the Missal in 875*
900–1000 A.D.	Composition of the antiphon *Regina Coeli*, dedication of Saturdays to Mary*
1000–1100 A.D.	Composition of *Hail Holy Queen*, start of the building Notre Dame Cathedral in Chartres, France*
1054 A.D.	Great schism between the church of the west (Catholic) and the church of the east (Orthodox)
1050–1150 A.D.	Compositions of the antiphons *Alma Redemptoris Mater* and *Salve Regina*, building of the church of Our Lady of Walsingham in England*

1100–1200 A.D.	Early versions of the *Litany of the Virgin Mary* and the first part of the *Hail Mary**
1100–1135 A.D.	Rupert of Deutz gives Marian interpretation of the *Song of Songs* and speaks of Mary's spiritual motherhood*
1100–1153 A.D.	Anselm of Canterbury and Bernard of Clairvaux highlight in addition to Mary's role in the incarnation her role in redemption*
1163–1235 A.D.	Building of Notre Dame Cathedral in Paris, France*
1225–1274 A.D.	St. Thomas Aquinas, author of the *Summa Theologica*
1230–1280 A.D.	Albert the Great uses the title *Mother of the Church**
1300–1400 A.D.	Institution of the Feast of Mary's Presentation*
1321 A.D.	Dante's *Divine Comedy* written
1326 A.D.	Founding of Oriel College in Oxford, England, and its dedication to Mary*
1350 A.D.	The beginnings of the Italian Renaissance
1379 A.D.	Founding of Saint Mary's College in Oxford, England, and its dedication to Mary*
1400–1500 A.D.	Composition of the *Memorare**
1423 A.D.	Institution of the Feast of the Sorrows of Mary*
1475 A.D.	Founding of the first Confraternity of the Rosary*
1495 A.D.	Approval of the Rosary by Pope Alexander VI*
1517 A.D.	Martin Luther posts his 95 Theses, marking the beginnings of the Protestant Reformation
1531 A.D.	Apparition of the Blessed Virgin Mary to Juan Diego at Guadalupe, Mexico*
1534 A.D.	Henry VIII breaks with the Catholic Church and establishes himself as the head of the church in England
1536–1541 A.D.	Michelangelo paints the Last Judgment in the Sistine Chapel in Rome
1538 A.D.	Destruction of the Shrine of Our Lady of Walsingham [by Henry VIII]*
1547–1563 A.D.	Council of Trent affirms Mary's immunity from every actual personal fault, and reaffirms the regulations regarding the veneration of Marian images*
	Saurez develops a first systematic teaching on Mary*
Seventeenth century	The French School of Spirituality brings about a renewal of Marian devotion: Mary at the heart of the Christian mystery; the first and most perfect Christian*

1754 A.D.	Proclamation of Our Lady of Guadalupe as patroness of Mexico*
1827 A.D.	Mormon Church founded by Joseph Smith
1830 A.D.	Apparition to Catherine Labouré in Paris, France*
1846 A.D.	Apparition at La Salette, France*
1858 A.D.	Apparition [to Bernadette] at Lourdes, France*
1879 A.D.	Apparition at Knock, Ireland*
1883–1902 A.D.	Pope Leo XIII: eleven Marian encyclicals, advocation of devotion to Mary and praying the Rosary*
1900 A.D.	Proclamation of Our Lady of Guadalupe as Patroness of the Americas*
1907 A.D.	Institution of the Feast of Our Lady of Lourdes*
1917 A.D.	Apparition at Fatima, Portugal*
1918 A.D.	Adding the invocation *Queen of Peace* to the Marian Litany*
1931 A.D.	Institution of the Feast of the *Divine Motherhood of Mary*￼*
1932/1933 A.D.	Apparition at Beauraing, Belgium*
1937 A.D.	Apparition at Banneux, Belgium*
1942 A.D.	According to Mary's wish at Fatima, Pope Pius XII dedicates the world to the Immaculate Heart of Mary*
1944 A.D.	Institution of the Feast of the *Immaculate Heart of Mary*￼*
1964 A.D.	Promulgation of the Dogmatic Constitution on the Church *Lumen Gentium* by Pope Paul VI at the Second Vatican Council: Chapter Eight of the Constitution addresses the Catholic Church's teaching on Mary's place in the mystery of Christ and the Church*
1973 A.D.	Publication of the U.S. Catholic Bishops Letter *Behold Your Mother*￼*
1987 A.D.	Proclamation of a Marian Year (June 7, 1987–August 15, 1988), Encyclical Letter *Redemptoris Mater* by Pope John Paul II*
1998 A.D.	Mary, the Mother of the Church, intercedes for the Christian people during the time of preparation for the great jubilee year, as presented in Bull of Indiction of the Great Jubilee Year 2000, *The Mystery of the Incarnation* by Pope John Paul II*
2002 A.D.	Pope John Paul II adds the Luminous Mysteries to the Rosary in his apostolic letter *On the Most Holy Rosary*

Appendix E

Marian Feasts

In the West

There are 14 Marian feasts in the general Western (Roman Catholic) Christian liturgical calendar:

January 1	Solemnity of Mary, Mother of God
February 2	The Presentation of the Lord in the Temple
February 11	Our Lady of Lourdes
March 25	Solemnity of the Annunciation of the Lord
May 31	The Visitation
Saturday after the Second Sunday after Pentecost	Immaculate Heart of Mary
July 16	Our Lady of Mount Carmel
August 5	Dedication of Saint Mary Major
August 14	Vigil of the Assumption
August 15	The Assumption of Mary
August 22	The Queenship of Mary
September 8	The Birth of Mary
September 15	Our Lady of Sorrows
October 7	Our Lady of the Rosary
November 21	The Presentation of Mary in the Temple
December 8	The Immaculate Conception of Mary
December 12	Our Lady of Guadalupe (in the United States)

The Society of Mary and several other apostolic congregations celebrate two additional feasts:

September 5	Mary, Queen of the Apostles
September 12	Most Holy Name of Mary

In the East

The Eastern Christian liturgy includes the following major Marian feasts:

March 25	The Annunciation
August 15	The Dormition of the Theotokos (Mother of God)
September 8	The Nativity of the Theotokos
November 21	The Entrance into the Temple of the Theotokos

The following are among the "lesser" Marian feasts:

October 1	The Protection of the Virgin
December 8	The Conception of Mary
December 26	The Synaxis of the Theotokos

Index

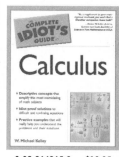